Planning, Deploying and Installing Data Protector 9

Greg Baker

January 2015

Contents

Part I

Background

1

Product Information

1.1 Why customers run Data Protector

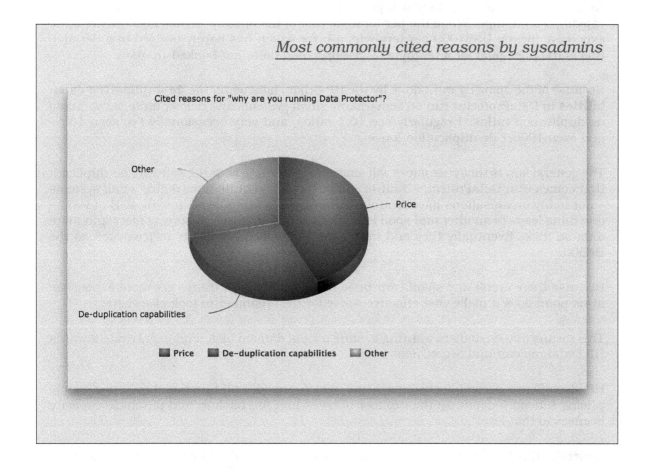

The most common reason given by customers as to why they chose DataProtector is: cost. DataProtector is positioned to be similar in price to Backup Exec, but to provide similar functionality to Net Backup, CommVault and Veeam.

Because DataProtector's classic licensing does not require licences for traditional file level backup it can often work out extremely **cost-effective**. Licensing for media agents (writing out to tape) is concurrency based, so organisations with servers spread across many time zones often also see very significant cost savings.

For example, a customer wanting to back up a few dozen servers to a small tape library with one drive in it would need to buy a licence to use the DataProtector cell manager. This license includes one concurrent drive license, and licensing for a small library (less than 60 tape slots) is free. Creating a bootable CD or USB stick is also free. Which means that the customer can get a very functional and effective backup solution for US$2000 or less, which might correspond to about $100 per machine.

As a customer scales up they will probably want to start backing up to disk and then copying it off to tape. While the per terabyte cost of the backup to disk licenses are quite expensive (nearly US$1000 per terabyte, a price which has barely budged in a decade), this is the price paid for a terabyte of *de-duplicated* data, not backed-up data.

Because of the amazing work done by the HP Bristol labs team, the **de-duplication capabilities** in DataProtector run on remarkably small systems and deliver quite outstanding de-duplication ratios. I regularly see 10:1 ratios, and very occasionally I've seen 100:1 and even 1000:1 de-duplication (once).

The general flow is that customers will start experimenting with the software de-duplication that comes with DataProtector built-in. Since it runs on quite remarkably small systems – not many organisations have troubles running up a Linux system with 4GB of RAM – one thing leads to another and soon enough they find themselves storing more and more data on disk. Eventually they end up buying StoreOnce hardware devices such as the B6500.

Because there aren't any significant price break points with things get more expensive, at no point does it make cost-effective sense for the customer to look elsewhere.

This means that customers wanting to store a lot of data on disk tend to gravitate towards HP DataProtector and StoreOnce.

HP also offers a second licensing scheme, which provides all functionality in one simple pricing scheme – count up the number of bytes in a full backup and purchase capacity licenses to that level.

Generally this is more expensive because the customer ends up paying for a lot of functionality that they don't use. But it can work out quite well for customers who want to take snapshots of a disk array, mount them on another machine, put the backup into deduplicated storage and be able to recover by either reverting the snapshot or reading from disk.

1.2 Past, present and future

Typical customers

- Most customers have used Data Protector for a long time
- Many have tried other backup products as well

DataProtector is a product with a long history.

When Hewlett-Packard acquired Apollo Computer in 1989, Apollo had written a backup system entitled the OmniBack Network Backup System. There was the OmniBack product (for filesystem backups), and there was the Omniback/Turbo product (for database backups). These got merged in 1996 – about the time I started being involved with the product – and called OmniBack II 2.0. Around 2000 OmniBack was renamed to Data Protector.

It shuffled around between different groups at HP. For a while it was part of the Open-View software group, then part of the storage group, before returning to software, being transferred into the new Autonomy entity.

The effect was a long period of what looked to the outside world like stagnation. DataProtector version 6 (released in 2006) was followed very slowly by version 6.1 late in 2009. A long anticipated replacement of the internal database with a proper relational database was reset when Oracle (whose database HP was going to use) undercut Itanium support. It wasn't until version 8 in June 2013 that customers began to see that HP was going to make good on their development promises.

This meant a number of loyal HP customers – many of whom had been running DataProtector for two decades or longer – had started looking at alternatives.

It's not appropriate in a book like this to say nasty things about other backup products, but many customers discovered that the grass wasn't greener on the other side of the fence. HP regained a few customers this way, and these are often quite high-value customers.

So, quite a few customers were using Data Protector before, went somewhere else, and came back again.

New Data Protector users

- Centralising their backups

- Replacing Backup Exec

- Generally have many other HP products

There is however, a surprising area of growth at the low end of the market. Customers who have a large number of remote sites with local backups are often wanting to consolidate to a centralised backup solution. Many customers switch to DataProtector as part of this process, often leaving BackupExec in order to save administration time. The low bandwidth replication technology in the StoreOnce systems let them have on-site disk copies, a central site disk copy and a copy written to tape for long-term storage.

In either case, the vast, vast majority of DataProtector customers are running DataProtector alongside many other HP products. A typical DataProtector customer runs it on a proliant server or HP blade server. It controls and HP tape drive in HP tape library which is filled with LTO tapes bought from HP. It backs up data residing on 3PAR or other HP storage. The **single vendor support** model is very compelling for these kinds of customers, as it avoids the problem of vendors pointing fingers at each other.

In the future though, I'm expecting to see the high-end enterprise backup market consolidate down to CommVault, EMC Networker and DataProtector. Leaving out IBM's offerings and NetBackup may seem surprising, but backup is going through a time of rapid change and the required research and development spending is going to be very significant. The upshot of this is that in the future will be seeing DataProtector customers who have little else in the way of HP infrastructure initially: for example as IBM loses customers, HP will be the obvious alternative.

1.3 Strengths and Weaknesses

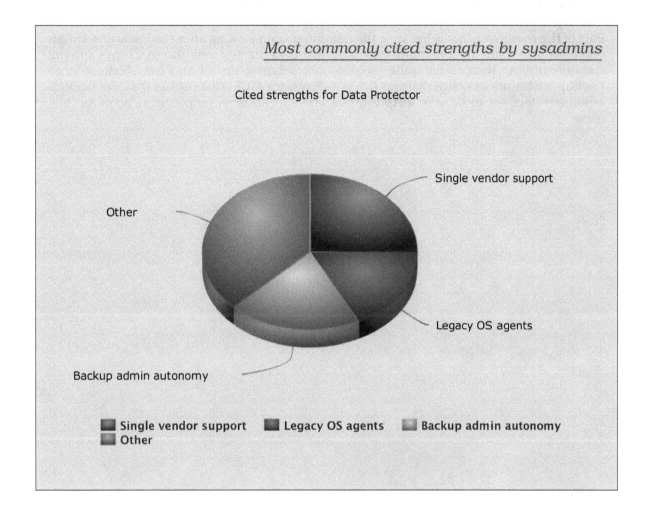

Most commonly cited strengths by sysadmins

Cited strengths for Data Protector

Single vendor support

Other

Legacy OS agents

Backup admin autonomy

■ Single vendor support ■ Legacy OS agents ■ Backup admin autonomy
■ Other

Apart from the single vendor support model mentioned in the previous section, the Store-Once de-duplication technology and the generally low cost of acquisition, there are a couple of other reasons that customers report as being DataProtector strengths.

Many customers buy DataProtector because they need to support very obscure or older operating systems. Because the backup protocol is backward compatible, anything that has had an agent in the past will generally still work. Thus there are customers running DataProtector to back up their SCO, SINIX, VMS and Windows NT 4 systems. The strength reported by customers use in the **universality** of DataProtector's coverage.

Anecdotally – and I would love to get some real data on this! – it appears that the **system**

administration effort involved in running HP DataProtector is much lower than that of other competing products. System administrators report that they have far more time for other activities when they switch to HP DataProtector.

Part of the reason for this is because the administrators looking after the backup solution don't need to login to the computers they are backing up, nor the machines driving the tape drives. Instead it's quite possible to configure, install and troubleshoot large backup environments entirely from the DataProtector GUI. This means that the backup administrators get to be very **autonomous** and can address problems as soon as they arise.

Areas of weakness

- Desktops, notebooks, tablets
- Archiving
- MySQL, PostgreSQL
- Google Apps, Office365, Salesforce, other cloud-hosted applications
- High availability

On the other hand, there are other parts to a good backup solution which DataProtector does not offer. For example if you put the client software onto a laptop or desktop workstation you can take backups. But there is no simple way for the laptop or desktop to initiate the backup when it comes online. (HP is pushing their Connected Backup solution for this kind of task.)

DataProtector does not make a good archiving system simply because it's not possible to create a backup specification which backs up files more than a certain number of days old. This is a curious oversight because it's certainly possible to backup files *newer* than a certain number of days old: it's called an incremental backup!

DataProtector also lacks support for the most common open source technologies. Even though the internal database is PostgreSQL and it can backup its own internal database, DataProtector cannot backup a PostgreSQL database on another system. Nor is MySQL supported. (Of course in both cases it's possible to configure a database dump job that is run at the start of the backup, and then to backup the dump files, but this is far from a neat solution.)

Infrastructure-as-a-service (IaaS) offerings such as Amazon EC2, Microsoft's Azure, HP Cloud and Google Compute Engine all run real operating systems which HP has agents for. Combined with low-bandwidth replication for deduplicated backups, backing up from these cloud solutions can work quite happily. But there is no way of backing up mail in Google Apps or Office365. Nor is it possible to backup Salesforce data either.

DataProtector's high availability offering is a little restricted. It's not possible to keep a second copy of the internal database live in another site, even though PostgreSQL has the technology to do this. Instead there are all sorts of workarounds required.

1.4 Related products

- DataProtector Express

- Media Operations

- Backup Navigator

- DP Management Pack

There are four other products commonly associated with Data Protector.

DataProtector Express This actually has nothing to do with DataProtector at all, other than sharing a name and causing vast amount of confusion. This was a very cheap application given away with tape drives and Pro-Liant servers. It has now been obsoleted and is essentially impossible to buy.

Media Operations This product keeps track of tape movements, boxing and archiving of tapes. It becomes relevant once an organisation has a few thousand tapes under management, or when there are multiple sites handling tapes is beginning to become a time-consuming issue. HP is not maintaining this software, and it does not work with recent versions of Data protector

Backup Navigator HP's long-term plans for DataProtector appear to be for it to be the centrepiece of their very well funded backup and recovery strategy. The roadmap for this strategy involves doing big data analysis on backups and making automated suggestions for improving backups and resolving any problems. DP Navigator is the first step in that process – collecting large amounts of information.

DP Management Pack This is a Microsoft SCOM component which monitors Data Protector.

2

Lab Environment

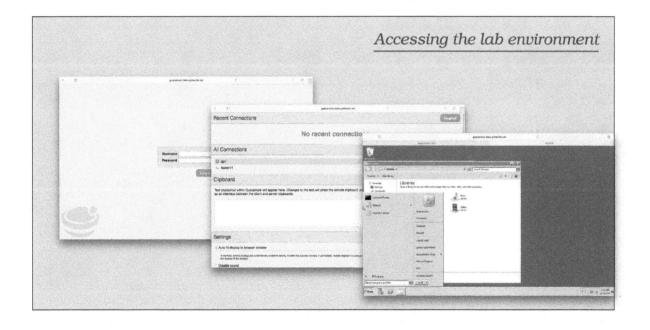

Accessing the lab environment

If you are using the IFOST-supplied lab environment, your instructor will supply you with usernames and passwords.

1. Go to https://guacamole.data-protector.net/guacamole

2. Accept the dodginess of the self-signed certificate.

17

3. Log in with your username.

4. Confirm that you can get to the Windows and Linux systems.

Part II

Deployment

3

Cell Roles

3.1   The Cell Manager and how to install it

The Cell Manager

- The cell is named after the computer running the cell manager software.

- This can be a virtual machine

The first computer that you install DataProtector onto becomes the cell manager. This computer will run the internal database and the scheduler. It will be the computer that initiates all backups in your environment.

DataProtector can be installed with the cell manager in a cluster. Very few customers do this, mostly because backups are very rarely mission-critical: few companies lose money if their backups are not running.

Starting with version 8 it has become very practical to run the cell manager as a virtual machine because the database performance and efficiency is so much better than it was in previous versions. This too makes high availability much simpler because it's possible to use VMware replication technologies such as site recovery manager to maintain DataProtector availability.

Ideally, customers generally put their cell manager in their disaster recovery site instead of their production site. This saves time in a disaster and has very little performance impact on day-to-day operations.

3.2 Windows Installation

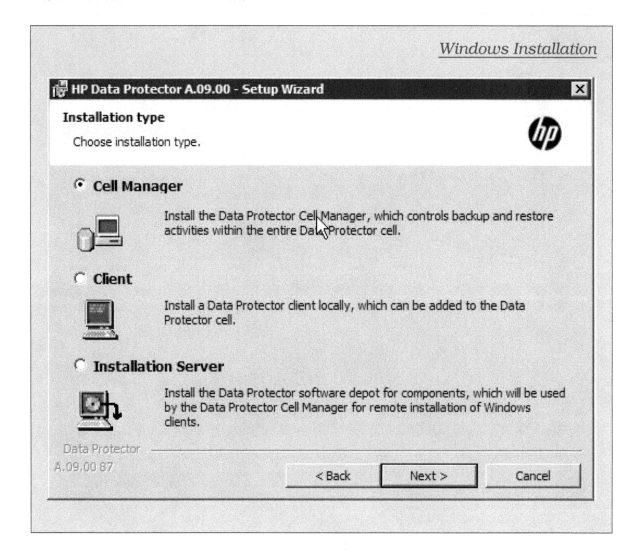

Installing on Windows is just a matter of running the setup program, which can be automated if necessary.

You will first be asked whether you want to install a cell manager, an installation server or a client.

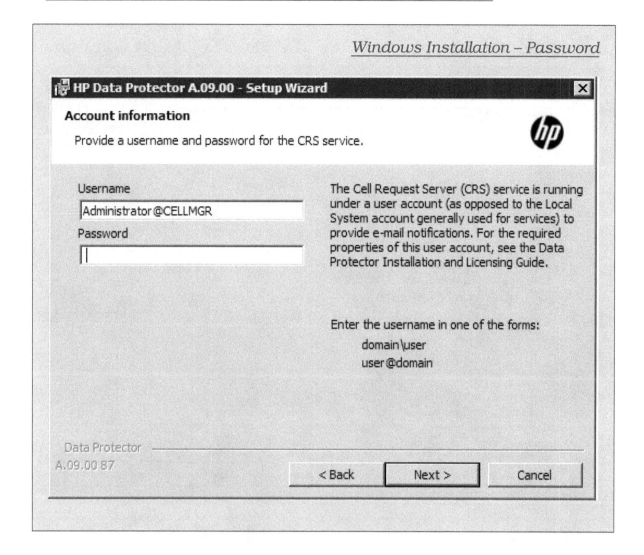

If you choose the cell manager option, then you will be asked for a password for an account to run the DataProtector service with. If possible, it is very convenient if this account has administrator rights on the domain because that will make installing clients via the *push* method much simpler.

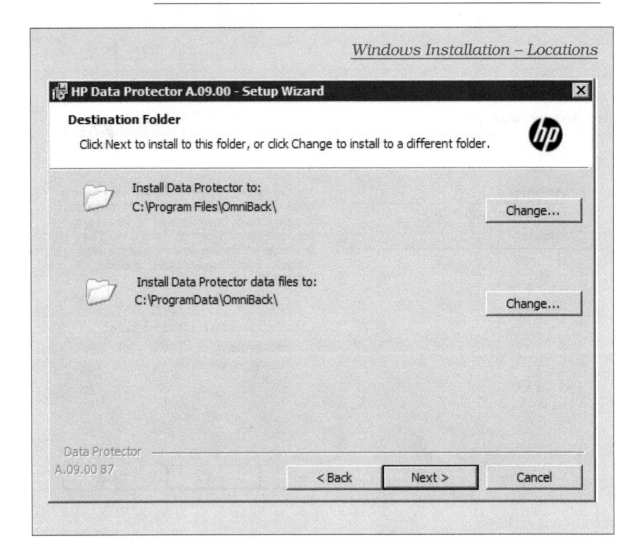

The binaries don't take up very much room and it doesn't really matter whether they are on the C drive or not. The database can be somewhat larger – and if the cell manager is also an installation server as it normally is, then the space required for the data files can be large as well. So it's best practice to install this on to another drive.

In fact, if possible try to store the database on flash drives as the bottleneck on backups involving many tiny files will sometimes be the seek speed of the disks on which the database is held .

In the screenshot above, I have been very lazy and not bothered to change the data file storage location.

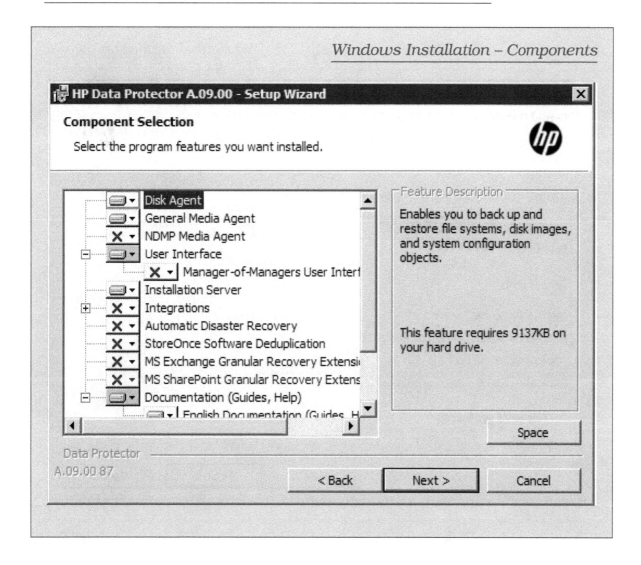

As long as you've installed the installation server, then you can add the other components later if you need to. The screenshot above just shows the defaults, but since many customers choose DataProtector for its de-duplication capabilities quite often they will choose to add the StoreOnce Software De-Duplication option onto the cell manager.

The other very common one is the Automatic Disaster Recovery module as this is required for bare metal recovery.

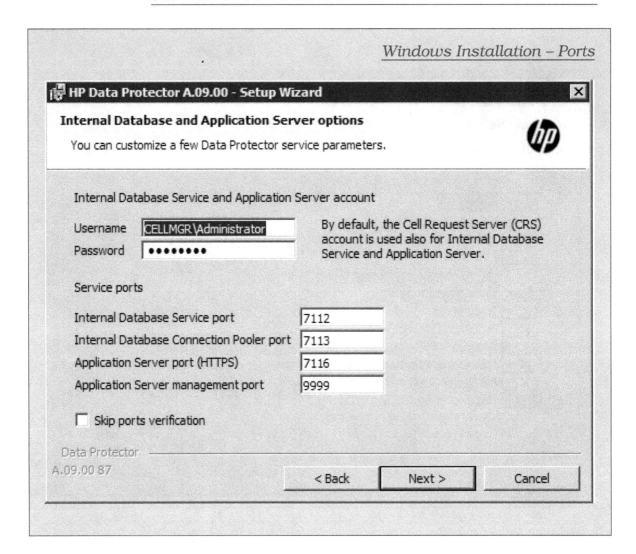

These are the default port numbers. I haven't seen a customer yet who needed to change them.

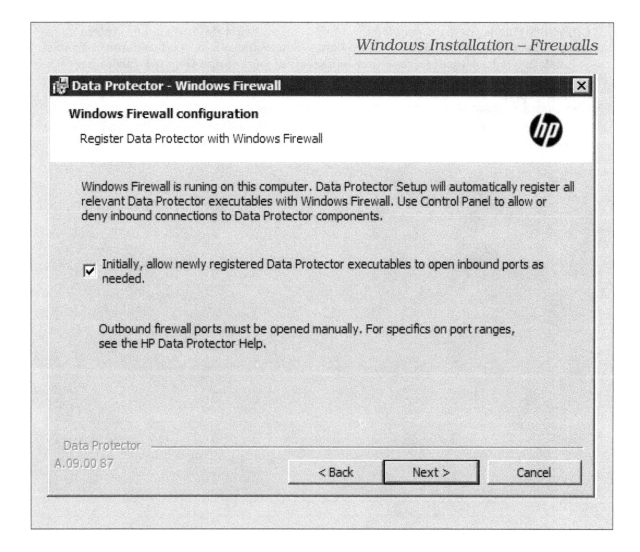

This is only looking at the Windows Firewall. Of course if you have other firewalls in your organisation then communication between cell manager and the clients could be interrupted by them as well.

A brief list of important port numbers to DataProtector:

TCP/5555 Any service running on a client computer (a disk agent, media agent, etc.) is initiated by the cell manager connecting to port 5555 on the client. Integration agents (e.g. Microsft SQL backups) also connect *from* the client where the agent is running *back to* the cell manager.

TCP/9387 This is the command and control port for the StoreOnce software de-duplication system.

TCP/9388 This is the data port for the StoreOnce software de-duplication system.

Random ports from Port 5560 and upwards Where there is a need to connect from a disk agent to a media agent this is the usual port range that the media agent is configured to listen on; therefore the port range that any firewall would need to have open.

TCP/45555 The cell request service (crs) listens on this port number. The Data Protector GUI and the omnistat program need access to this in order to report on the messages

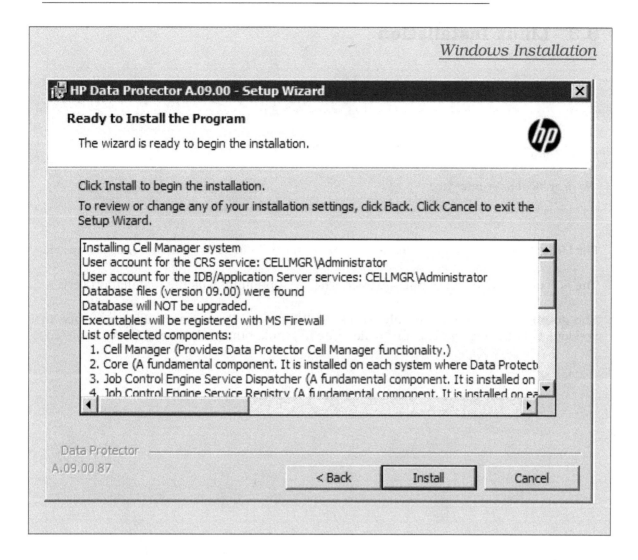

The installation takes only a few minutes.

There are a similar set of screens for performing an upgrade, but the upgrade from version 7 to version 8 is much slower as it has to dump the entire database and then re-import it afterwards.

Upgrading to DataProtector 8.1 is very, very slow because an index not being created at the right time causes a large number of nested sequential table scans.

3.3 Linux Installation

Linux Cell Manager Installation

- `useradd -m hpdp`
- `yum install xinetd`
- `omnisetup.sh -CM -IS`

No graphical user interface

For Linux (and HP-UX) machines the installation media includes a script `omnisetup.sh`.

The `-CM` option installs the cell manager. The `-IS` option installs the installation server.

The graphical user interface only works on Windows. There was a Java interface in versions 6.11 through to version 7 which ran on Linux, but this has been since obsoleted.

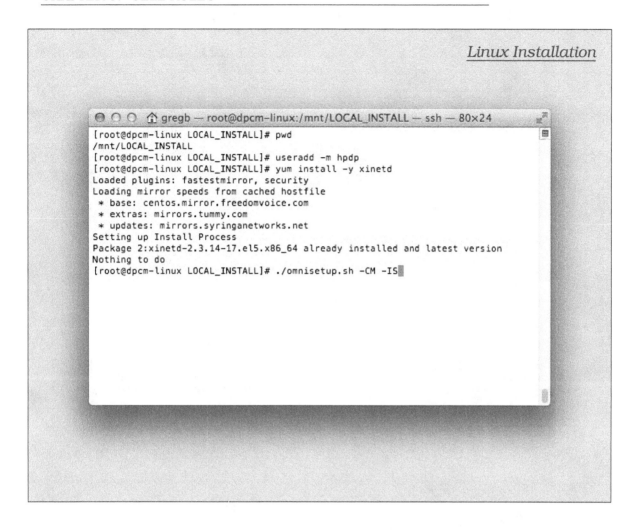

The `useradd` step was not required in earlier versions of DataProtector. But in version 8 and version 9, the internal database is a copy of PostgreSQL running as the user `hpdp`. This can be changed by modifying the `omnisetup.sh` script.

RedHat does not install `xinetd` by default, and in the screenshot above I installed it manually.

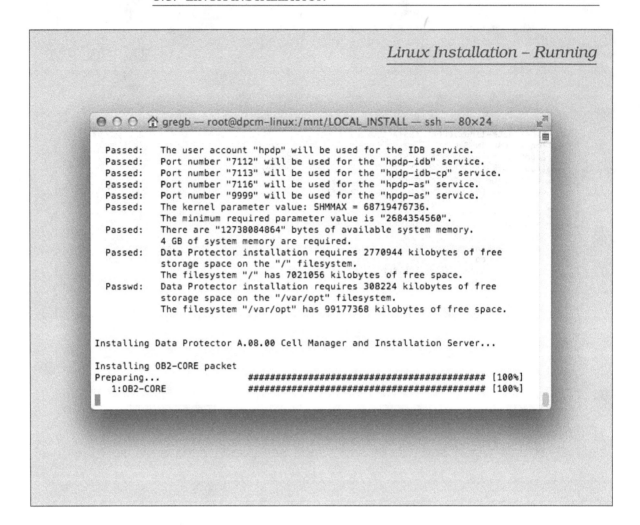

The installation script runs some checks and then begins installing the RPM packages.

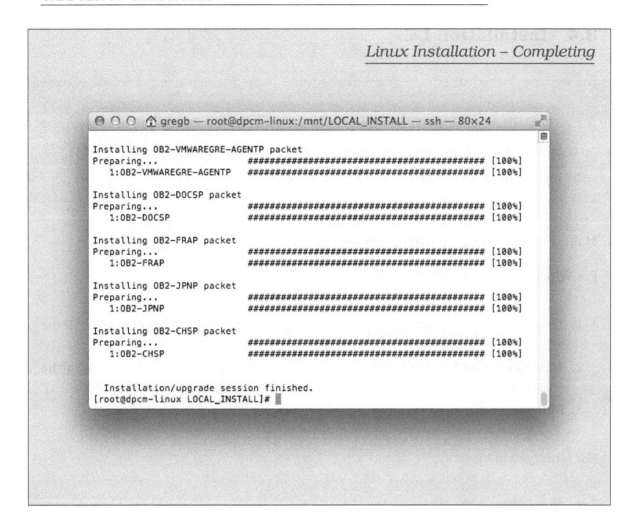

The script takes several minutes to run, and shows progress along the way.

3.4 Installation Lab

> *Installation Lab*
>
> 1. You will be assigned a cell manager dp-cell*N*.data-protector.net
> 2. Install the DataProtector cell manager software.

Make a note of which cell manager you will be using.

For Windows cell managers:

1. There will be a .zip file in the Administrator's *My Documents* folder. Extract all the files from this.

2. Windows 2008R2 (and Windows2012) can use the 64-bit installer, so look in the x8664 folder.

3. Run setup.exe

For Linux cell managers:

1. There will be a file Software_HP_DP_9.00_for_Linux_TD586-15021.iso in root's home directory.

2. mount -o loop /root/Software_HP_DP_9.00_for_Linux_TD586-15021.iso /mnt

3. cd /mnt/LOCAL_INSTALL

4. yum install xinetd

5. useradd -m hpdp

6. ./omnisetup.sh -CM -IS

4

Installing the agents

4.1 Installation Servers

> *DataProtector can push out client software*

- **Push installation** requires an installation server.
- The cell manager includes an installation server by default

	Windows client	**UNIX client**
Windows install server		✕
Linux or HP-UX install server	✕	

Almost every DataProtector cell has access to an installation server. Unlike every other component, an installation server can be freely shared between cells.

Normally there would be a Windows and Linux installation server at every remote site and data center. The Linux installation server will push the agent out to all Unix-like clients (Linux, HP-UX, Solaris, etc.) and the Windows one will push to all versions of Windows.

Not only does the installation server push out initial installations, they are also used for upgrades and for patch deployments.

This will mean that the installation binaries will only be copied over any wide area networks once each.

There are a few exceptions to this:

- Organisations that are Windows only, or UNIX only would not bother having installation servers of the flavour that they'll never use.

- A very small remote site with only one server in it would derive no benefit from having an installation server.

- If your organisation still needs to back up and recover legacy systems (for example Windows 2000 servers) then you may want to keep a DataProtector 6.11 installation server running in order to install the agent to these legacy machines.

- If your organisation has some other very convenient way of deploying software packages quickly, then there may be no advantage to having an installation server to perform this task. (Installation servers can be used for checking a client installation, though, which can be useful in troubleshooting and debugging.)

- Organisations with multiple independent trust domains (for example several Active Directory forests which do not trust each other, or development and production environments which use different secure shell key infrastructure) might need more than one installation server to function.

Installing more installation servers

Windows Run `setup.exe`, choose *Installation Server* option
Linux/HP-UX Run `omnisetup.sh -IS`

Installation servers don't have to match the version number of the cell manager

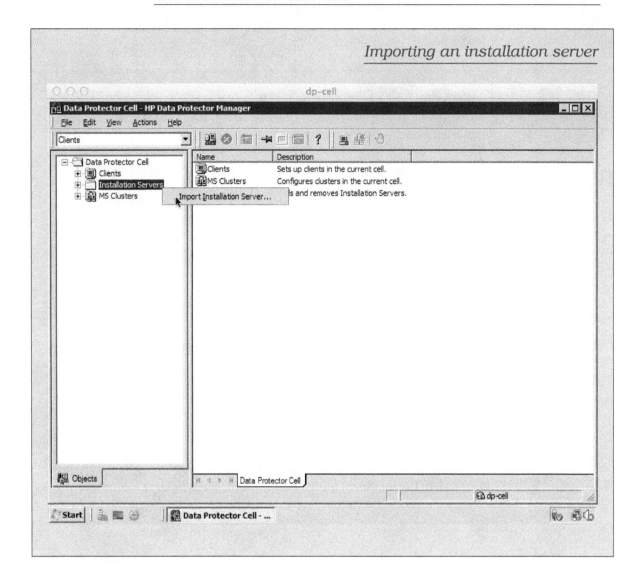

This was a right click on the Installation Servers area in the Clients section of the user interface.

You will then be asked to supply a hostname.

The Linux command line equivalent is: `/opt/omni/bin/omnicc` -import`is` *hostname*

What that just did was to check that the other server was genuinely a DataProtector installation server, and then to add a single plain-text line to the installation servers file:

Linux/HP-UX `/etc/opt/omni/server/cell/installation_servers`
Windows `C:\ProgramData\OmniBack\Config\cell\installation_servers` (unless installed elsewhere).

4.2 Installation Servers Import Lab

LAB: Import an Installation Server

- If you are on Windows, import a Linux installation server
- If you are on Linux, import a Windows installation server

Use either the command-line or the GUI as appropriate.

Look at the `installation_servers` file afterwards.

4.3 Agents

The most important agents

Disk agent What you want to backup

Media agent Where you want to backup to

Cell console Where you want to control it and monitor it from

There are 3 important agents which will be installed in every cell. In fact, they will be on almost every computer.

The **disk agent** (which can be installed as many times as you like on as many machines as you like because it is free) reads files off disk for disk backups. It is also used whenever you are selecting a file or directory for some operation. It also includes the software for performing restores of file level backups.

The cell console is software which you can install on as many machines as you like because it too is free. This is the graphical user interface (on Windows) and the command-line interface on all platforms for which it is available.

The media agent is software which interacts with tape drives and other backup devices. There is no licensing cost associated with installing the media agent, but if you are using the traditional licensing model then you can only run a certain number of media agent processes concurrently. Essentially, in the traditional licensing model you pay for the number of tape drives and tape drive equivalents which are running concurrently.

The next most important agents

Disaster recovery Prepare for bare-metal restores
StoreOnce Because it's awesome

The next most common agents are also installed on nearly every computer in the cell where they are supported.

The automatic disaster recovery module is free as well, and there is really no reason not to install this whenever the disk agent is installed on a Windows or Linux system. On a Windows system when you run a backup of the registry, if the disaster recovery module is installed then DataProtector also captures the information required for disaster recovery: master boot records, partition information, IP address and network information. On Linux systems, a backup of the root filesystem of a system with the automatic disaster recovery module automatically triggers capturing that same information.

The StoreOnce Software System Software System is worth installing on any supported platform (HP-UX, Windows2K8R2 and newer, 64-bit Linux systems). Even if the computer is not going to have a de-duplication storage area, it can interact with storage systems on other computers using low bandwidth protocols. These systems can also act as gateways to allow other (older) computers to make use of the advantages of the StoreOnce system.

VEAgent

One *virtualisation agent* for:

- VMware

- Hyper-V

The virtualisation agent is what is used to backup VMware and Hyper-V servers.

For Hyper-V, generally the virtualisation agent will be installed on the Hyper-V host.

But since it is impossible to install anything onto a ESX host, for VMware backups you install the virtualisation agent onto some other servers (possibly including a virtual machine running inside the VMWare cluster) and it initiates the backup and restore over the network (and over the SAN if it can).

There is no licensing for the virtualisation agent, but there is licensing for whatever it is that it backs up. For example, you need an online extension agent for each ESX host whose VMs you are backing up. (Or, if you are using capacity licensing, then the total size of the VMs that you are backing up needs to be included in your capacity count.)

VMware backups are discussed in more detail later in this course.

The only other supported virtualisation platform is Xen. There is no special integration agent for this, it just consists of pre-exec and post-exec scripts and a traditional disk agent.

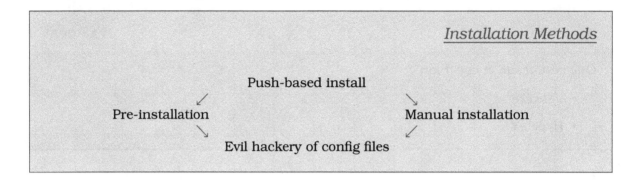

The quickest installation method is pushing from an installation server. This has numerous advantages: you can push the agent out to hundreds of machines simultaneously, you can enter just one set of user names and passwords, and the installation guarantees that future patch upgrades will work correctly.

Alternatively, if you have some other mechanism for installing software in your environment, you could use that to push the software out. The DataProtector software will wait, listening on port 5555 for the incoming connection from a cell manager asking to take control. The incoming connection is known as an import request. You can then use either the GUI or the command line to import the machines you just installed.

It's common that computers in a DMZ may be unable to be pushed to, and also be out of range of any other automated software installation method. For these, often the simplest method is to take the DataProtector CD to them, or just the binaries from the relevant installation folder. As we saw when we were installing the cell manager, there is an option to choose to install a client. You get prompted to provide the name of the cell manager. If you supply this, then the installation process will try to register with the cell manager. If you leave it blank, it will wait for the cell manager to initiate connection to perform an import.

Occasionally you might encounter an environment where no easy option is available to you. Ultimately any trick that can get the software installed, a service listening on port 5555, a client knowing its cell manager and the cell manager knowing the existence of the client is sufficient.

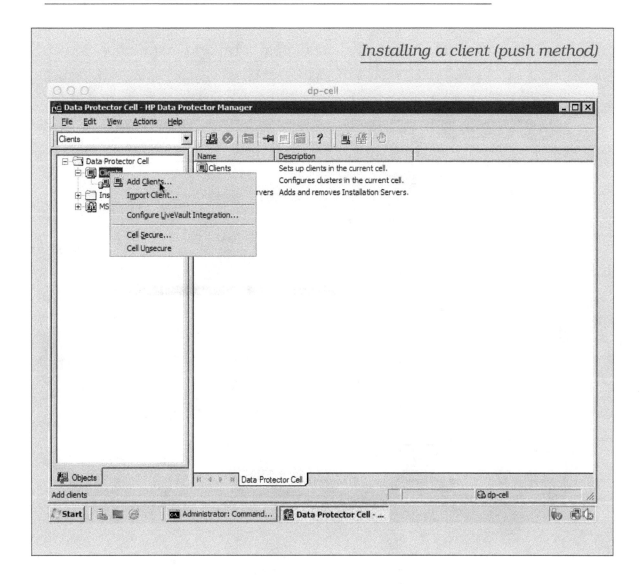

Right click on Clients to bring up this menu.

Add Clients will push out software using an installation server.

Import Client is the menu item to trigger the import of a computer that has already been installed.

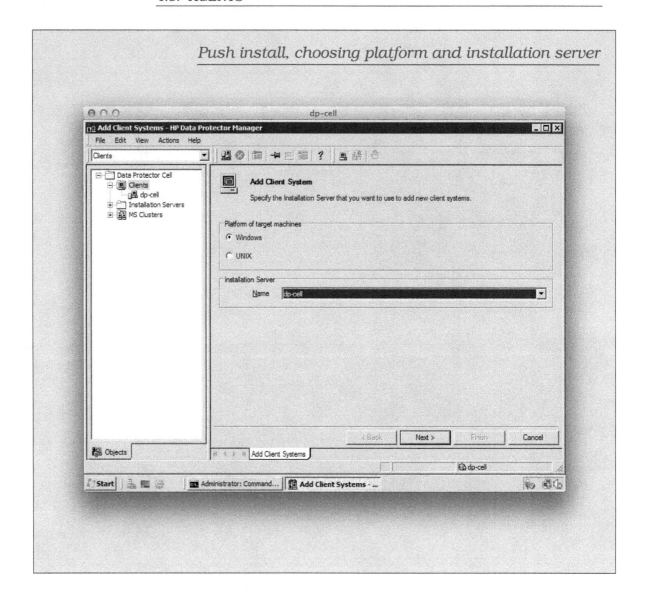

Push install, choosing platform and installation server

One push installation job can only push to one kind of platform. That is, an installation job can simultaneously push to (say) a Windows 2012 machine, some WIN2K8 machines and a Windows 7 desktop; but that same job could not also be pushing to a Solaris machine. Conversely a single installation job can push to Linux, Solaris and HP UX boxes at the same time, but could not include a Windows server in the job.

Specifying the installation server platform changes the drop-down list of installation servers.

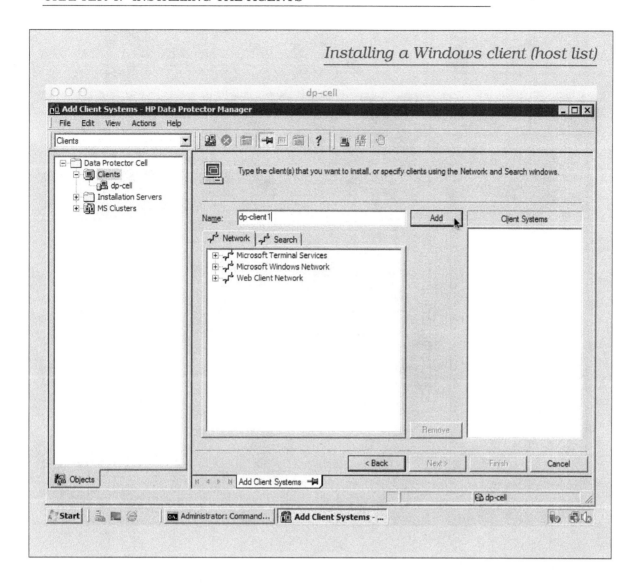

You can enter the hostname and press add. Or you can browse through the network of Windows machines, or search. You can repeat this as many times as you need to.

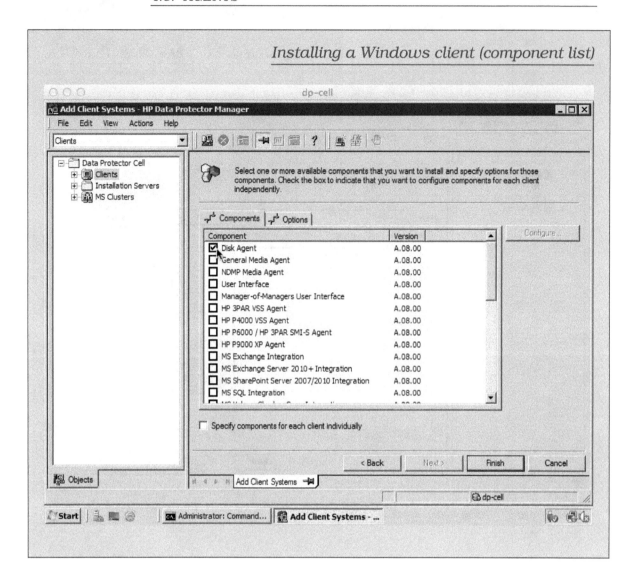

Installing a Windows client (component list)

You definitely want to install a disk agent; add other agents here as required.

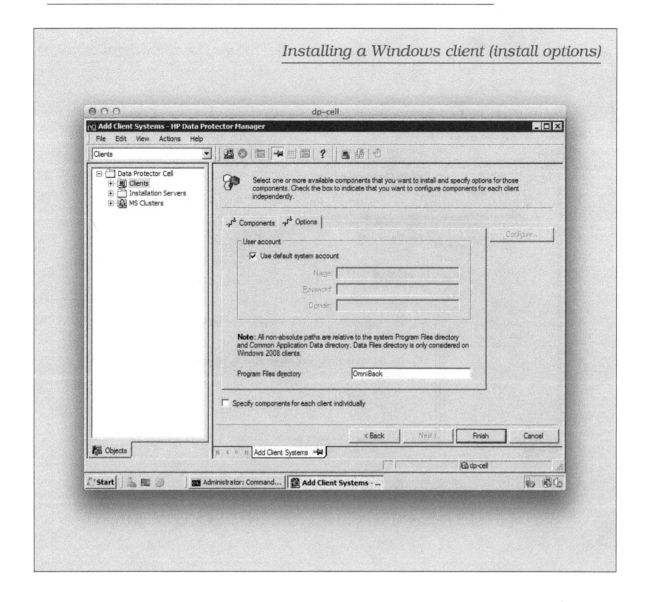

Note that I clicked on the options tab to get here. If you are installing across a domain (i.e. the target machine does not give administrative rights to the user account that you are running DataProtector with) then you can set the username and password for the connection here.

You can also choose an alternate directory for the installation binaries.

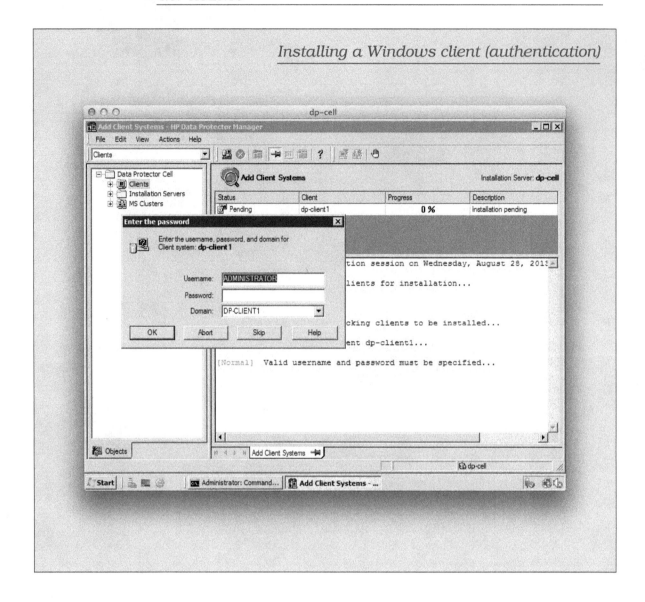

Installing a Windows client (authentication)

If there is a permissions or authentication problem you will be prompted for a username and password individually for each machine that had an issue.

Common reasons for this:

- You are running DataProtector with a local account. Obviously this doesn't have domain privileges. - You are running DataProtector with a domain account, but the machines you are installing to do not trust that domain. In the example above, the target machine is actually in its own workgroup.

- Firewalls are blocking port 445, which is preventing DCOM from working properly.

- You are trying to install to a WIN2K8 system which has UAC turned on. You give the right credentials, but since there is no way for the UAC prompt to appear, it fails.

- You are trying to install to a Windows desktop system running in simple share mode.

  You can also use the `omniinetpasswd` to provide default credentials for all installs

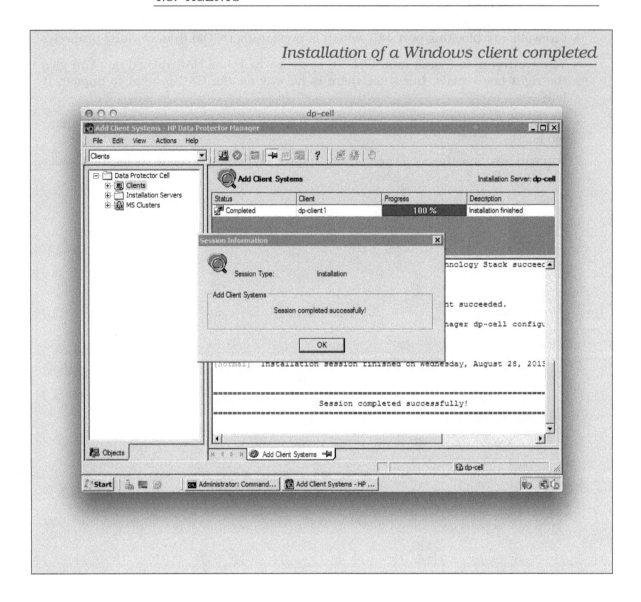

Installation of a Windows client completed

This has updated both the client and the cell manager.

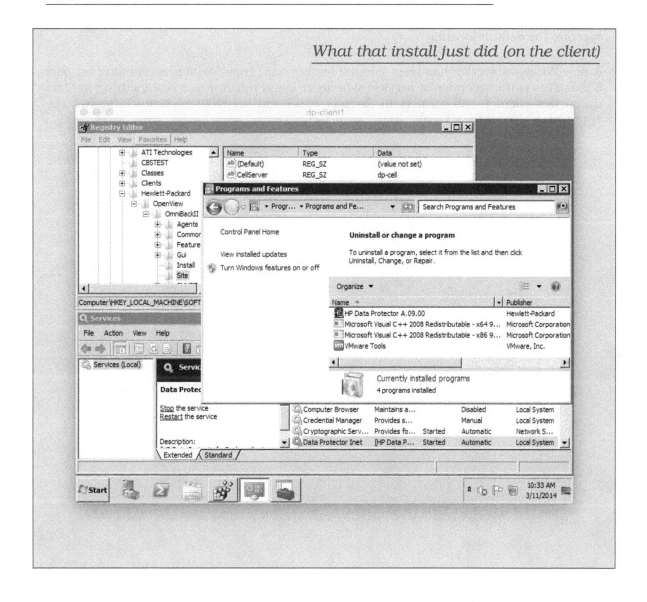

What that install just did (on the client)

As part of the install process the installer sets the registry key on the client `HKEY_LOCAL_MACHINE` `\SOFTWARE\Hewlett-Packard\OpenView\OmniBackII\Site\CellServer` to the hostname of the cell manager: `dp-cell`. This is the only place on the client where the cell manager defined. (There is an optional `cell_secure` file used for security as well which could happen to have the cell manager in it as well.) If you want to move a client from one cell to another, essentially this is the only registry key that needs to be modified on the client. Also if this registry key is missing (or deleted), the client will be happy to see itself imported into another cell.

The binaries have been installed into `C:\Program Files\Omniback`, because we did not override the default location.

A new Windows service has been created (called `OmniInet`), which is listening on port 5555. This is the *receptionist* service: whenever DataProtector needs something to start up on this client it will connect in via port 5555 and the INET service will spawn the appropriate process.

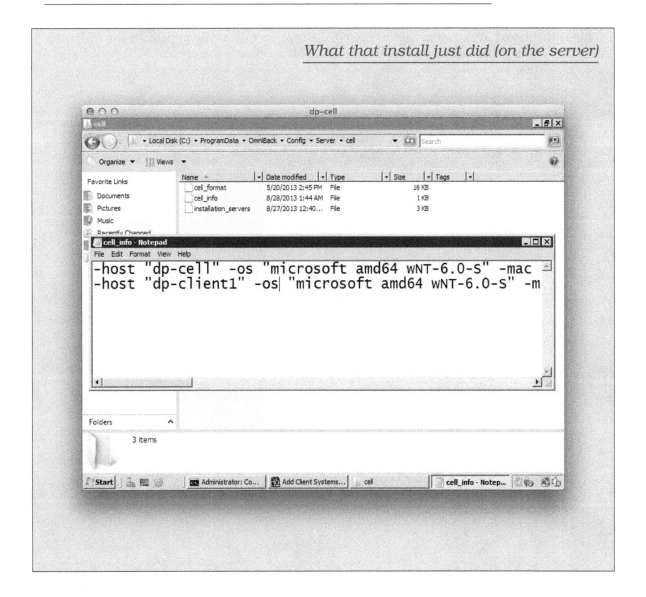

What that install just did (on the server)

The cell info file is the master list of all members of the DataProtector cell.

Windows cell managers C:\ProgramData\OmniBack\Config\cell\cell_info
Linux/HP-UX cell managers /etc/opt/omni/server/cell/cell_info

Importing a client simply adds the relevant registry entry (as discussed on the previous page) to the client and adds a line into the cell_info file on the cell manager.

This file also records the ethernet MAC address of the client (so that wake-on-LAN packets can be sent) and the versions of each component which is installed on the client.

This is displayed in the client list in the GUI. Changes to this file appear in the GUI after the GUI is disconnected and reconnected in order to clear its cache.

Importing pre-installed clients and evil hackery

- `omnicc -import_host` *hostname*
- Or GUI (right click on Clients)
- Or edit the `cell_info` file.

These are used when:

- You have an imaging system (such as Altiris) or an automated network boot installer which creates servers pre-populated with software. You add the relevant DataProtector agent software packages to the build, and then you can import them into the cell later when you need them.

- If you use VMware templates, or if you run servers in the cloud that get built from block images you can automate these servers being added to and removed from the cell.

Where the Windows media is

\\ *installserver* \OmniBack = `C:\ProgramData\OmniBack\Depot`
i386 folder For 32-bit Windows systems
x8664 folder For 64-bit Windows systems (Windows 2008R2 and newer are all 64-bit only)
ia64 folder For Itanium Windows systems (very rare)

Ignore the DR folders; they are only used when preparing disaster recovery media.

4.4 Installation Lab

Install a Windows client

- You will be assigned a client `dp-clientN.data-protector.net`
- Use either the GUI or a local install to install this system.
- Import if necessary
- Look at the client-side registry key and the cell manager's `cell_info` file.

Registry key `HKEY_LOCAL_MACHINE\SOFTWARE\Hewlett-Packard\OpenView\OmniBackII\`
   `Site\CellServer`

Windows cell manager's cell info file `C:\ProgramData\OmniBack\Config\ cell\cell_info`

Linux/HP-UX cell manager's cell info file `/etc/opt/omni/server/cell/ cell_info`

Linux / Unix install prereqs

- `OB2_SSH_ENABLED=1` in `/opt/omni/.omnirc` on **installation server**

- Install `inetd` or `xinetd` on client

- Copy install server's `root/.ssh/id_dsa.pub` to client's `root/.ssh/authorized_keys`

- Make sure SSH doesn't give any prompt (e.g. accepting host keys)

The default installation method that Data Protector uses is the very ancient and insecure `remsh` protocol (also known as `rsh`)!

To tell Data Protector to use SSH instead, add a line `OB2_SSH_ENABLED=1` to the file `/opt/omni/.omnirc`. Create this file if you need to, or you can copy `/opt/omni/omnirc.TMPL`. You do not need to restart any services to make this take effect.

Data Protector assumes that the client you are installing to already has `inetd` or `xinetd` in place, and will simply fail if they aren't. Many modern Linux distributions don't include this, so it can be an issue. Use whatever method you would normally use to install this (e.g. `yum install -y xinetd`).

The installation server needs to be able to SSH to `root` on the client system, so set up SSH equivalence. If there is no `.ssh/id_dsa.pub` or `.ssh/id_rsa.pub` file on the installation server, create a new set of keys with `ssh-keygen -t dsa`.

Usually what happens know is that you will test that the SSH session works, and you will be prompted to save the client's host keys. This is sufficient to let the installation server proceed. But sometimes the easiest way of making sure that you aren't prompted for keys is to add a line `StrictHostKeyChecking no` to the top of the installation server's `root/.ssh/ssh_config`.

The binaries are transferred via SCP, so tunnels (e.g. with `corkscrew`, `netcat` or others) work fine.

After the installation is completed you can remove the SSH key on the client.

Linux / Unix GUI installation

- Initated from Windows console

- Same process as for Windows, except no password prompting

Once the Linux or HP-UX installation is set up, you can initiate installations to Linux or UNIX systems by walking through the Windows console GUI just as if it were an install to a Windows system. Simply select a UNIX installation server and then proceed.

Linux / Unix command-line push

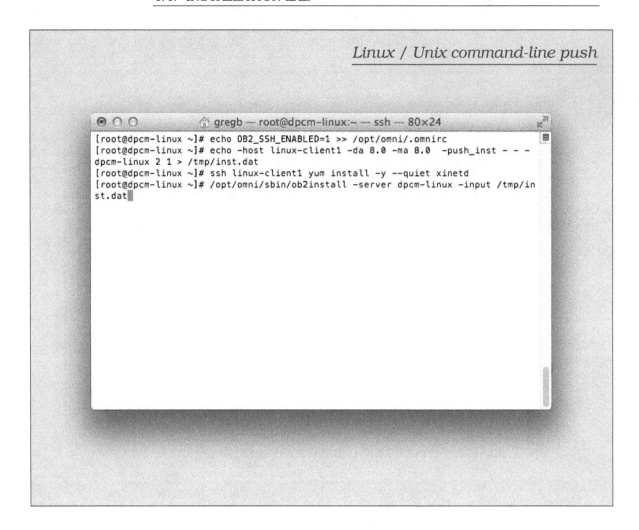

```
[root@dpcm-linux ~]# echo OB2_SSH_ENABLED=1 >> /opt/omni/.omnirc
[root@dpcm-linux ~]# echo -host linux-client1 -da 8.0 -ma 8.0  -push_inst - - -
dpcm-linux 2 1 > /tmp/inst.dat
[root@dpcm-linux ~]# ssh linux-client1 yum install -y --quiet xinetd
[root@dpcm-linux ~]# /opt/omni/sbin/ob2install -server dpcm-linux -input /tmp/in
st.dat
```

The syntax of the file given as an argument to -input is documented in the ob2install man page.

Linux / Unix command-line local pull install

```
omnisetup.sh -install cc,da,autodr
```

The media used for a Linux or HP-UX cell manager can also be used to do a local installation of a Data Protector agent.

The common components to install are:

cc The command-line tools (the same cell console software as exists for Windows except for the GUI)

da Disk agent

ma Media agent

autodr Disaster recovery module

StoreOnceSoftware The StoreOnce software system, available only on 64-bit Linux systems

veagent Virtualisation backup agent

Linux media location

Media is in `/opt/omni/databases/vendor` on the install server:

agent	vendor	arch	os	version	This is an RPM!
↓	↓	↓	↓	↓	↓
da/	gpl/	x86_64/	linux-x86-64/	A.09.00/	packet.Z

Agents to include: `omnicf` + `da` + ...

Bizarrely enough, the `packet.Z` file for Linux is actually an RPM file which can be installed independently. It *isn't* a file compressed with traditional Unix compress.

Likewise, the HP-UX `packet.Z` is actually a gzip'ed software distributor-format file, ready to be installed with `swinstall`.

Part III

Backing up

StoreOnce

5.1 Background

StoreOnce De-duplication technology features
• Low-memory
• In-line, real-time
• Global

StoreOnce is a de-duplication technology developed by HP in their Bristol labs. It is noted for its very low memory consumption, which means that larger amounts of data can be stored on low-end equipment.

It is an in-line technology; as data is written to the StoreOnce device (or software store) it is immediately processed. It is not like the older low-end D2D technologies that HP used to sell where the de-duplication was done after the backup completed.

It is also a global de-duplication, which means that if the same block of data appears in 2 totally independent backups (for example a block in a VMware VMDK backup and inside a file in a file system backup) that the data is only stored once. (Unlike some competitor products – such as Veeam where the de-duplication only occurs within a backup, or within a backup of the same type.)

It is a disk-only system; there is no deduplication on writing to tapes.

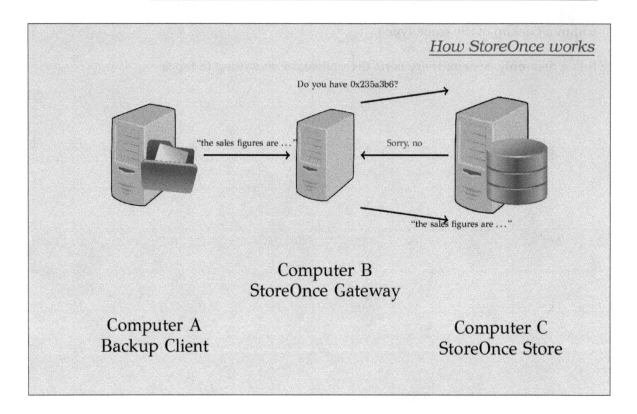

One of the interesting aspects of HP's StoreOnce technology is that the engine that calculates checksums can be run on servers away from where the actual data restored.

The de-duplication pipeline looks like this. Computer A reads from its disk and sends that data in raw form to computer B. Computer B calculates various checksums of the data it was sent and then sends just those checksums to computer C. Computer C checks to see whether it already has stored any data with that checksum, and if it has then it tells computer B not to bother sending the data. Only if the checksums don't match anything previously stored at computer C will C tell B to send the data.

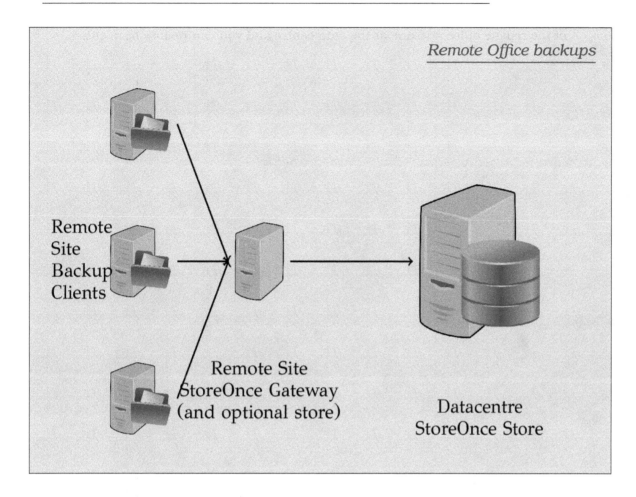

The most common use of this StoreOnce technology is to support backing up of remote branch offices. There are several variations of this.

- If there is no concern about restoring data over the WAN link then one or more servers at the remote site have the StoreOnce software installed on them and they act as gateways to a store in the central data centre. Since the only data being sent across the slow link during day-to-day backup operations is only the data which is not previously been sent, a full backup only sends about as much data as an incremental would.

- If you have less than 20 TB to backup, and have sufficient storage at the remote office – and it can be very low tier storage, such as external USB hard disks – then one server at the remote office acts as a StoreOnce store. Then you create a copy job that runs automatically at the end of the backup to bring that data back to the data centre. Again, each full backup being copied will only send roughly the same amount of data as an incremental would. You end up with 2 copies of the data, one of the remote office and one at the data centre and you can restore from either.

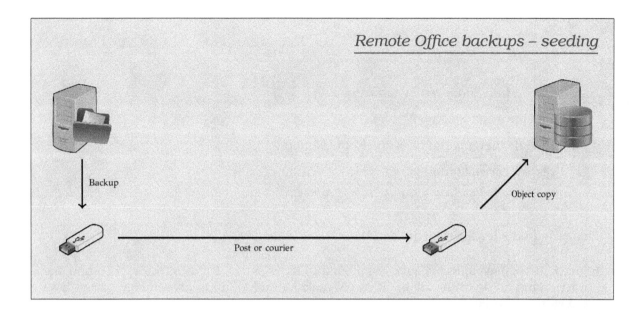

Remote office backup will often involve pre-seeding the data centre's copy of the data. This is done by running a backup at the remote site targeting some kind of removable media.

For example, if there is already a tape drive at that site this could be used. Alternatively, DataProtector supports using removable USB storage with the File Jukebox device.

The removable media is brought back to the datacentre and copied (using a copy job) into the StoreOnce store.

It doesn't particularly matter if there is a delay between the removable media backup and the beginnings of the low bandwidth WAN link backup, since the copied media will have most of the data and therefore most of the next backup will not need to be sent across the slow link.

Copying is discussed later, on page 171 (in section 9).

Remote office – Incremental forever

1. Turn on *Use Enhanced Incremental*

2. Schedule a full backup.

3. Schedule incremental backups from then on.

4. Create a consolidation job to synthesise full backups

This only works for file systems.

It used to be used quite regularly for small offices when DataProtector only had file libraries (and no de-duplication). It rarely makes much of an improvement against low-bandwidth deduplication.

When you shouldn't use StoreOnce

- Remote office Exchange servers

- Remote office File shares

- Audio and video data

- Scientific data (scans, measurements, etc.)

While it might look sensible to backup Microsoft Exchange servers in remote offices using StoreOnce technology, there are usually better alternatives. (Apart from the obvious ones of replacing a branch office Exchange server with Office 365 or Google Apps.) A remote branch office server is a single point of failure and you would sensibly want to have its availability group replicated back to your datacentre anyway. The Exchange agent can be configured to backup a specific availability group, or the availability group with the greatest replication latency (which will almost always be the most distant server).

Similarly, it usually does not make any sense to backup the file shares from a remote office using StoreOnce technology. A better strategy is to use Microsoft's DFS Replication as it supplies redundancy and availability in the event of the remote site office server failing. Of course, if the remote site is not part of the same Active Directory environment this would be impossible; and it still makes sense to use StoreOnce technology to keep a copy of important system files (for example the C: drive and registry).

If you do not have any duplications in your data then StoreOnce is very inefficient. It will cost far more than the writing out to tape. If the data is unchanging (for example audio recordings of telephone calls, recorded video footage for a television studio, or data from scientific instruments) then a strategy of having a few major full backups, a few major incremental backups and numerous differentials in between them all being sent out to tape is a much better strategy.

Having said that, early in 2013 I went to help one of the universities in Brisbane with backing up the enormous amount of data they were collecting from their imaging systems. It turned out that they were doing such original research that there was less duplication in the file shares devoted to LaTeX documents then there was in the file share devoted to their imaging data, because they were often imaging overlapping sections of the same object!

5.2 Preparing for StoreOnce

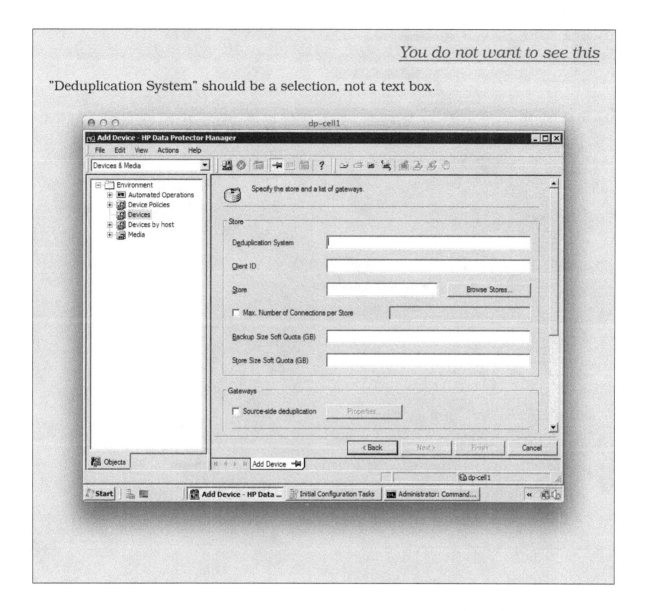

This DataProtector cell has no computers which have the StoreOnce component installed.

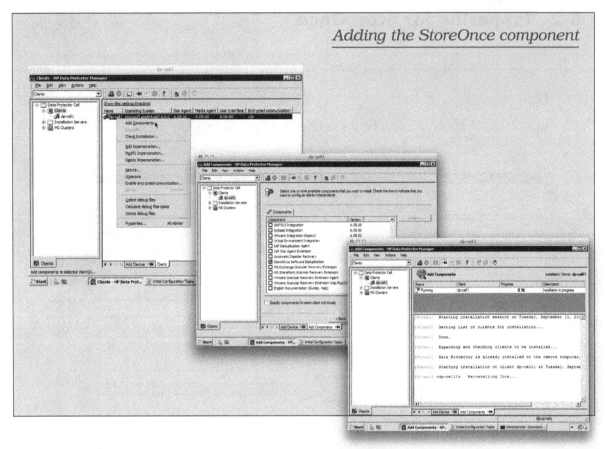

Adding the StoreOnce component

Adding a component is usually quite simple:

- From the Clients context, right click on the computer you want to use.

- Select Add Components.

- Choose an installation server (if there is more than one)

- Select the StoreOnce component

- Hit Finish

It becomes slightly more complicated if you cannot push the agent out. This could be because you don't have an installation server or because the server you want push to cannot access any of the installation servers that you do have.

For isolated Windows servers, you can always rerun the setup program from the DataProtector media. You are given the option to modify an existing installation.

For isolated Linux servers, you can run `omnisetup.sh -install StoreOnceSoftware`

5.3   StoreOnce Prep Lab

LAB: Install the StoreOnce component

- Find out if any computers in your cell have the `StoreOnce Deduplication` software installed on them. (e.g. right click and get the properties of each computer)

- Add the StoreOnce component to your cell manager if it is not already there.

5.4   Creating a StoreOnce Device

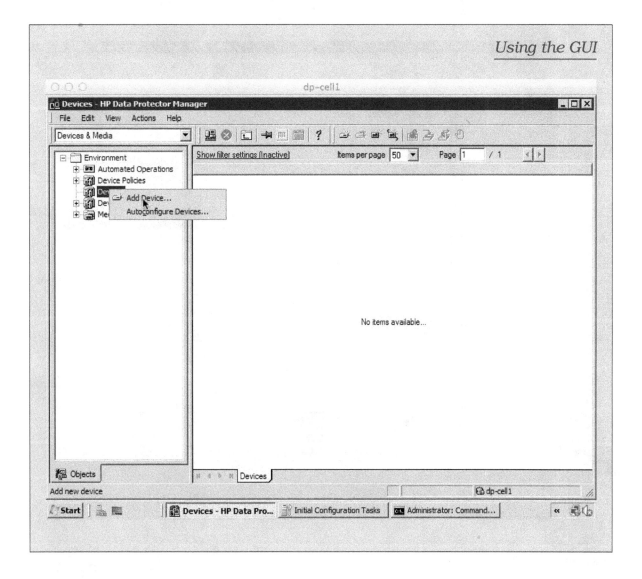

This is a right-click on Devices.

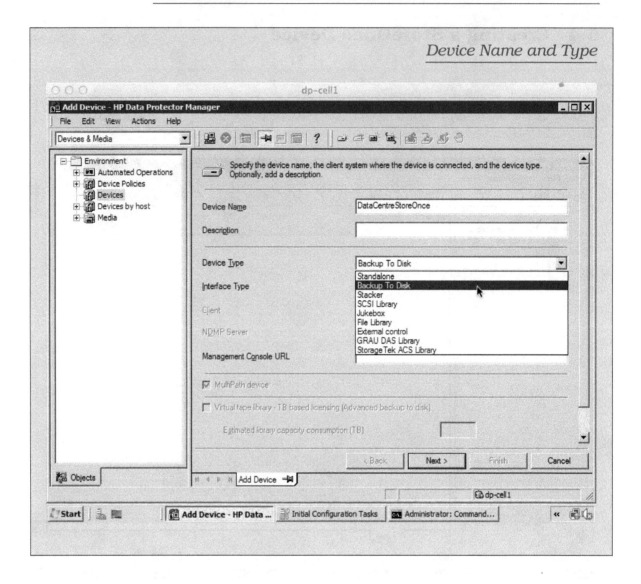

Device Name and Type

We filled in the Device Name. It can have spaces in it, but it is convenient for command-line applications for it to be a single word.

The Description field is blank; there is no good reason for this, it was simply that I couldn't think of any interesting description to put here.

Importantly, we need to select the Device Type to be Backup to Disk.

A brief description of the other alternatives:

(Backup to

Standalone A single stand-alone tape drive.

Stacker An ancient tape library where the only robotic command understood was *use next tape*.

SCSI Library Almost every tape library. Generally you would create this by autoconfiguration, which is what we'll do later.

Jukebox This is used primarily to support backup to USB hard disks. The general idea is similar to a SCSI library, but where the management of which media is used is controlled by a human being rather than a robot.   :File Library Generally this is legacy: prior to StoreOnce devices being available, this is how backup to disk was done. :External control This is used in the HP Cloud and in Amazon's EC2 in backing up to their volume store. :GRAU DAS Library Essentially unused. :StorageTek ACS Library Essentially unused. :SmartCache (Not shown in the screenshot above). Introduced in version 9, this uncompressed format makes file-level recovery from VMDKs much faster.

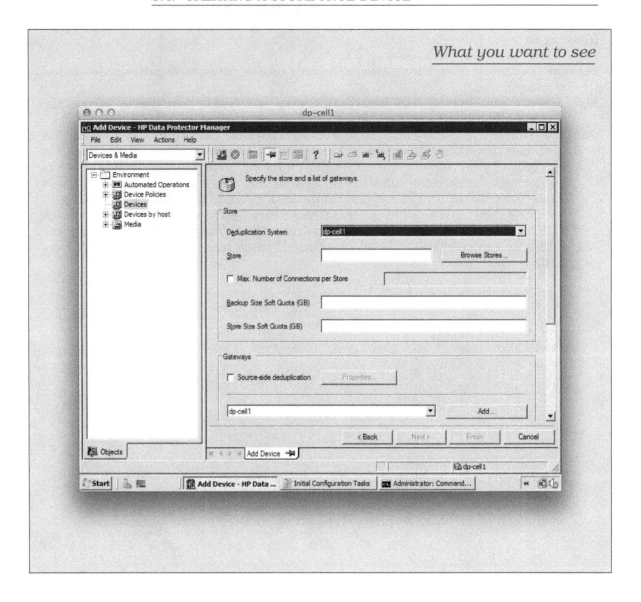

Note that the Duplication System is now a selection pulldown. Also you will see that the Gateways section has more entries in it. Compare against the screenshot on page 75 (in section 5.2).

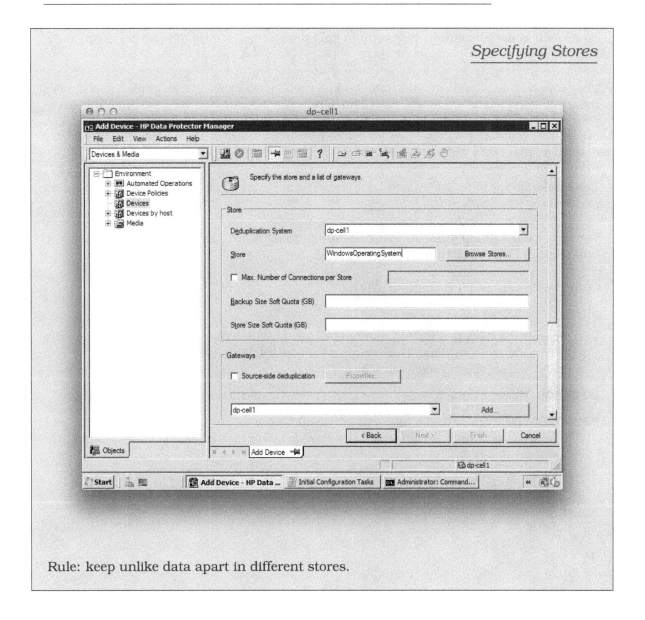

Rule: keep unlike data apart in different stores.

The *Browse Stores* button will do nothing because there are no stores in place yet. You simply enter a name here.

Smaller stores are more efficient than larger stores.

There will be a noticeable performance difference between 1 x 20 TB store versus 20 x 1 TB store – the latter will be much faster.

So while it is not absolutely necessary to split data across stores, it is a very good idea if you can.

There are certain islands of data that you know will not overlap: for example, no Windows binary is going to be the same as a Linux binary. It would be very surprising if there were even a couple of moderate sized chunks within binaries that were common across operating systems. So these can be backed up into different stores without losing any de-duplication. This will lead to better performance as well.

The total amount of data that can be stored in a software store is 20 TB per machine no matter how you divide it up.

For larger amounts of storage, you can either create more stores on other machines or buy some of HP's other solutions.

In increasing order of price, these are:

VSA StoreOnce This is a virtual machine which provides the same functionality as the HP hardware solutions. These support up to 100TB of raw storage space, but you must supply the storage yourself.

D2D4500 These are the low-end physical hardware solutions for deduplicated storage.

B6200/B6500 These are the high-end physical hardware solutions for deduplicated storage, when you need petabytes of raw storage space and have very high I/O requirements.

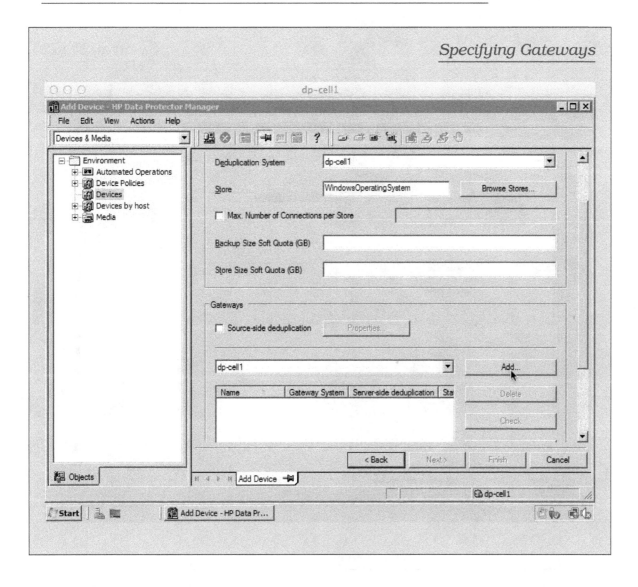

Refer back to the diagram on page 68 (in section 5.1).

In the lower half of the screen we are defining which machines will calculate checksums of the data; the server listed as the Deduplication System is server where the data is stored.

It is fairly common to want to have a gateway on the same machine where the store is, not least because it makes debugging network issues much easier!

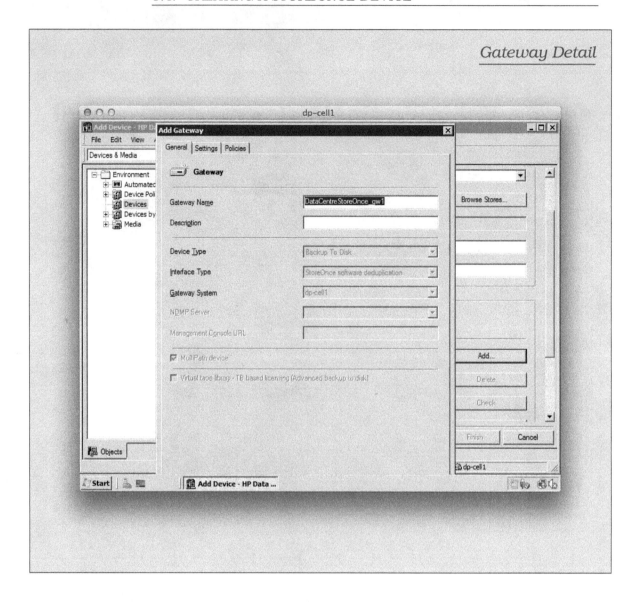

For a gateway which is running on the same machine as the store, the default parameters work well enough.

I prefer to change the name of the gateway to something like *storename*`via`*servername*, because it makes it very clear and more consistent for low bandwidth replication later. In the example above I have not changed anything.

(There is an OK button at the bottom of the active window which cannot be seen in the screenshot.)

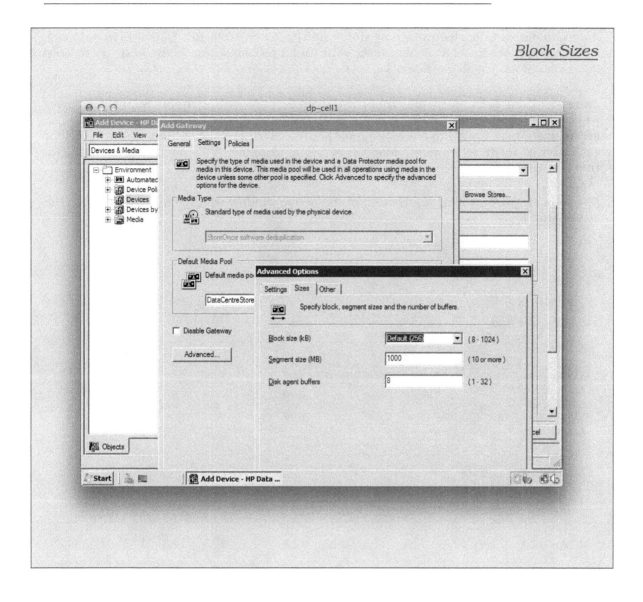

We reached the screen above by selecting the Settings tab and then hitting the Advanced button.

The StoreOnce technology has a varying block size and will de-dupe chunks smaller than the block size listed here if there is a fragment which is in common with data that has been seen before.

However, when we're copying to and from tape the block size becomes very important as LTO tapes perform very badly with smaller block sizes. Also there is a performance hit associated with repackaging from one sized blocks to another.

A good block size for deduplication stores is 512 kB or 1024 kB. LTO-5 drives do well with that sort of size as well. Whatever your initial testing shows is the best, try to keep it consistent across all your devices.

The other thing to be aware of is that the clients that are writing to this StoreOnce device will need to allocate at a shared memory segment `Disk-agent-buffers * Block-size` kB in size. There are quite a few common platforms which have a limit of only 4 MB for each shared memory segment: Mac OS X is one example. This isn't a major problem: these parameters can be overridden for each backup specification.

(There is an OK button at the bottom of the active window which cannot be seen in the screenshot.)

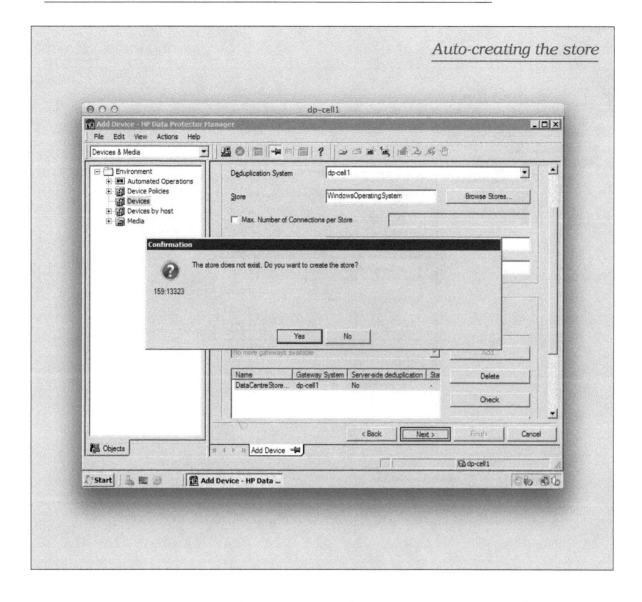

DataProtector correctly identifies that this is the first store ever to be created on that server and prompts us to create it and to configure the StoreOnce software.

After we have done this step, the *Browse Stores* button will work and will show us one store: *WindowsOperatingSystem*.

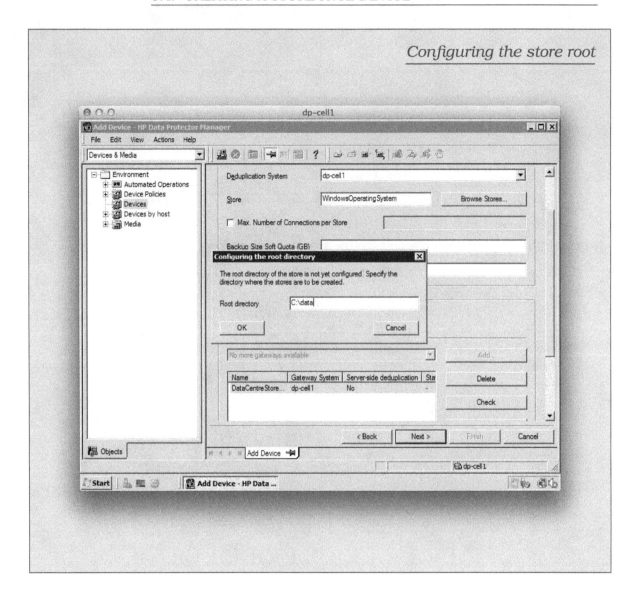

Configuring the store root

It is very unusual to put the store on the `C:` drive. Since the StoreOnce store cannot spread across different volumes make sure that the folder that you are choosing here is one that can be resized and extended. For Windows systems a `D:` drive backed by a storage array is ideal. For Linux systems make sure this is an LVM logical volume – but if anyone plucks up the courage to try this with btrfs I'd love to know how you get on.

You only set this path once for each server running the StoreOnce software. In fact if you change your mind and want to move to another volume there is no way of doing this through the user interface.

The folder you choose will have a folder created in it entitled *StoreOncelibrary*.

For reference, here is the procedure for relocating the StoreOnce root folder:

1. Stop the StoreOnceSoftware daemon / service. On Windows, go into the Services MSC, locate the StoreOnceSoftware service and then stop it.

   On Linux systems run: `/opt/omni/lbin/StoreOnceSoftwared stop`

   Backups to this device will now fail.

2. Manually move the data to the new directory. Since no backups are writing to it, this is safe to do.

3. Run `StoreOnceSoftware --configure_store_root --path=` *new-directory* `--force`

4. Restart the StoreOnceSoftware daemon / service. On Windows, go into the Services MSC, locate the StoreOnceSoftware service and then start it.

   On Linux systems run: `/opt/omni/lbin/StoreOnceSoftwared start`

5. Backups will now work again. Try a tiny backup first to confirm it.

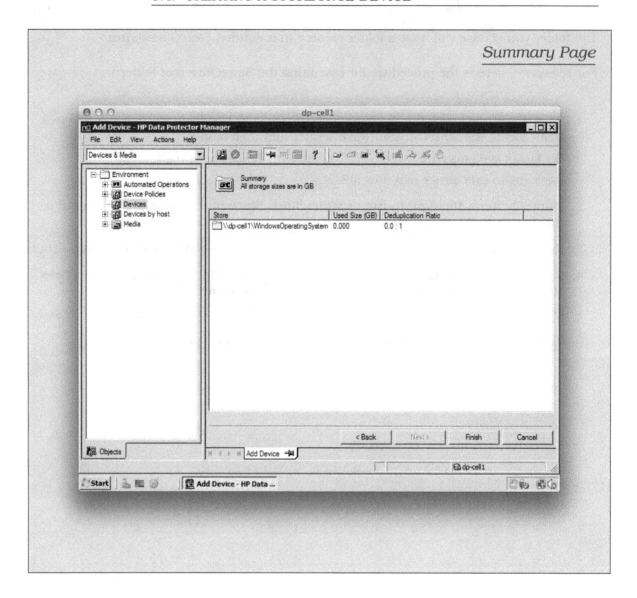

When you press finish, the store will be created.

5.5   StoreOnce Device Lab

LAB: Create a StoreOnce Device

- Create a folder on your cell manager called `D:\data`

- Create a backup-to-disk device on your cell manager called *OSBinariesB2D*. Create the store name as *OSBinariesStore*.

- Create a second backup-to-disk device called *DataB2D* which has a store name of *DataStore*.

- Look inside `D:\data`

- Run the command `StoreOnceSoftware -list_stores`

If you haven't already added the StoreOnce component to your cell manager, do so now.

Filesystem Backups and the Scheduler

6.1 Using the GUI to create a specification file

Kinds of backups

- Filesystem
- Internal Database
- SQL
- Oracle
- Exchange
- ...

HP DataProtector began its life as 2 products in a company called Apollo, which HP bought in the mid-1980s. The 2 products were called OmniBack (which was a product designed to backup large numbers of workstations) and another called OmniBack Turbo (which backed up databases).

As a result even today different kinds of backups cannot be mixed into the same session. That is a file system backup cannot also contain an Oracle backup, and an Oracle backup cannot contain any Exchange backup objects.

Only 2 kinds of backups can spread over multiple servers: file system backups and SharePoint backups (and they are still backups within the same farm).

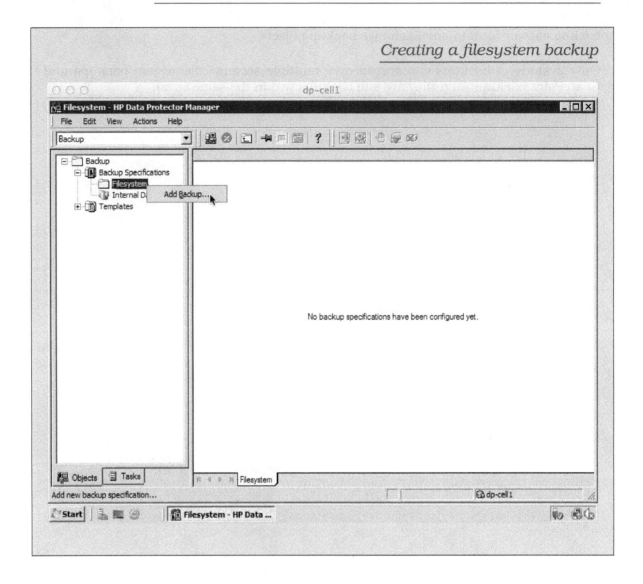

Creating a filesystem backup

If you have not installed the SQL agent on any computers then you will not see an option for creating a new SQL backup. Likewise for Exchange, Oracle, SharePoint and all the other backup integrations.

Since you cannot have DataProtector cell which does not have a cell manager, and cannot do anything unless there is at least one disk agent installed somewhere, you are guaranteed to at least have the option of creating file system backups and internal database backups.

In DataProtector version 7 and earlier the internal database backup was a kind of file system backup. The upgrade process from DataProtector 7 to DataProtector 8 automatically creates an internal database backup based on the definitions found in the configuration being upgraded. Unfortunately, the initial release to market version of DataProtector 8 didn't always do this upgrade correctly and in particular if you had set an owner of the file system backup then the internal database backup created by the upgrade process would have an owner as well, which is invalid.

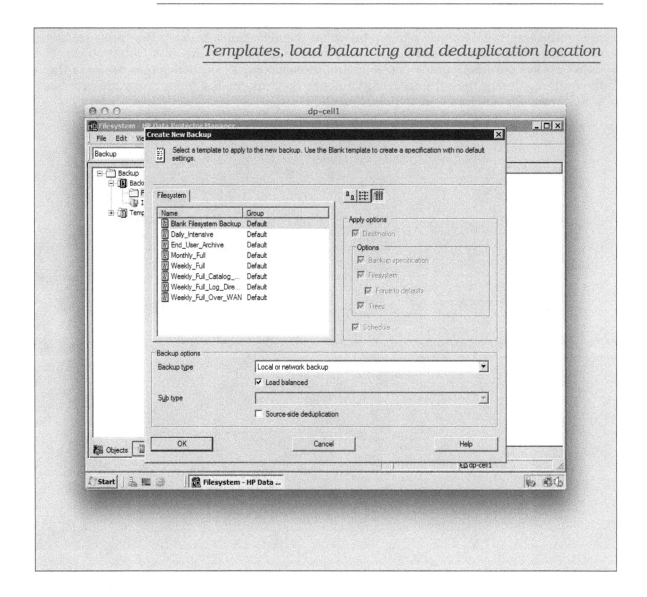

Out-of-the-box DataProtector comes with a selection of **templates**. You can add to these yourself. They are simply stored in plaintext files in:

MS-Windows cell managers `C:\ProgramData\OmniBack\Config\dltemplates`
Unix/Linux cell managers `/etc/opt/omni/server/dltemplates`

The defaults only offer templates for the schedule for when the backup is going to run.

However, templates can be applied to a backup once it has already been created. This particularly useful when you want to apply changes to a large number of backups. For example if you have just bought a new tape drive, you can create a template which sets that new tape drive as the destination and very quickly apply that template to all of your backups. This is much faster than manually editing each backup specification.

You will almost always want to enable the *Load balanced* option: this lets DataProtector handle the allocation of tape drives itself, rather than relying on you to explicitly allocate which file system is going to be backed up to which tape drive.

If your backup job consists entirely of machines that have the StoreOnce de-duplication component installed on them, and will only write to StoreOnce devices (i.e. it won't be writing to a tape drive) and you concerned about bandwidth, then you can enable the *Source-side deduplication* option. Generally though it is easier and more flexible to create additional deduplicating gateways.

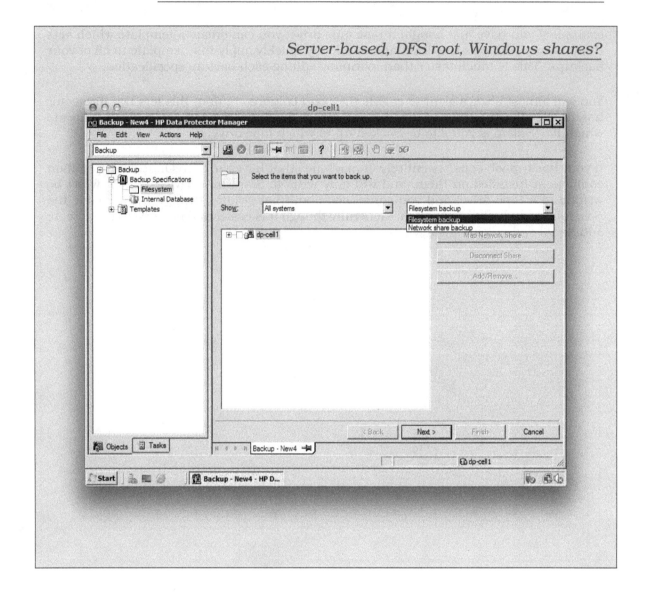

Generally it makes sense to do server-based backups as there are all sorts of optimisations that can be done. Data is still going to be sent across the network regardless of the method chosen here.

However, it can be easier to be confident that you have backed up all important company documents if you start at the DFS root.

You can also back up a file share which happens to be accessible to a machine in the DataProtector cell. DataProtector does not charge for disk agents, so it is no cheaper to backup file shares in this way instead of installing an agent.

One thing to be aware of: unless your files are stored on a fabulously fast disk array and the server which is sending the data to the backup device is connected by a very high-speed network, then any modern tape drive will be much faster than the other bottlenecks in the dataflow.

We will back up to the de-duplication store, so we're probably not overly bothered about how long it takes: it's not as if this backup is monopolising scarce hardware. So for us here it would make little difference to the performance of the backup which starting point we chose.

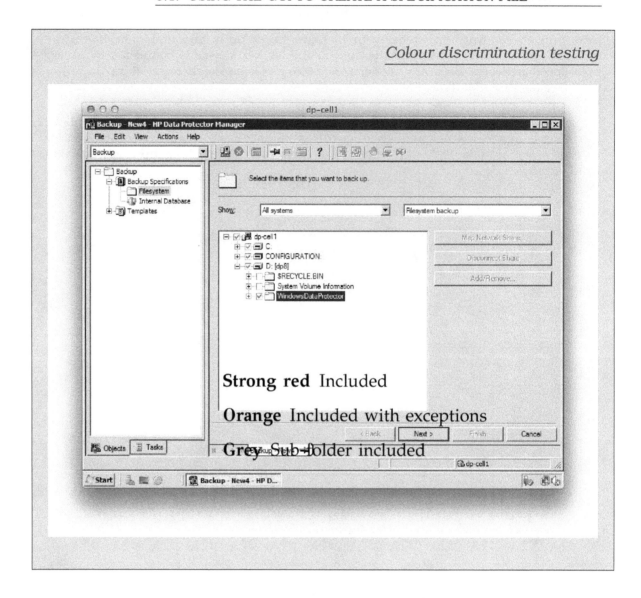

Different coloured ticks have different meanings. You will also see:

Black included because a parent folder has been included.

The exceptions on the C: drive would have been created by selecting the top level of the C: drive, expanding out that to show the files and folders within it, and then deselecting some of them.

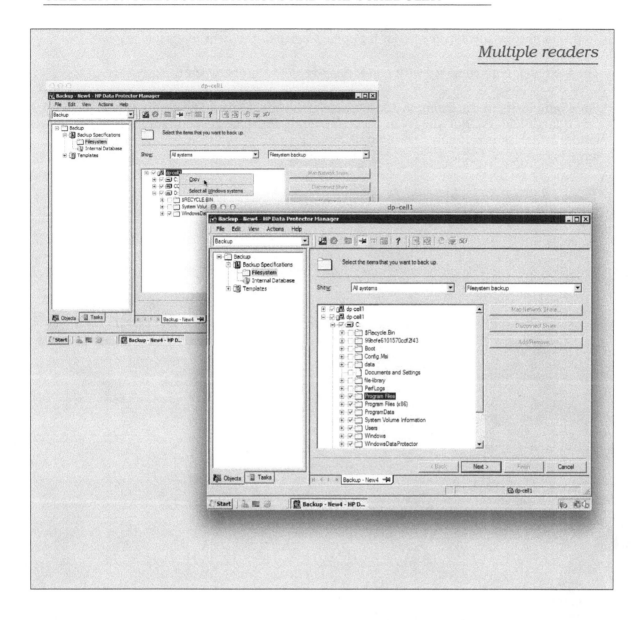

Occasionally for very fast servers with very fast filesystem access, it can make sense to have more than one process reading from the filesystem at the same time. It can also make sense where you want to spread one large file system over many different devices (for example if your tape library has more than one drive in it).

The way this is expressed in DataProtector is to have multiple copies of the same server in the backup specification.

In the screenshot above we obviously wanted to have 2 readers for the C: drive. The first step was to copy the server so that it appears twice in the user interface.

The next step is to come up with some clear-cut division between the 2 readers.

For example (as in the example above) the second reader could be configured to backup seven large folders. Not shown in the screenshot above is the configuration of the first reader which is presumably configured to backup all of the C: drive *except* for those 7 large folders.

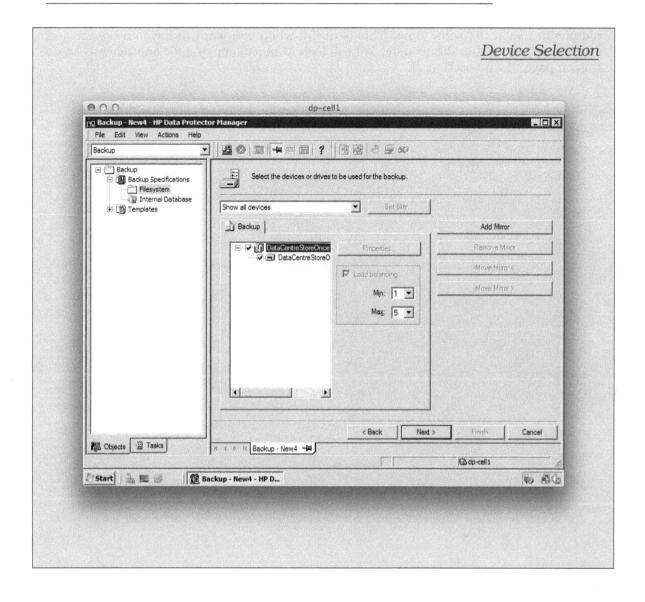

Note that the Load balancing checkbox is ticked (and is unable to be un-ticked). This was selected on the screen with the template choices. Changing it will require editing the backup specification's text file.

This backup will only run if there is at least one device available (minimum equals 1) and will try to use up to 5 devices if they are available. This is obviously very relevant for backing up to tape libraries, but is irrelevant here as we are only going to back up to one device (our StoreOnce device via the one StoreOnce gateway that we have defined).

Note also that it is possible to have mirrored backups: for a backup to have two destinations in use at the same time. This is useful when you want to have an on-site and off-site copy made simultaneously. We will look at object copying for another way to do this on page 171 (in section 9).

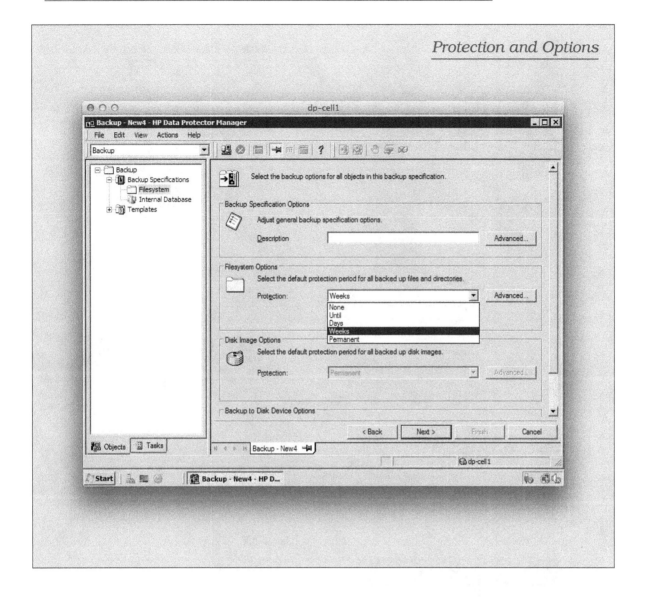

The default protection is permanent – DataProtector will make sure that that data is never lost. Particularly when writing to a StoreOnce device this is very inefficient!

On the day that the protection expires, the next backup job that runs with the destination of the same StoreOnce device will cause the space associated with this backup to be freed. If the *catalogue* protection is set to the same as the data protection (as it is by default) then the internal database will drop the rows which store the file names and their corresponding media.

The description field is optional.

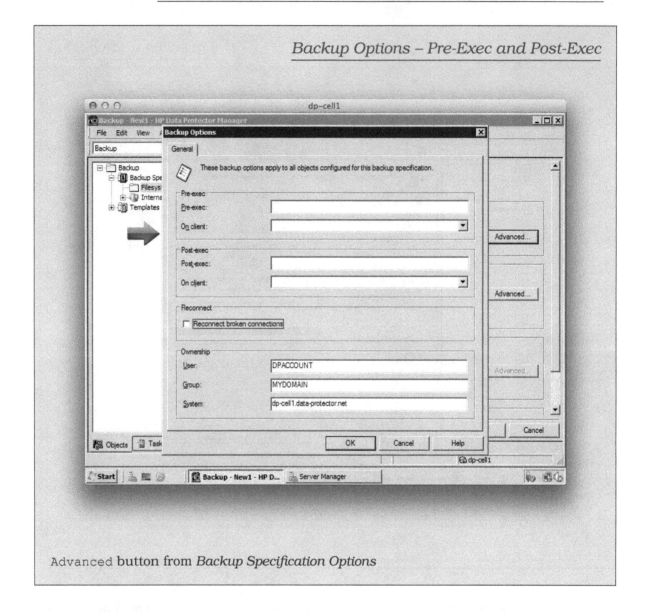

Advanced button from *Backup Specification Options*

To keep things confusing, on the options page there are two buttons marked `Advanced`. The screenshot above shows the window which pops up from pressing the first of those buttons (the one beside the Backup Specification Options).

None of these options are particularly important.

The **pre-exec and post-exec** command commands can run on any machine in the cell – including computers that have nothing to do with the backup itself.

There are 8 global options relevant to pre-exec and post-exec commands:

ExecScriptOnPreview By default these scripts are on the run when a genuine backup is taking place; by default they will not run when a backup administrator is previewing a backup.

BackupPreexecBeforeDevLock By default the scripts run after the devices have been acquired by the backup.

PrePostExecOnEveryVolume By default the scripts are run just once at the very beginning and very end of the backup. This option will run the script for each file system object in the backup.

PostExecOnAbortHost By default if you abort the backup job the post-exec script will not run.

ScriptOutputTimeout By default the script needs to produce output at least once every 15 min.

SmDisableScript You can disable all scripts.

UsePanScripts If set to 1 (the default), then the pre-exec and post-exec programs have to be in `C:\Program Files\OmniBack\bin` for Windows systems or `/opt/omni/lbin` on UNIX and Linux systems. There can be symbolic links to other locations though. If set to 0, they can be anywhere.

ScriptUser By default scripts will run as the user `omniback` on UNIX if it exists (and root otherwise).

There is also an omnirc parameter called OB2FORCEPOSTEXEC which will mean that a post-exec will get run even if the session was aborted and there wasn't a pre-exec.

Of interest on Unix / Linux systems is that there is a program which will let a pre-exec or post-exec script appear to finish but still carry on in the background. It is already in the `lbin` directory: `/opt/omni/lbin/utilns/detach`

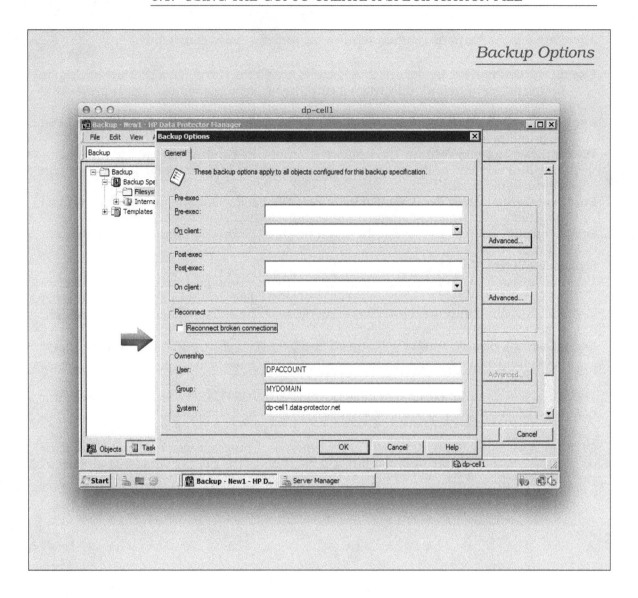

The option to **reconnect broken connections** is appropriate when there is an unreliable network link between the cell manager and the machines acting as the disk agent and media agent. In other words, whenever you are running a local backup of a small remote office.

As this doesn't have a performance impact in any backup that is working, the only reason ever to have this off is if there is a firewall between the cell manager and the remote site which was going to block connections back from the remote site to the cell manager.

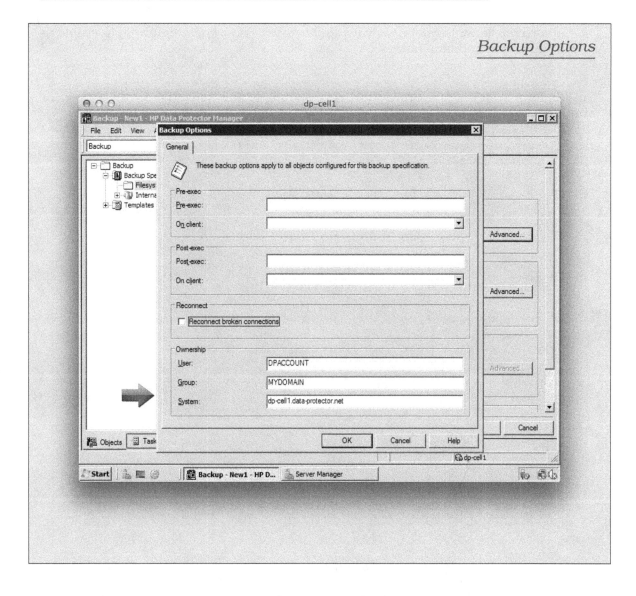

Ownership does not have to be specified. It is useful for two reasons:

- If you run a backup interactively it will run as your user ID if the ownership is not set. If the next scheduled backup is an incremental it will be incremental not against your interactive backup, but against the scheduled backup before it. If the ownership is set, then all backups will run as that username.

- If you want to have some backups visible to certain users so that they can restore from them (presumably without special privileges) you can select that the backup is private and will then be only visible to the user specified here and to any DataProtector administrators. Private backups with no ownership are only visible to DataProtector administrators.

On Windows systems, the Group field corresponds to the Active Directory domain or workgroup.

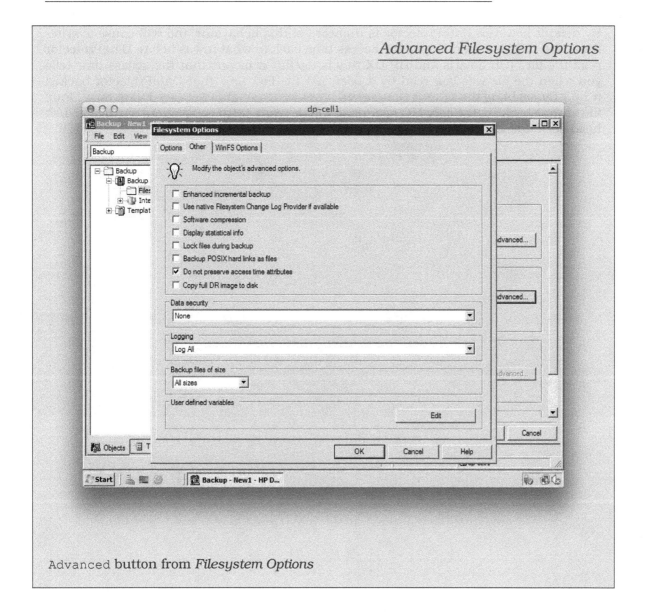

Advanced **button from** *Filesystem Options*

Most of these options are essentially irrelevant in DataProtector 8 environments using StoreOnce devices. For full details the online help describes what each option does.

If you are backing up Linux systems enable the option "Do not preserve access time attributes". Modern Linux systems mounted filesystems with the option `-o relatime` which means that the access time is only updated if the access time is older than the modification time – in other words, it only gets updated the first time after a file is modified.

By default however, DataProtector is unaware of this behaviour and will cause a write-back into the file system to put the access time back to what it was before DataProtector read the file. (On Solaris and HP-UX this is useful: it means that the access time tells you when the file was last read by a *user*, not the last time that DataProtector backed it up.) By enabling the `Do not preserve access time attributes` option on a Linux file system backup, the only I/O occurring will be reads (with consequent savings in disk head seek times).

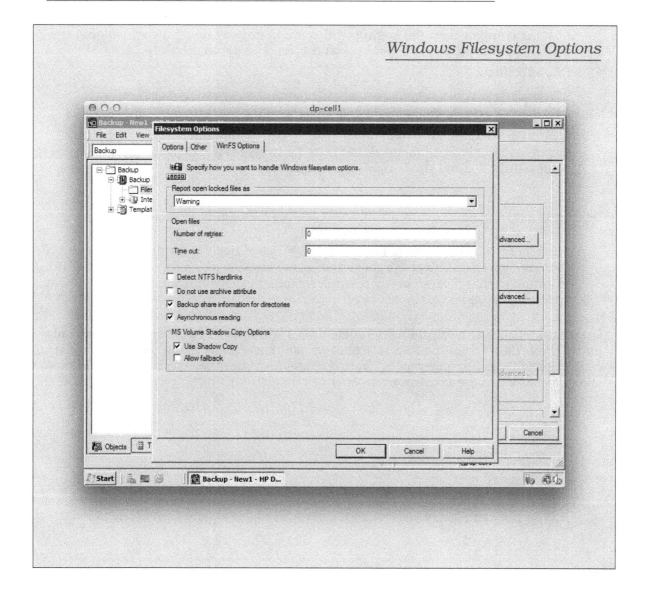

Windows Filesystem Options

The options *Backup share information for directories* and `Use Shadow Copy` are on by default.

It is a pity that *Asynchronous reading* is off by default, as it seems to generate a reasonable performance improvement on any Windows server after Windows 2003.

There are two matters to be aware of in using VSS snapshots.

- There is a minimum amount of disk space required. If you enable the `Allow`

`Fallback` option then the backup will proceed anyway doing a conventional tree walk. Then the `Number of retries` and `Time out` parameters are used.

From Technet:

> For volumes less than 500 megabytes, the minimum is 50 megabytes of free space. For volumes more than 500 megabytes, the minimum is 320 megabytes of free space. It is recommended that least 1 gigabyte of free disk space on each volume if the volume size is more than 1 gigabyte.

Source: http://technet.microsoft.com/en-us/library/ee692290(v=ws.10).aspx

- There is no way of knowing how much disk space really does need to be free. If there is a job that runs at the same time as the backup which copies large amounts of data into that filesystem, then Windows might remove the snapshot (for lack of space) in the middle of the backup.

One of my customers encountered a problem with Windows 2012 R2 servers which only had 4GB of RAM, where the VSS snapshot would appear to be taken, but then no data could be read (and the only way of clearing it was to reboot the server). In the end they added memory and the problem went away.

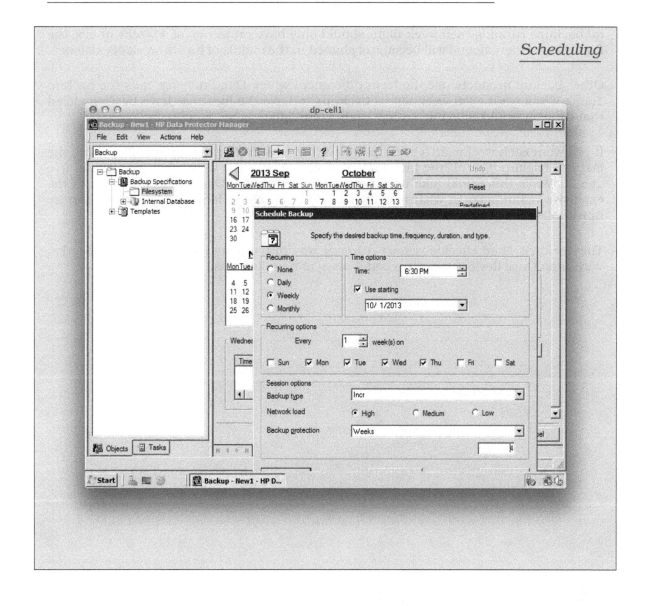

The Windows user interface provides a simplified view of what the DataProtector scheduler can do.

Once the schedule has been created, the user interface provides very few options for changing it. Changing a backup to start later or earlier generally involves editing the scheduling text files.

One thing to be aware of when scheduling incremental backups: and incremental backup should have a protection shorter than the full backup that it references. So for example, if the full backup has a protection of 5 weeks and runs each weekend, then incremental backups running each week night should only have protection of 4 weeks or else the Friday night incremental will become orphaned in the middle of its 5th week of existence.

Other backup products use the term *differential* where DataProtector calls the backup `Incr`. If you want each weeknight's backups to have the files that have been modified that day you would schedule an *Incr* each weeknight.

If you want each weeknight's backup to have the files that have been modified since the last full backup (i.e. all the files that have changed in the week) then you would use `Incr1`. While this would take up no extra space in a StoreOnce device (because of the extensive redundancy in what is being backed up) it also offers no advantages: restore times will still be essentially the same.

The `Network Load` checkboxes are a legacy way of handling low bandwidth networks. With StoreOnce devices there are better ways of handling this.

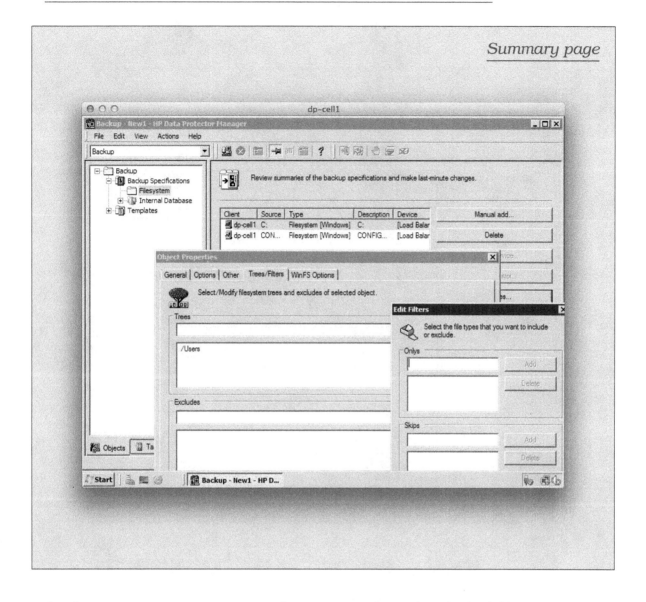

Summary page

On the summary page you can set the properties for each individual file system. You might want to skip certain file patterns (`*.avi` for example), or create a backup that only backed up Microsoft Office documents (`*.docx`, `*.xlsx`, " `*.pptx`"). Or perhaps a particular file system does not need a VSS snapshot taken.

It is also possible to include or exclude particular folders. Normally this is done through the user interface on the opening page of the backup, but can be done here as well. Note that even on Windows the file names are given with forward slashes (/) as the directory separator.

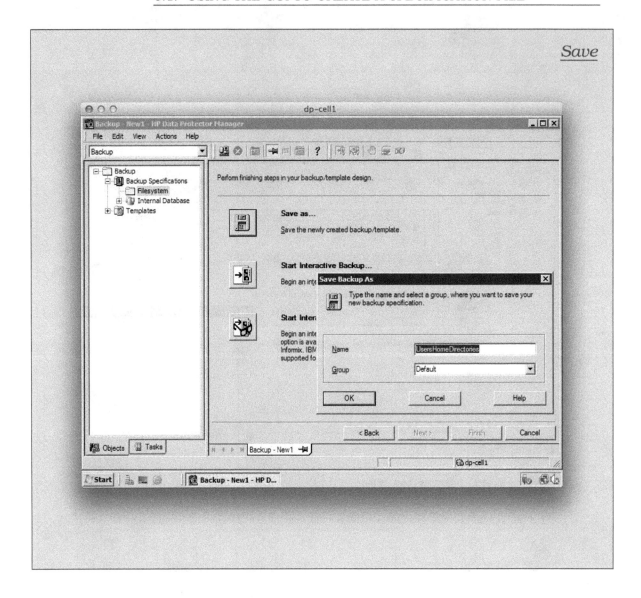

Finally, you are presented with the option to save the backup, run the backup interactively now or to run a preview of the backup.

6.2 Specification and Scheduler Internals

Backup Specification Text File (Datalist file)

```
DATALIST "UsersHomeDirectories"
DYNAMIC 1 5
DEFAULTS
{
  FILESYSTEM
  {
     -no_storedrim
     -vss no_fallback
     -async
  } -protect weeks 52 -keepcatalog weeks 8
}
DEVICE "DataCentreStoreOnce_gw1"
{
}
WINFS "C:" dp-cell1:"/C"
{
   -trees
       "/Users"
}
```

The graphical user interface has simply provided a front-end for creating this text file
(the datalist file) and the schedule text file (discussed next).

We called this backup *UsersHomeDirectories*, so it would be in a file called `C:\ProgramData\`
`OmniBack\Config\Server\Datalists\UsersHomeDirectories` if you are using a Windows cell manager (the first parts of that path would differ if you had put the database
on a different drive), and `/etc/opt/omni/server/datalists/UsersHomeDirectories`
if you were using a Linux or HP-UX cell manager.

You can manipulate this text file with a text editor, rename it and move to different
cell manager. Sometimes the graphical user interface caches information so the see the
effects of your text file changes sometimes you need to disconnect and reconnect from
the cell manager in the GUI.

If you want to rename a backup specification, you can do it through the GUI by copying
and deleting, or you can do it on the command line or file manager by simply renaming

this data list file and the corresponding schedule file after altering the DATALIST argument. Watch out for any copy or consolidation jobs that might reference the old file name.

Schedule Specification Text File

```
-incr -protection -weeks 4
    -starting 1 10 2015
    -every
        -day Mon Tue Wed Thu
        -at 18:30

-full
    -every
        -day Sun
        -at 05:00
```

We called this backup "UsersHomeDirectories", so the schedule specification files would be saved in `C:\ProgramData\OmniBack\Config\Server\Schedules\UsersHomeDirectories` for a Windows cell manager and `/etc/opt/omni/server/schedules/UsersHomeDirectories` for a Linux / HP-UX cell manager

The schedule specification shown in the specification that defines a full backup every Sunday at 5 AM and an incremental backup on Mondays through Thursdays at 6:30 PM (starting on 1 October 2015) where each incremental backup will be protected for 4 weeks. (Presumably the full backup is being protected for longer.)

Changing times or days or backup types is simply a matter of editing this schedule specification file with a text editor and saving it. There is a DataProtector service on Windows (`omnitrig`). On Linux and UNIX the installer creates a cron job for the root-user which runs `/opt/omni/lbin/omnitrig`. When this is woken up each minute it rereads all the schedule specification files to see if any match the current time.

First Saturday of the Month

```
-full
  -day 1 2 3 4 5 6 7
  -at 17:00

-full
  -exclude
  -day Mon Tue Wed Thu Fri Su
  -at 17:00
```

The way to read this is that there is going to be a full backup at 5 PM on the 1st through 7th of the month of each month. Then there is an exclusion which says that they will not be a backup at 5 PM on any day except Saturday.

Since the first Saturday of the month will always be in the first 7 days of the month therefore this schedule will only fire on the first Saturday of each month.

There is no way of expressing this in the GUI, however if you view the GUI it will greatly show all the dates on which this schedule will fire.

Last Sunday of the Month

```
-full
  -every
    -day 25 26 27 28 29 30 31 -month May Jul Aug Oct Dec Jan Mar
    -at 21:00

-full
  -every
    -day 24 25 26 27 28 29 30 -month Jun Sep Nov Apr
    -at 21:00

-full
  -every
    -day 22 23 24 25 26 27 28 -month Feb
    -at 21:00

-full
  -exclude
    -day Mon Tue Wed Thu Fri Sat
    -at 21:00
```

This specification does not work correctly in the year 2032 when the final Sunday of February is the 29th instead of the 22nd.

Other ways to schedule backups

- Advanced scheduler

- `omnib -datalist` *UsersHomeDirectories* `-no_monitor` (can be triggered from `cron` or Windows scheduled tasks)

We will see the advanced scheduler on on page 128 (in section 6.4)

The `-no_monitor` option says to run the job and then disconnect from it and exit while letting it carry on in the background. Without that option, the command will only return once the backup job is complete.

6.3 Backup Lab

LAB: Backup

1. Create a backup job for a small folder on your cell manager.

2. Run it to confirm it works.

3. Check the created datalist and schedule files.

4. Change the schedule using a text editor. Confirm that this appears in the GUI.

6.4 Advanced Scheduler

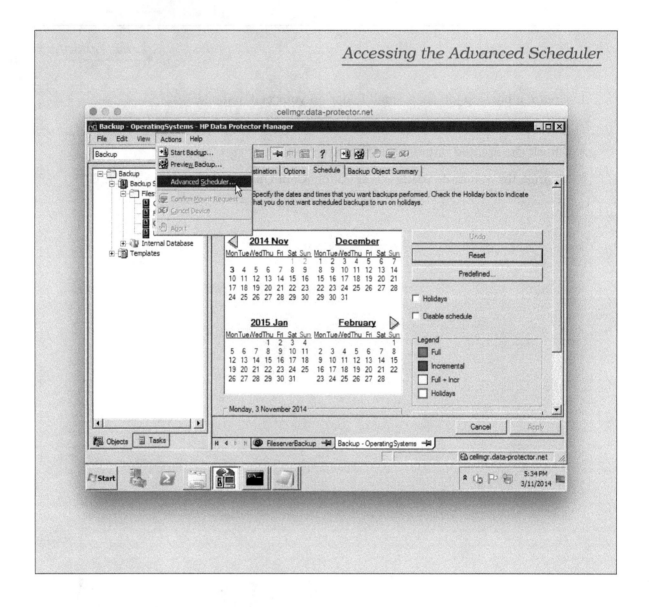

There is a second scheduling mechanism available in Data Protector which was introduced in version 8.1. It is known as the advanced Scheduler.

Unlike the traditional schedule which stores information in text files, the advanced Scheduler stores them in the internal database. The application server uses the Quartz scheduler (http://quartz-scheduler.org/) which is an open source job scheduling library.

This is configured to store its data in the `hpjce` database instance, where there are tables `qrtz_triggers` and `qrtz_cron_triggers`. The actual backup specification to trigger is stored in the byte array column called `job data` in the `qrtz_triggers` table.

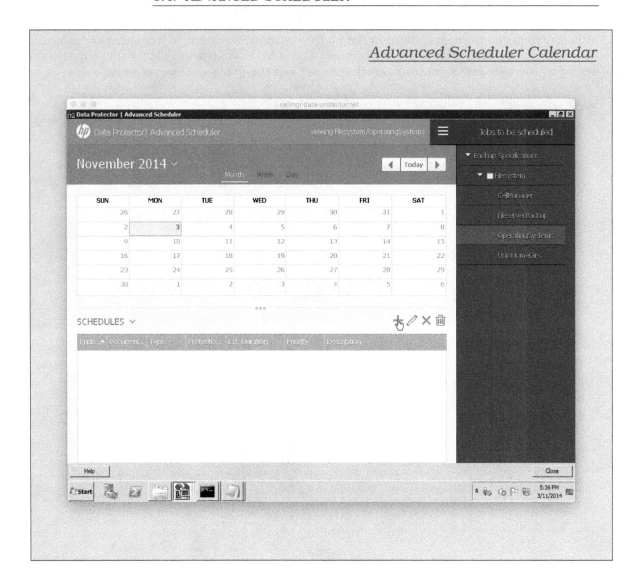

This screenshot is showing that there is nothing scheduled in the advanced Scheduler for this backup specification. It would not show any classic-scheduled jobs if they have been defined.

The priority of a backup job only gets used in one situation. If two backup jobs are queueing unable to start because a tape drive that they both needs is busy, then the backup job with the best priority will start even if the other job was scheduled earlier.

In this way if there was a hold-up early in the evening that caused a delay in backups being started the most important jobs will still get completed, at the expense of less important backup jobs.

The estimated duration does nothing other than make the calendar look better. It is not based on historical data for this backup job and does not impact priority scheduling.

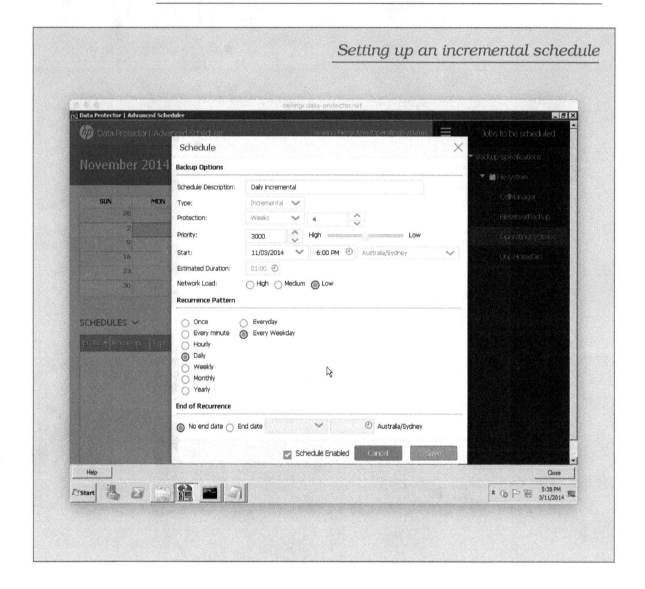

The default network load is medium, which is quite strange. Normally the goal is to complete a backup as fast as possible, rather than reducing load on the network.

If you really wanted to have a minimal network impact then you would choose low as in the screenshot above.

The remaining fields are hopefully self-explanatory.

Setting up a full schedule

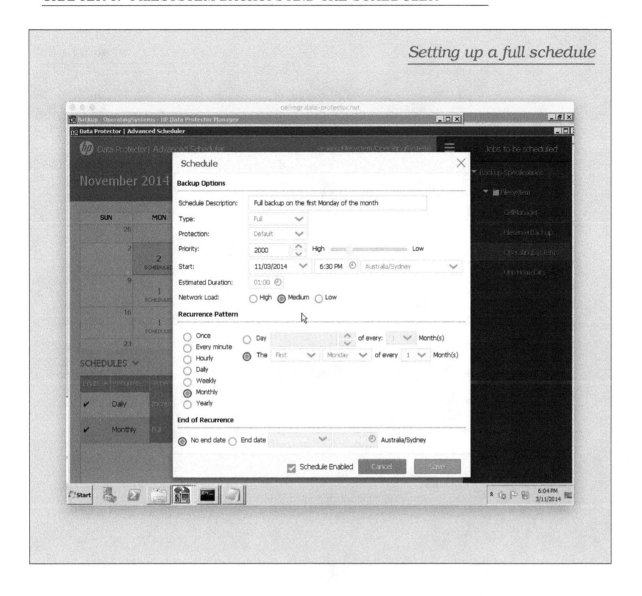

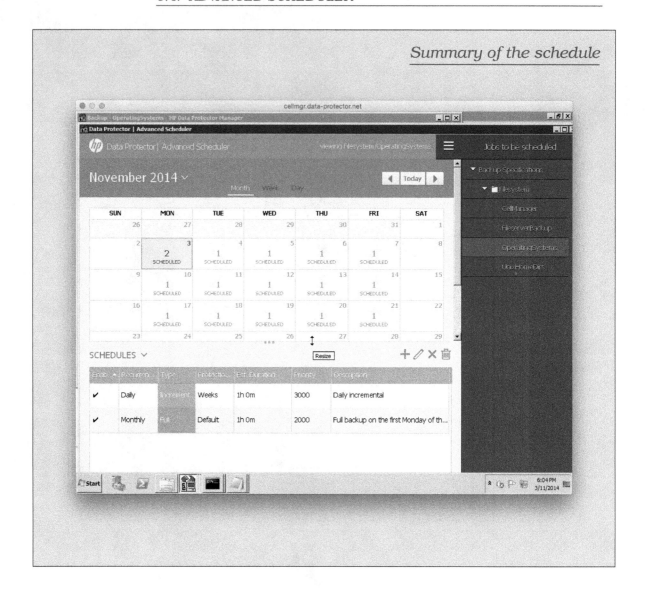

Notice that there is a conflict at 6:30 PM on the first Monday of every month. The advanced Scheduler does not have the concept of exclusions, nor does it have the concept of a full taking priority over an incremental.

As it stands, this schedule would launch two backup jobs simultaneously of the same backup specification.

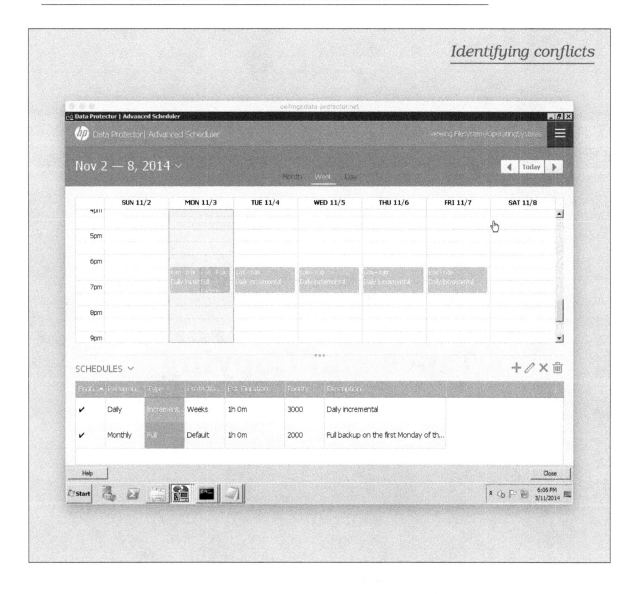

Part IV

Tapes and Copying

7

Tape Drives

7.1 Configuring

The media agent software can do a hardware scan in which it walks through every attached device (USB, SCSI, iSCSI and Fibre Channel) looking for devices that respond as a tape drive or as a tape manipulation robot.

Behind the scenes it actually running a program called `devbra -list_devices` which you can run as well to diagnose why something might be missing. It is included as part of the media agent software.

It's not doing anything that you can't see in Windows Device Manager, through the Linux command `lsscsi -g` or through the HP-UX command `ioscan`.

Occasionally in Windows 2003 it can be necessary to turn off the Removable Storage Manager service to make the discovery work correctly.

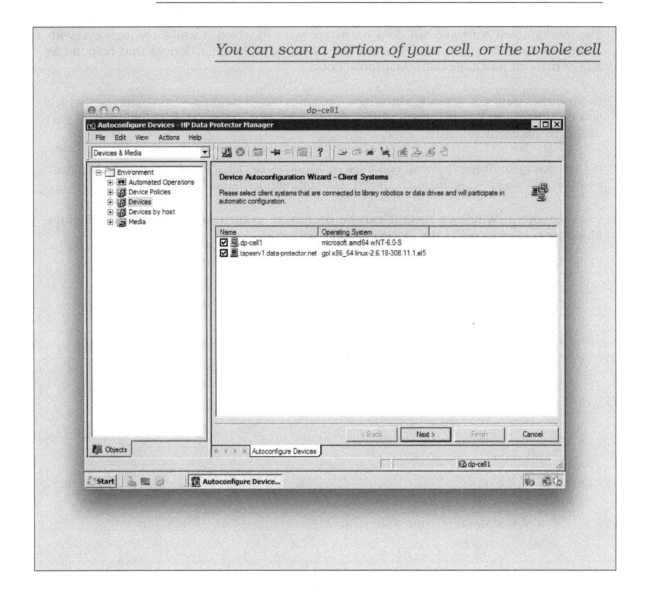

Fibre Channel and SCSI tape drives and robots are often deployed on SAN fabric. This means that several computers might have access to the same drives. In fact, for performance you almost definitely want to have this sort of configuration.

Two tape drives are considered the same if they have the same serial number when probed. If this happens, the drive will be set up as a multipath device. If you are using traditional licensing in which you pay for the number of drives concurrently in use, then this will cause the device to consume a top tier agent licence. A low tier licence is included with Windows and Linux cell managers: all top tier licenses need to be purchased separately.

You can use the `sanconf` program on the command-line from the cell manager to find out what the DataProtector GUI is working from.

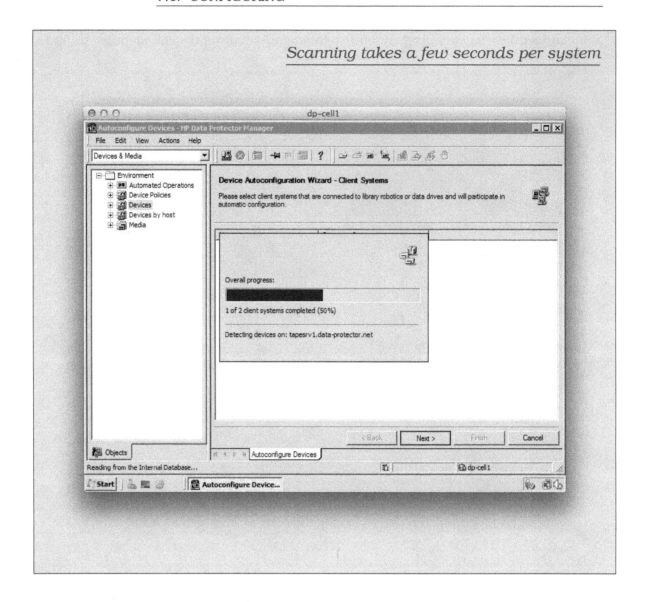

Not all hardware works perfectly all the time. If the progress bar seems to freeze for a long time (more than a few seconds) and you don't have some enormous Superdome system with hundreds of PCI adapters in it, then perhaps there is a hardware fault somewhere. Try again and exclude some servers until you find the problem.

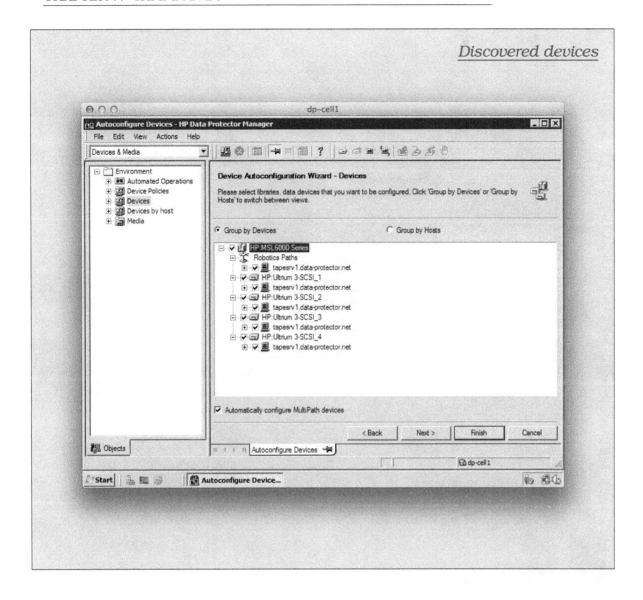

Discovered devices

You will be presented with all the devices that DataProtector was able to find on all the computers that you selected. If it found some devices which were connected to more than one computer then it might make sense to view the devices by host (what each computer was connected to) or by device (which computers were connected to a device with that same serial number).

Simply by enabling all checkboxes, you can create everything that DataProtector needs in order to use that device.

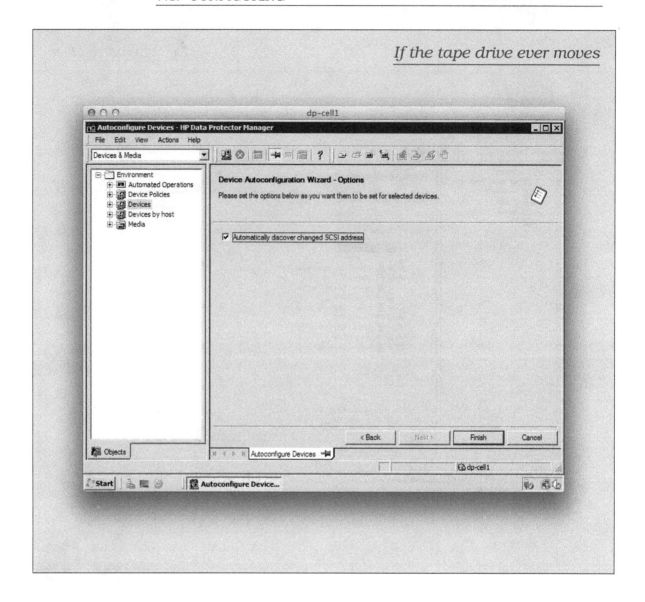

If the tape drive ever moves

Various changes can occur which might mean that a tape drive's hardware address changes. Here is a short list:

- Somebody could unplug a pair of cables connecting two tape drives to a server and then put them back in again the wrong way around.
- An upgrade is performed to the firmware on a fibre channel switch.
- Your organisation migrates their SAN infrastructure.

If DataProtector attempts to open a device and receives a file not found error or similar, and the *Automatically discover changed SCSI address* option is enabled here, it will first assume that the device still exists but has moved. It will initiate a scan of all devices and look for a device which has the same serial number as the one it was trying to open. If it finds one it will update the device information to refer to the correct device.

Also, every time it successfully opens a device it will record the serial number of the device that was found there. In this way it will correctly handle the replacement of a tape drive at the identical location without operator intervention.

Of course, if a tape drive gets replaced and ends up at a different address then DataProtector has no way of knowing that was the drive that you wanted to use and will report an error.

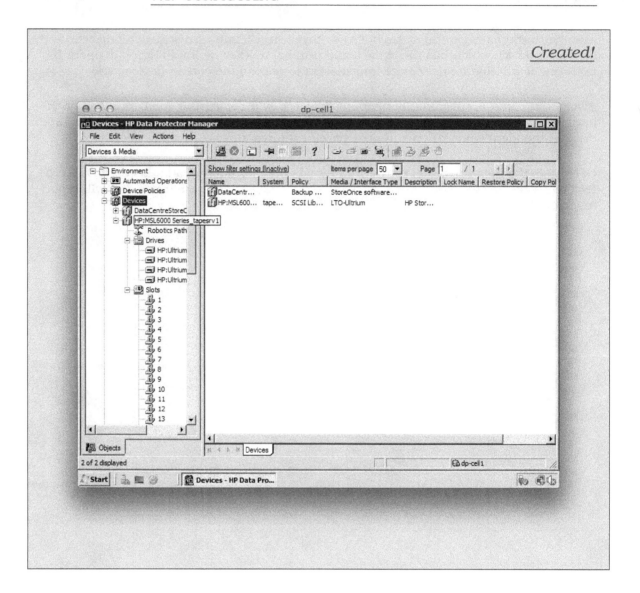

The slots in the tape library will all show as being Unknown media and with no barcodes recognised because we have not yet run a barcode scan.

Right click on the library to bring up a menu of commands such as ejecting tapes, running a barcode scan, loading and unloading tapes through the mail slot and scanning and importing tapes.

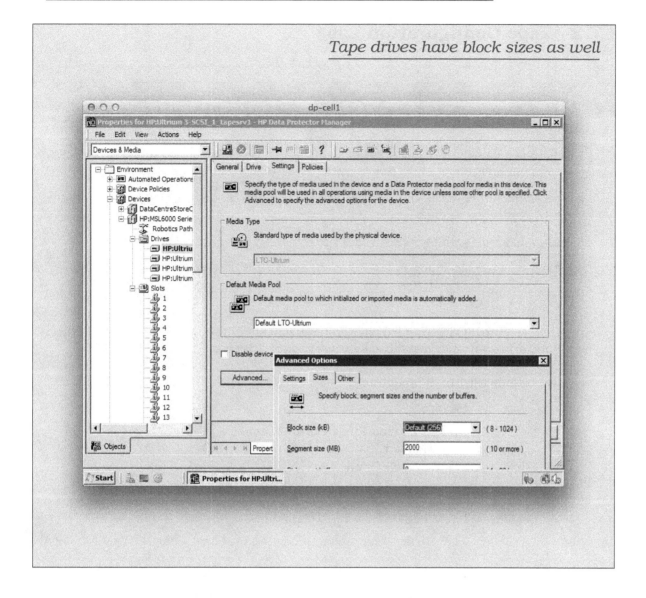

In version 8 and 9 DataProtector defaults to having a 256 kB block size. If you intend to use this tape drive to copy from a de-duplication store, make sure the block sizes match for best performance.

Generally, the larger the block size, the faster the tape drive will run. However, the effect is quite small – small enough that it is often unmeasureable.

7.2 Tape Configuration Lab

LAB: Tape Configuration

1. There is a server `tapesrvX.data-protector.net`. Import this into your cell if it is not already.

2. Run autoconfigure. It should find a large HP tape library. If it doesn't, create a SCSI library manually.

3. Run a barcode scan to confirm that the robotics are working correctly

4. Make sure the block size is 256KB to match your StoreOnce device.

If you are using the IFOST supplied environment, you should see a MSL6000 tape library. The robotic arm control device file will be `/dev/sg6` with serial number 80000090.

There will be four Ultrium 5 tape drives:

Device File	Serial Number
/dev/nst3	80000094
/dev/nst2	80000093
/dev/nst1	80000092
/dev/nst0	80000091

Media Pools

- Distinct groups of media

- Backup and copy jobs are configured to fetch from a media pool

- Have nothing to do with retention policies

Unlike Backup Exec or some other products, media pools do not have their own retention. Backup objects (file systems, databases, etc.) have a retention and it is quite possible to have two different retentions on different areas of the same tape. If the media pool is appendable and the data on the second part on the tape has expired then that space will get reused.

Each device in each backup job is configured to fetch tapes from a media pool. They can be given an allocation list (a specific list of tapes to use first) or they can fetch the next available good tape.

Geography	Virtual tape versus real
Media Generations	Barcoded versus non-barcoded
Isolation	WORM vs non-WORM

... and other reasons

Here is my methodology for working out what media pools to create.

Geography Make sure each site has separate pools for everything. Otherwise an operator might be told to place a tape currently in Melbourne into a Sydney tape drive.

Virtual tape versus real If you are using a VLS6000 (or similar) to emulate DLT tapes, then you will need different pools for the real tapes and the virtual tapes. Otherwise you might get asked to put a virtual tape into a real tape drive!

Barcoded versus non-barcoded In an ideal world, every tape has a human and machine-readable barcode. In reality, tapes that aren't in a tape library tend just to get handwritten labels. These would have to be in a different media pool, so that DataProtector doesn't start asking for a non-barcoded tape to be put into a tape library device.

Media Generations DDS1 tapes can't go into DDS4 tape drives, so separate the pools of these tapes. This gets tricky for compatible generations of tapes.

WORM vs non-WORM Some tape technologies support special write-once media. Obviously these will need to be treated differently to your standard multi-write tapes.

Block size You can have tapes with different block sizes in one pool, but if you have a backup with one block size on it, no backups with a different block size can be appended to it. DataProtector will load the tape, reject it, and then try the next best tape until it finds a tape that can be used. You could have a lot of tapes each with a tiny backup on it with a 64k block size, giving you a pool with vast amounts of free space which is unusable for any other backups. If you want to be very sure that you know your tape capacities and usage, you might want to create a pool for each different block size in use. Watch out for MS-SQL backups in 6.2 where you can set the block size to $2 * * n + 4$ kB instead of the $2 * * n$ kB block size for file systems and any other kinds of backups.

Archiving reasons If tapes have to be left in a tape library, and the pool has to be appendable because you have multiple backups configured to go into it, but you don't want the next day's backups on the same tapes, then there's little alternative to creating another media pool. Or beg HP to add a 4th usage option: *appendable within 24 hours of the first protected write.* I tend to create a media pool called *Tapes for Restore* which I move tapes into when an off-site tape is brought back into the pool. This way it won't get written to accidentally. (The write-protect tab is good for this as well, but watch out that it doesn't get marked as *bad* by a tape drive failing to write to it.)

Financials Maybe it's because of chargeback costing, control, or security. Usually these reasons are quite pathetic, but if it's too hard to battle against the bureaucracy in the name of common sense, well ... maybe the easiest way to solve the problem is to let each division pay for and manage its own pool of media.

Isolation If you have different tape retention cycles for different data – e.g. backup X must stay on-site for 4 weeks, but backup Y must go-offsite the next day, then you don't want these two backups on the same tape. You can create separate pools to keep these backups isolated. However, usually, the problem is better solved by keeping all originals on-site and creating copies to send off-site where necessary.

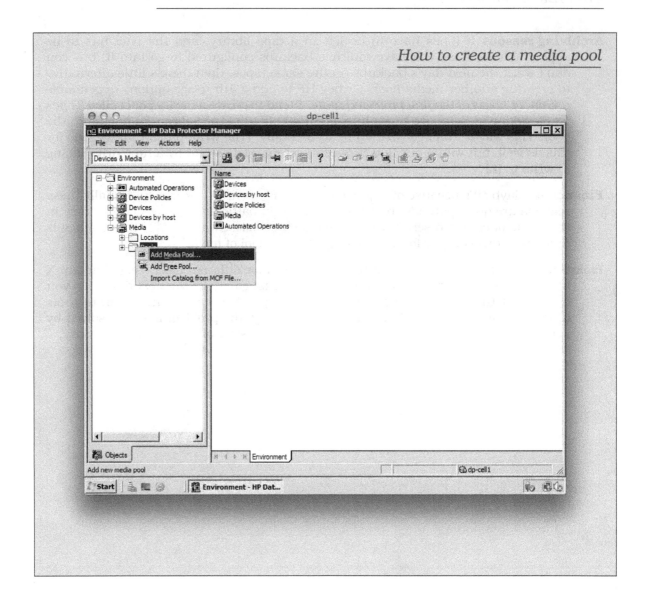

This is a right click on the Pools folder inside Media in the Devices and Media context.

Choosing a pool type, name and description

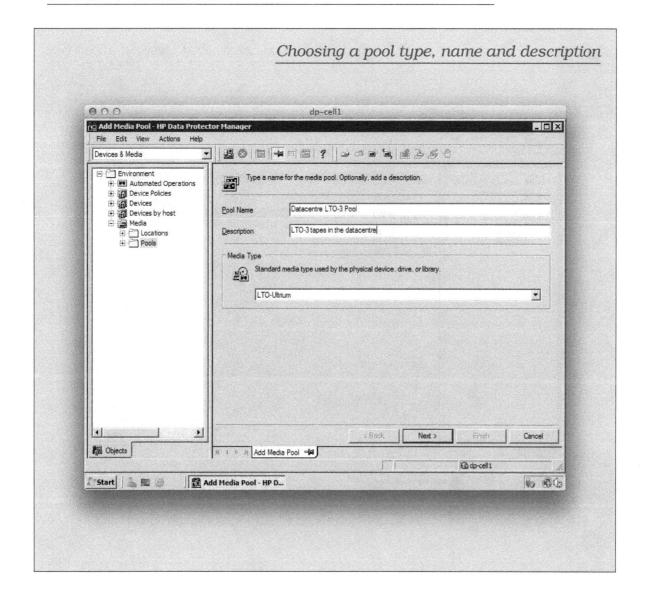

The selection drop-down box contains all the kinds of media that DataProtector understands. There is no option for creating additional types, but the list is quite comprehensive, covering almost everything that has been on the market in the last 30 years.

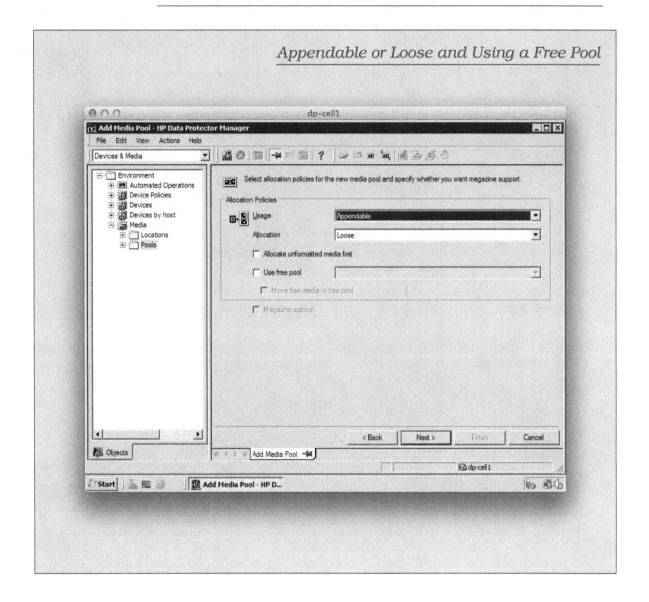

Almost every media pool I see is created as Appendable and Loose.

The alternatives to being *Appendable* are:

Appendable on Incrementals This works quite well if you have a large backup with regular incrementals that you want to write directly to tape and take off-site at the end of the week.

Non-appendable It almost always it works out better to split backup jobs into different media pools (in order to isolate certain file systems to live on their own tapes) than it is to make tapes non-appendable.

The alternative to being Loose is to be Strict. This will guarantee that DataProtector will take the first priority tape from the media pool: it is not available the backup will be blocked waiting for a Mount Request. Since the Loose allocation policy will try to take the first priority tape if it can – but fall back to the next best if the best is unavailable – there is almost no advantage to using the Strict allocation policy.

If some reason you have several media pools of the same type in the same location (and even in the same library) it might be convenient to create a Free Pool. A Free Pool contains media with no protection that has been returned from other pools. Those other pools can call on tapes from the Free Pool when they need extra media.

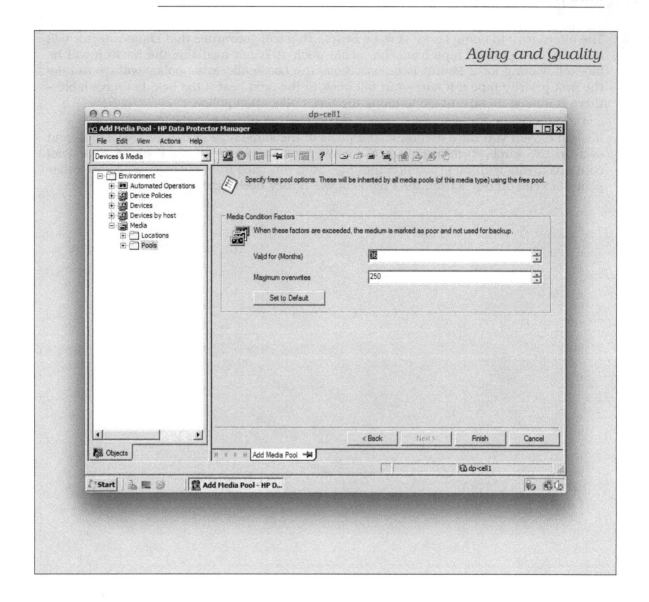

Tapes that are more than 3 years old are probably not the ideal media for writing backups to. Nor is it a good idea to write to tapes that have already been written 250 times. The magnetic media will have degraded, making errors in reading and writing much more likely.

You may vary these. For example, if you are verifying tapes (which means that each tape is getting rewound twice for each overwrite) you might want to halve the maximum overwrites parameter.

When a tape hits these limits it is marked Poor. This cannot be reset. When it reaches

80\% of these limits is marked Fair. Fair tapes can be written to, although if there are any available unprotected Good tapes, the Good tapes will be used first. Poor tapes never get written to.

There is another way that a tape can be marked as Poor. If during a backup, restore or copy job the device reports and I/O error, DataProtector always assumes that the tape is at fault. This means that if you have a tape drive which is faulty you may find that hundreds of your tapes get marked as being poor. This can be fixed with the command `omnimm -reset_poor_medium`.

And of course, if a tape has a write protect tab on it – a physical marker that stops the tape drive from writing to it – then that tape will be marked as Poor in older versions of Data Protector if ever DataProtector tries to put a backup on it. (In newer versions it detects the write protection.)

File media – such as the media in a StoreOnce device – are ephemeral. After the protection on a backup expires, the media is destroyed with it. In this way even though a StoreOnce media pool may have a maximum number of overwrites it will never have tapes marked Poor because of this. (In odd situations media can be marked as Poor for other reasons in a StoreOnce device.)

- Can be over-ridden for each backup or copy job

- If not over-ridden, job will take from the device's default media pool

- There is a default default for LTO drives: `Default LTO-Ultrium`.

- Two drives in the same library can have different defaults

The media pool for each device is defined in the device section in the backup specification file. It applies consistently for that device across any file systems or other objects in that backup session. Different devices can have different media pools in the one job – which makes sense as you could be backing up simultaneously to take and to a StoreOnce device, and these 2 could not possibly have the same media pool.

Between different backups the same device can use different media pools. You might choose to write your monthly backups to WORM media for legal provably reasons, but your weekly and daily backups would go to non-WORM media. (Note that to do this you would have to create 2 different backup specifications and keep them synchronised somehow when you make changes to them.)

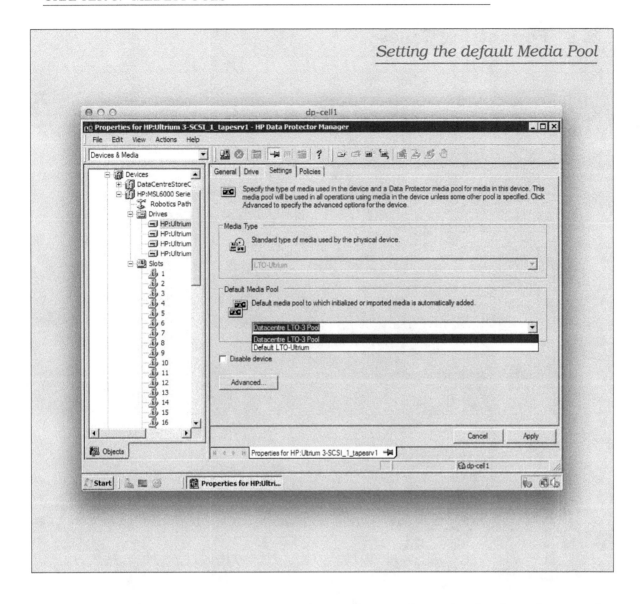

This is often the only manual step required to configure a device that has been discovered by the autoconfiguration process.

8.1 Formatting Tapes

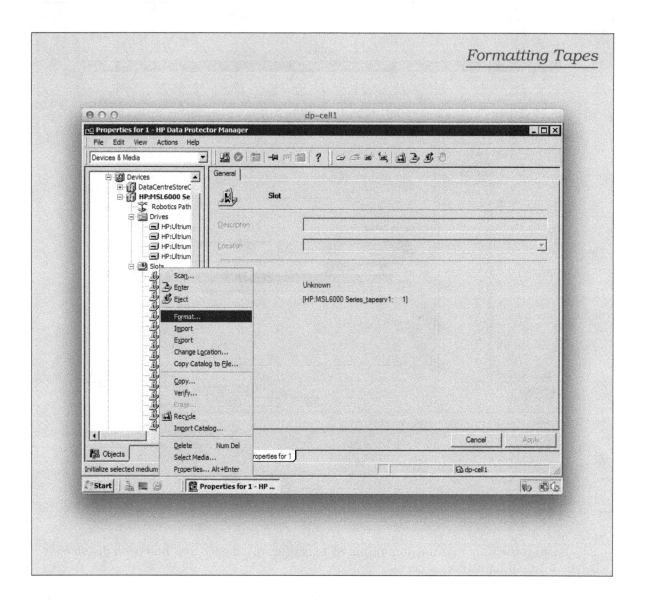

Formatting Tapes

Now that we have defined a media pool we can format a tape and put it into a media pool.

In the screenshot shown I have right clicked on one slot. I can also select several slots at the same time, which would have launched formatting jobs for each tape one after another.

It also possible to format tapes with the `omniminit` command. For example, if you have a device called `Drive1`:

```
omniminit -device Drive1 -slot 1
```

Another possibility is to create the media pool and use the option `Allocate unformatted media first`.

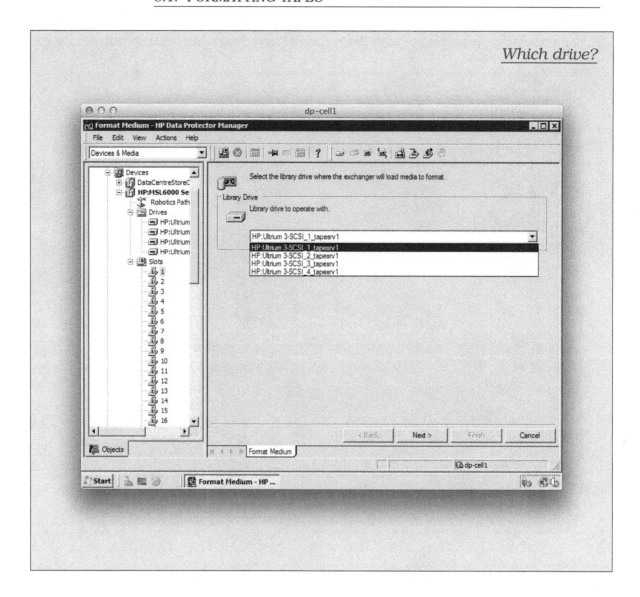

The first question is which drive you wish to use to format this tape.

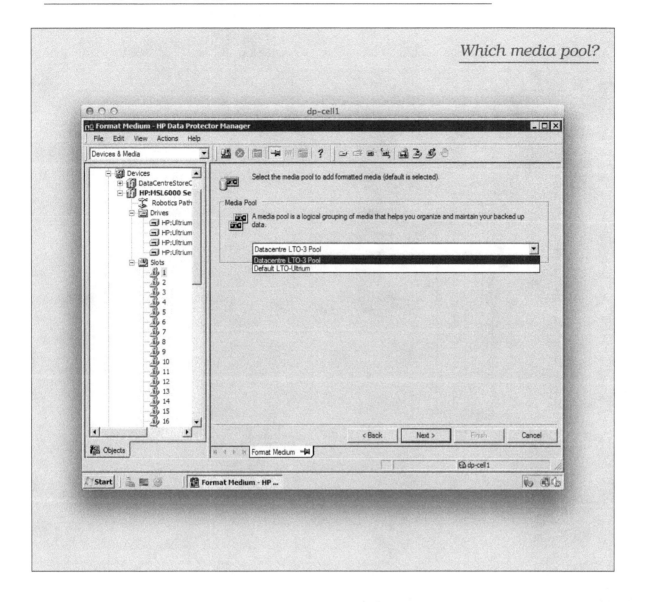

The reason we did not do this step previously was because we hadn't created a media pool for the tapes in this library. Now we can select the media pool that we created.

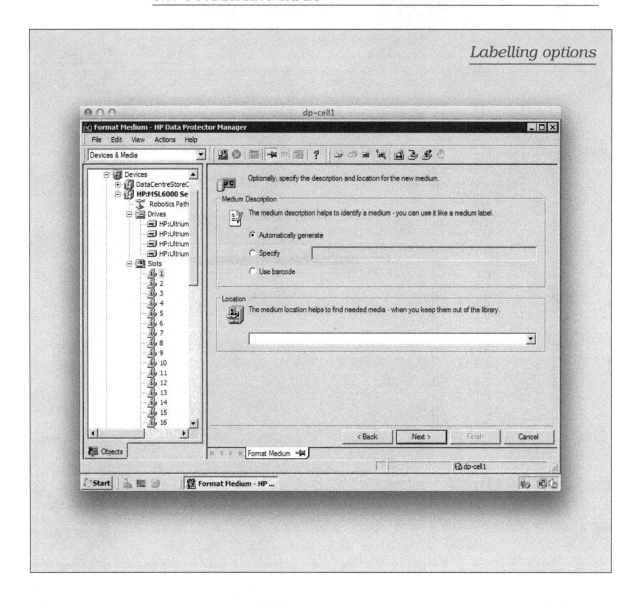

Tape management is much easier when your tapes have barcodes.

If you let DataProtector generate its own medium description, the description will begin with the barcode, followed by the name of the media pool and the next sequential number.

DataProtector has a locations database and every tape can have a location (it is optional).

Barcodes are surprisingly easy to work with nowadays. You can get USB barcode readers – they act like a funny kind of keyboard which types in a string of letters when they zap a code. There are many programs for reading barcodes on mobile phones – the excitingly named "Barcode Scanner" for Android is very reliable. Finally, it is also possible to scan barcodes using the web cam in a laptop or desktop computer; in fact there are websites that use the HTML 5 media API to fetch images from your web cam and process them in JavaScript!

I wrote a small program which lets a user scan tapes with a barcode scanner or mobile phone produce a list of commands to run to update the DataProtector internal database with the box or location of tapes. Access it here: http://www.ifost.org.au/cgi-bin/tapescan.py

The actual source code is available too: http://www.ifost.org.au/Software/dp-tools/tapescan.py

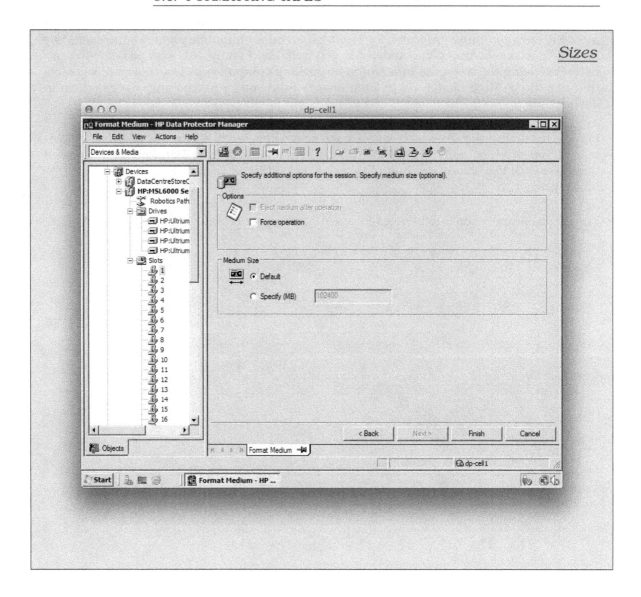

Because tape drives do hardware compression it is entirely possible that a 1 TB tape might store 2 or more terabytes of uncompressed data. Likewise, encrypted or random data will compress very badly. DataProtector has no way of knowing what the compression algorithm on the tape drive is achieving; it only knows when the tape drive reports that it has reached the end of the tape.

Thus, the medium size is almost entirely irrelevant. It provides an estimate for reporting purposes only, and not a very useful one at that.

Forcing a format is only required when you want to format a tape that already as a

DataProtector header on it. It might make more sense to import the tape instead in this case anyway, to find out if there was anything important on that tape.

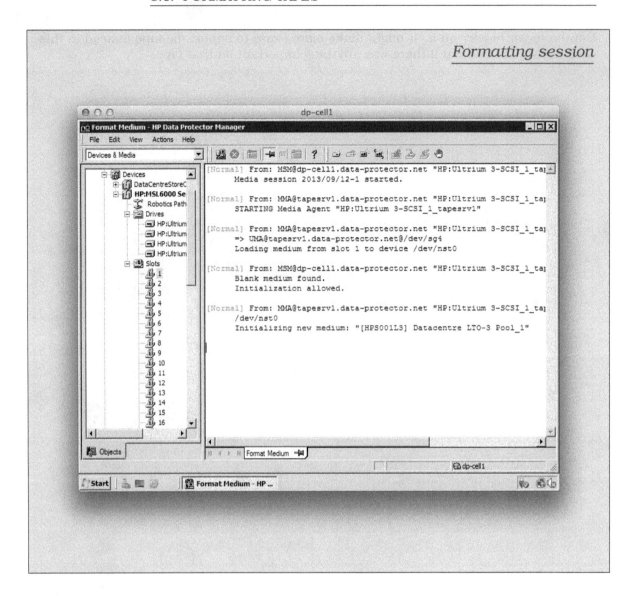

A media session is recorded in the database and can be reviewed later.

A DataProtector formatted tape begins with the letters OMNIBACK (the original product name for DataProtector) followed by a unique, randomly generated 12 byte sequence. That 12 byte sequence is the primary key for the database tables that keep track of media.

This formatting session is simply writing that header onto the tape.

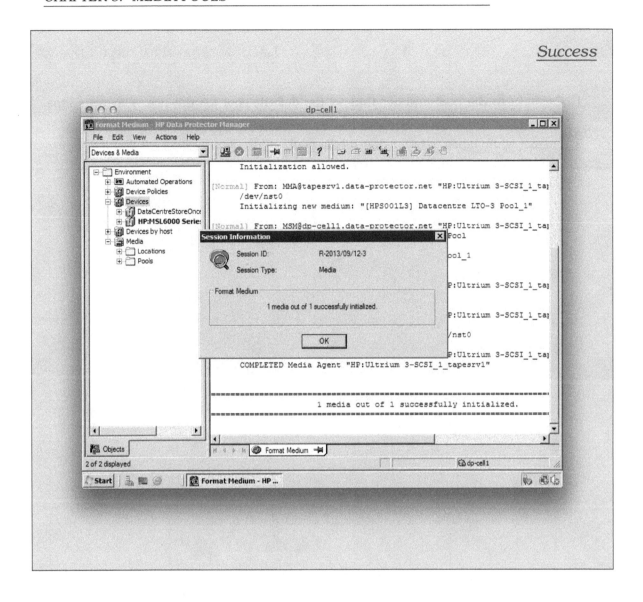

That media can now be used in backups and for copy jobs.

LAB: Working with media pools

1. Create a media pool and set that as the default pool for the drives in your tape library

2. Format some tapes to be in that media pool.

Object Copying

9.1 Copying to Tape

Why copy to tape?

- Legal requirements

- Cheap, long-term storage off-site

Tape isn't dead yet, it just smells funny.

Tape has some advantages and some disadvantages compared to disk storage. Tape has very poor retrieval time, which makes it a poor choice for backing up something that needs to be restored quickly.

On the other hand tape stores very well; you can expect to pull tape off a shelf where it has been sitting for several years and reasonably hope to read it. It's harder to be confident about this in dealing with disk drives that are very old.

Also there is no equivalent of WORM storage for disks. A tape that can be written to once and only once is the gold standard for auditable records.

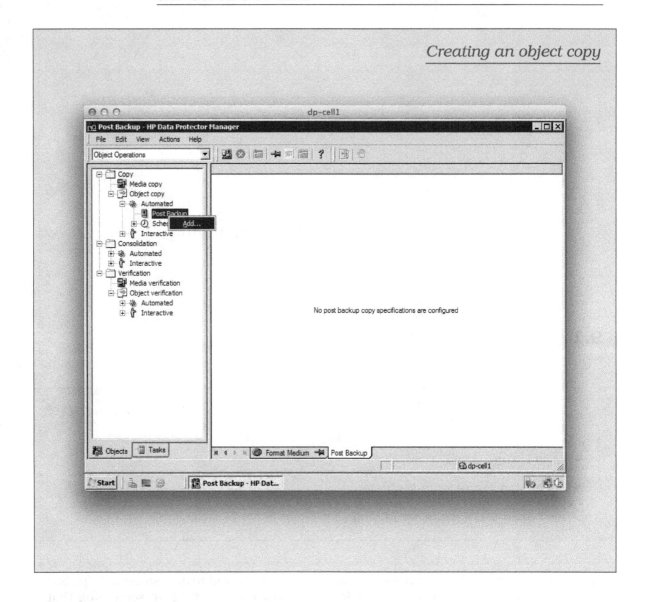

Creating an object copy

Our goal is to set up DataProtector so that we can backup efficiently to a StoreOnce device and then have DataProtector automatically copy these jobs to tape.

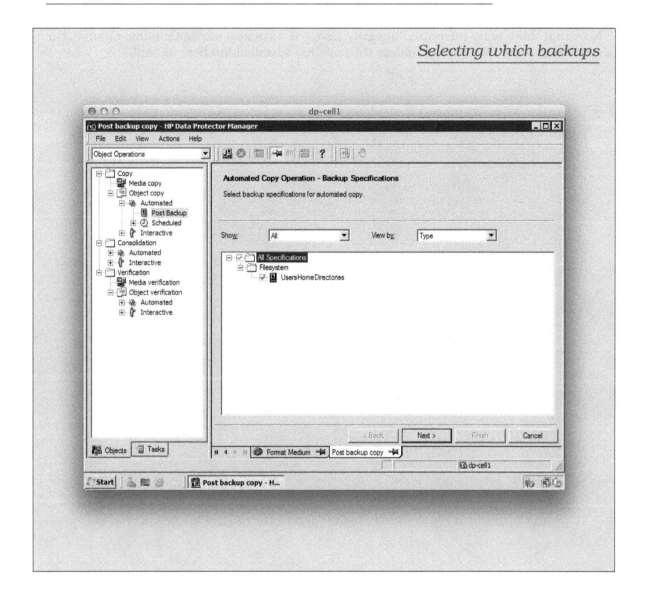

DataProtector provides two convenient ways of triggering copy jobs.

1. Automatically triggered at a particular time (a scheduled copy job)
2. Automatically triggered after something else has completed (post-backup copy job)

In this screenshot we simply tick the check boxes beside the backup that would like this copy to be triggered after. This is a very simple backup environment and only has one backup defined in it. However, post-backup copy jobs can be triggered to run after as many backup jobs as you like: the general idea "after I finished backing up to the StoreOnce area, trigger the copy to tape" is generic.

Note that there is no referential integrity here – if a backup job has a name change, the administrator would have to update the copy job specification here as well.

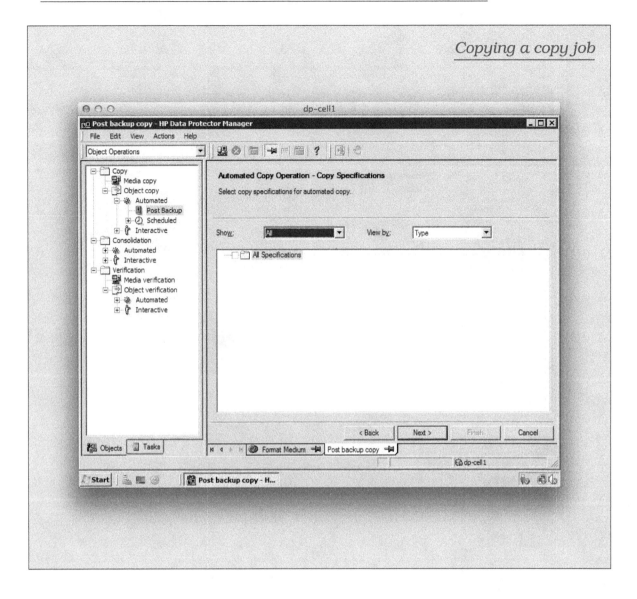

This screenshot shows the possibility of triggering a copy job after another copy job. We will show some examples of this later.

But be careful: it is quite possible to create infinite loops here with copy jobs!

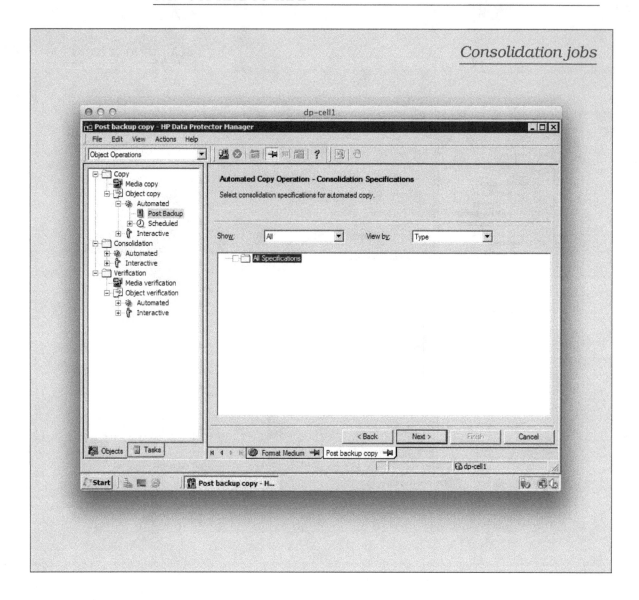

Consolidation was a very useful technique before StoreOnce de-duplication. It meant that it was possible to take continual incremental backups and synthesise full backups at a central location, and thus save a lot of bandwidth.

This is still possible to be done using a StoreOnce device, but in practice the bandwidth savings are minimal.

In any case, we have no consolidation jobs that we want to trigger a copy after.

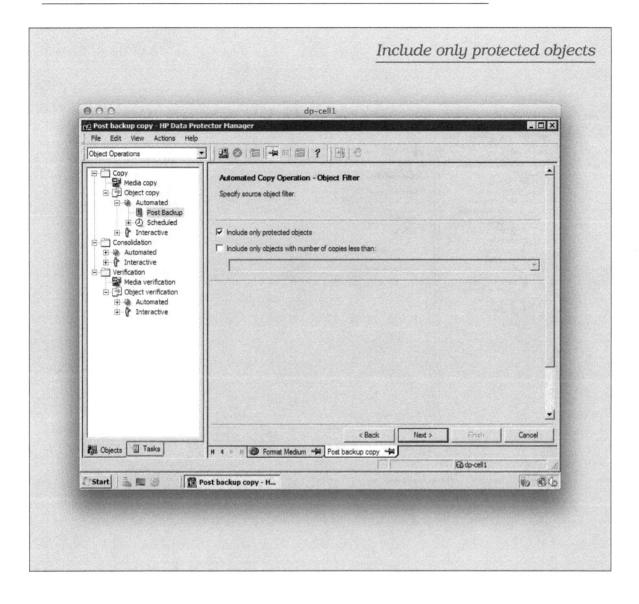

If a backup object is not protected then it is very unlikely that is worth copying out to tape.

Another interesting option (more often used with scheduled copy jobs) is to select backup objects (filesystems, databases, etc) which do not already have a copy. This can be used as a periodic confirmation that all data is in two locations.

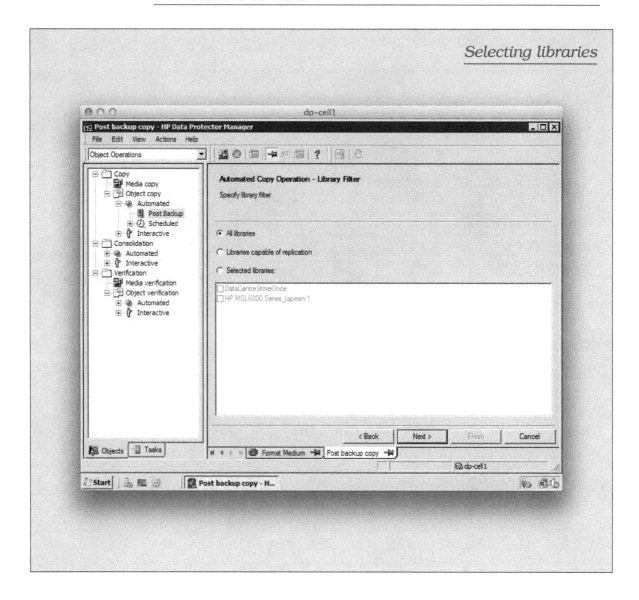

Remember that we have already constrained the copy job just to the backups selected on the first screen.

If we know that these backups can only ever appear in a particular library, then we could constrain the copy job only to look at that library but it is not going to make any difference.

So for a post-backup copy job constraining by library is probably irrelevant. It does sometimes makes sense for scheduled copy jobs: for example you could have a copy job which looks for objects lacking redundant copies which are saved in a StoreOnce store in your datacentre and decide to replicate them a StoreOnce store in your disaster recovery site.

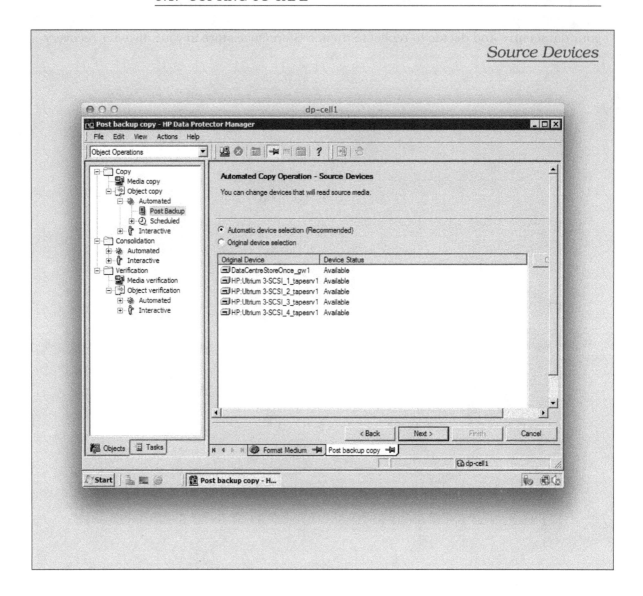

By default whenever DataProtector needs to read something from tape or from a Store-Once device it will try to read it using the same device that did the writing. Most of the time this is the right choice. When we discuss low bandwidth replication we'll see a situation where it is not.

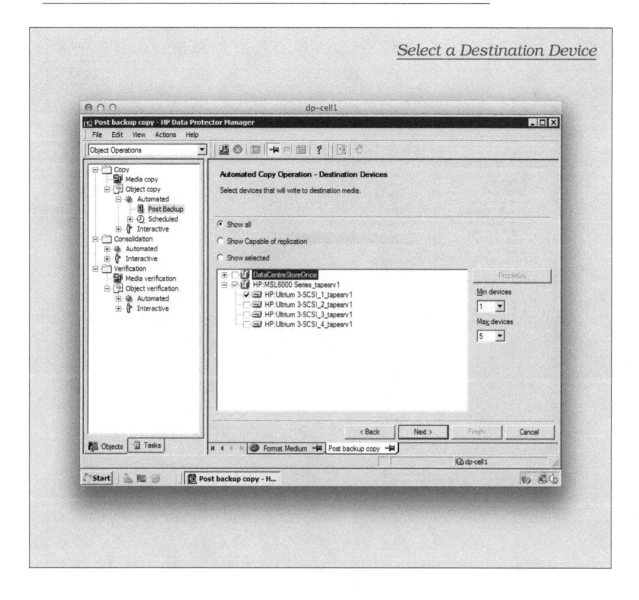

Finally we come to screen that requires us to make a decision: where would we like this copy job to write its data?

Clicking on a device activates the *Properties* button which can be used to set properties for this copy job such as which media pool it is going right to, whether or not to encrypt, what block size to use and so on.

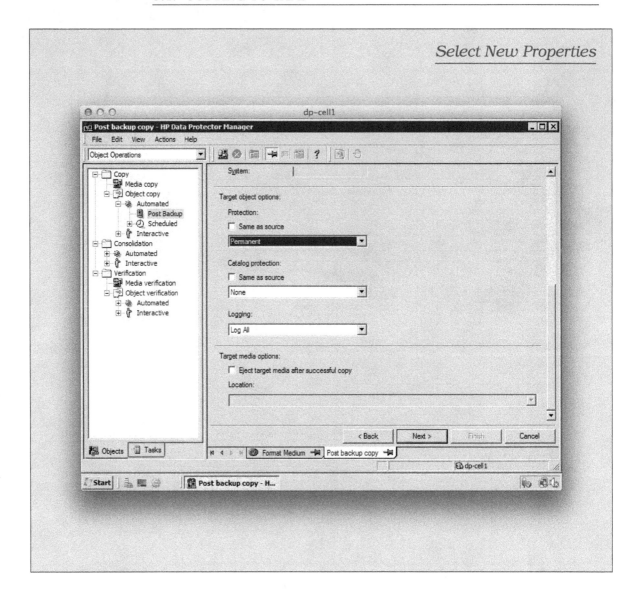

In the screenshot, I have chosen to give the copy job a different protection to the original backup. This is not unusual: you may want to preserve your StoreOnce storage just for backups taken in the last 4 weeks, back periodically writes a tape out for monthly storage and archiving.

In such a scenario, you are probably not expecting to be restoring from tape very regularly. The archival tapes will almost never get read, and will only be used once or twice to fetch some important document or database from the distant past. So there would be no point in keeping a complete catalogue of all the files that were backed up in that job ready at hand in the internal database after the protection has expired on the StoreOnce storage's copy. we can do this by setting the catalogue protection to None.

There are also options (not shown because of the scrolling) for recycling the original. This is appropriate when you are tidying up tapes that have a mixture of protections on them, or when you are using some kind of staging area that needs to be reset.

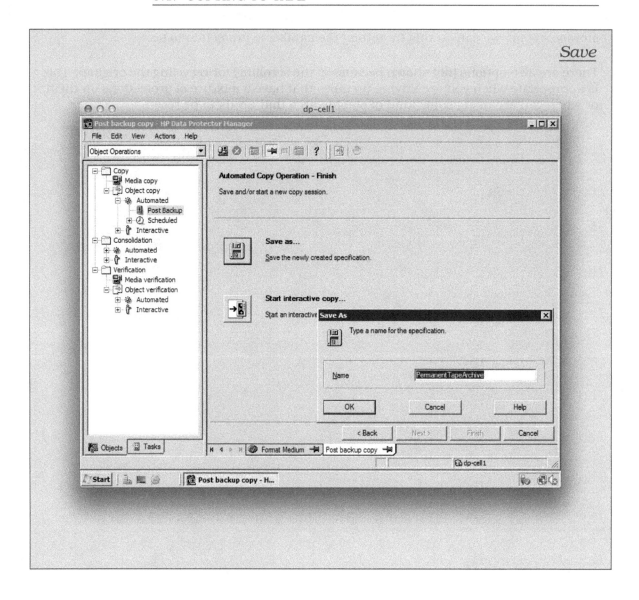

Object copies are defined in plain text files – just like file system backup specification data lists are. Scheduled object copies store their schedules in plain text files in almost exactly the same format as the scheduling file for a backup.

Windows cell managers C:\ProgramData\OmniBack\Config\copylists (unless DataProtector was installed elsewhere)

UNIX / Linux cell managers /etc/opt/omni/server/copylists

Testing a post backup copy job

- Right-click on the job to bring up a session selector
- Just try the backup

The kinds of things that go wrong in a post-backup job test are:

Block size mismatches If this does not stop the job from going ahead, it will give a warning.

Incorrect media pool This is why it is usually best to set up a sensible default for a drive rather then specifying a media pool for each job. The copy job will block waiting for a mount request if there are no tapes available in the pool selected.

General stupidity Blame a lack of coffee or your interrupting coworker, but one of the most common things to go wrong is selecting some option that you never wanted to select in the first place and don't even remember doing.

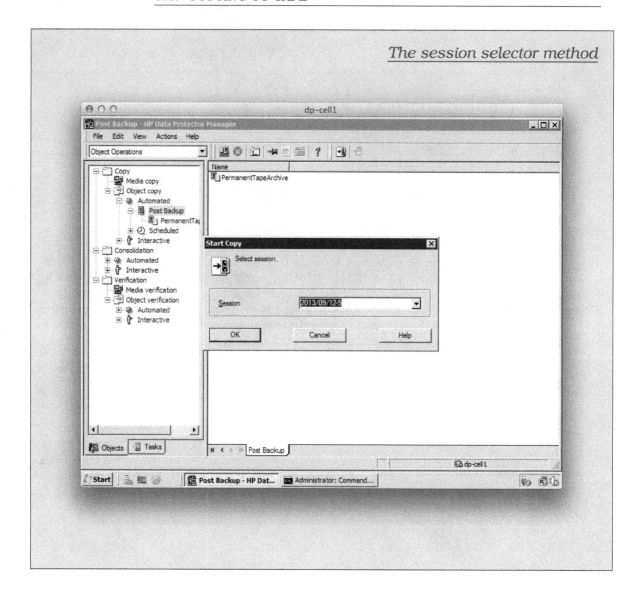

The session selector method

This session selector should only show backup sessions created by backup specifications that you selected as triggering this post-backup copy job. (Or copy your consolidation sessions that you had selected as being triggers.)

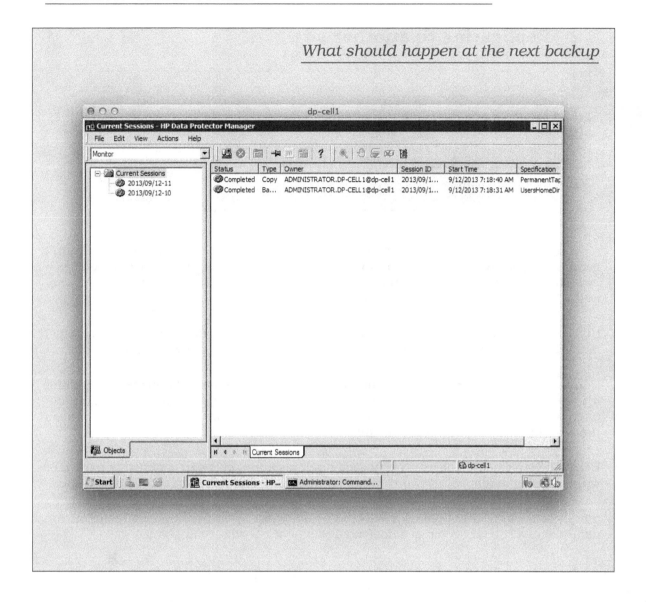

If you run a backup interactively, the post-backup copy job will still run however you will only see it if you happen to be looking at the monitor context at the time that your backup finishes or soon afterwards while the copy job is still running.

9.2 Replicating to another site

Site-to-site replication

- StoreOnce sends changed blocks and little more
- Data off-site without tape movements

A common problem that customers have which DataProtector elegantly solves is around getting remote sites backed up to tape. Loading and unloading tapes at remote sites – particularly when it is done by staff who are not full-time IT staff – never works out very well.

But it is often the remote sites which most desperately need to have reliable backups; and it is often at remote sites where the oldest and furthest restores have to be done.

I don't have any good answers to the question of why this often happens, but I think it's often easy to overlook small sites during upgrades and organisational changes; and often at small sites staff have the longest term relationships with their customers and so the requirements for the deepest recall.

Because StoreOnce is able to do very good de-duplication on cheap commodity hardware without using much memory, it can be very appealing solution for handling small sites.

Simply make sure that there is a WIN2K8 or Linux server at the remote site and at the data centre a similar server or a dedicated StoreOnce hardware appliance.

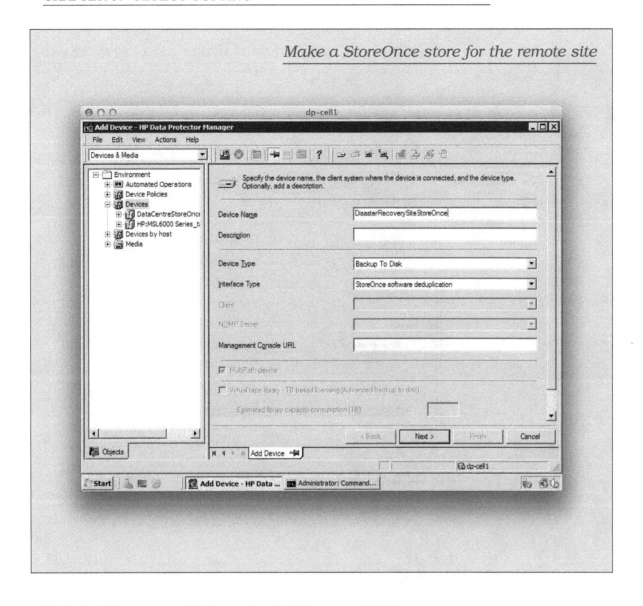

Refer back to on page 79 (in section 5.4) for more detail.

We choose a different name for the device this time, something that makes it easy to know where the data will be.

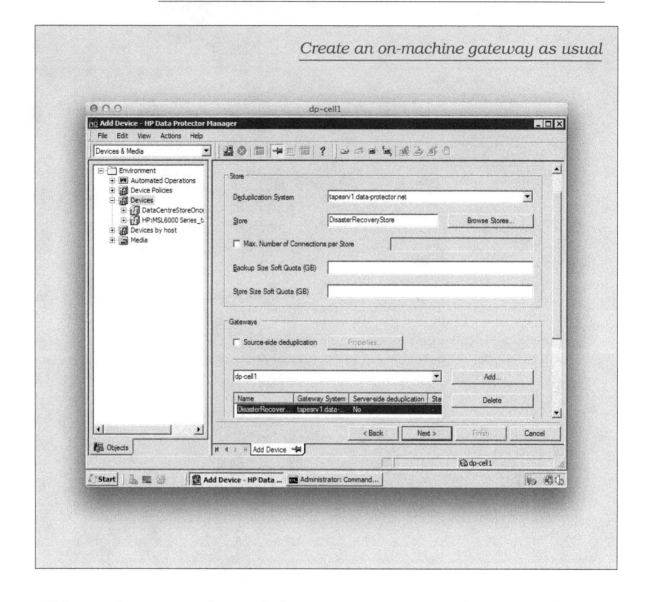

Create an on-machine gateway as usual

Following the same procedures as before, we create a gateway on the machine where the store is.

Notice now that the selection drop-down box beside the `Add` button now lists the hostname `dp-cell1` which is not the same as where the store is (`tapesrv1`). We have 2 computers installed with the StoreOnce component, so the user interface is offering to create a gateway for the other one.

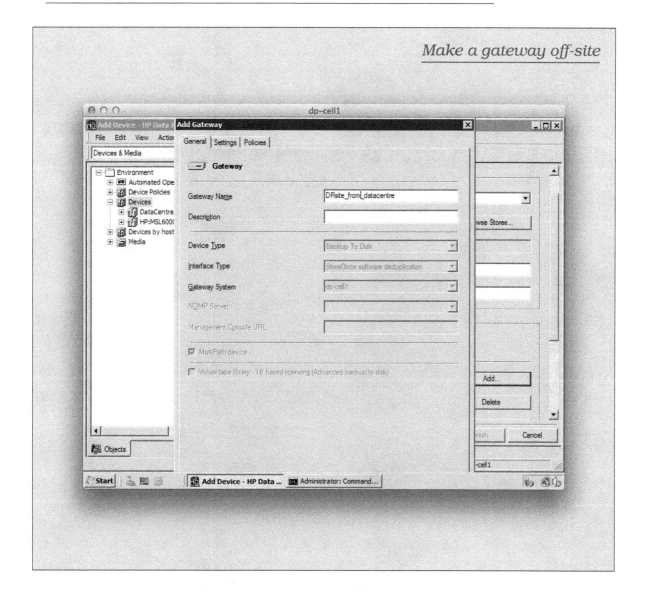

When we hit the *Add* button on the previous screen, the Gateway Name defaults to something uninformative. To make it very clear what we will use this gateway for I have changed the Gateway Name to be DRsite_from_datacentre. In other words this device is the device that you will use if you are in the datacentre and you want to write to the disaster recovery site.

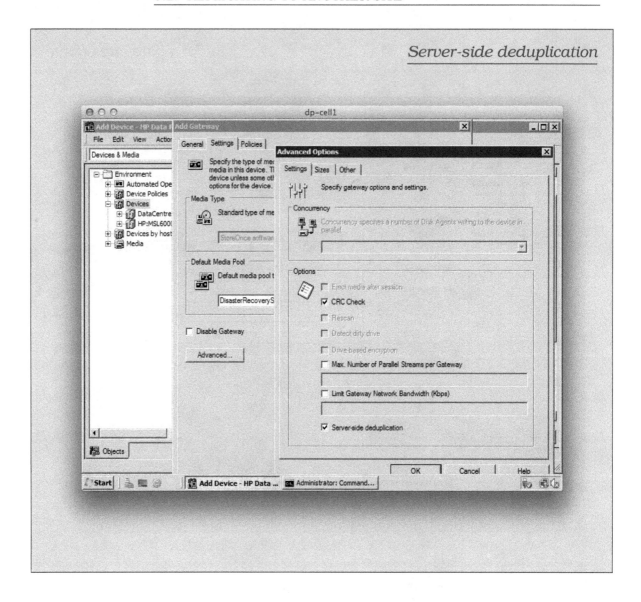

This is perhaps the most potentially expensive checkbox to get wrong. It defaults to unchecked which means that data is de-duplicated at the store server not at the gateway. I once left this disabled for a customer who had a lot of large backups and completely saturated their internal WAN bandwidth for several weeks.

I have enabled this checkbox because that is not the behaviour that I want: I want the de-duplication to occur at the *gateway*. This will ensure that the bandwidth is used most efficiently. If there is a block of data at the disaster recovery site and a computer sends an identical block of data to the gateway in the datacentre, I want nothing to be sent across to the other site.

There are some other parameters that can be set here. For example we can limit the bandwidth to ensure that there is spare capacity in the network link for other applications using the Limit Gateway Network Bandwidth parameter. In practice I rarely use this parameter. One thing I've noticed is that the actual bandwidth consumed is often much lower than what is specified here; this is an upper bound and no guarantee that data will be transferred at that speed.

Instead I work with the network engineers and ask them to de-prioritise traffic on TCP port 9388 , which is the data port for the StoreOnce software system. I asked them to let it use any other available bandwidth but for it to be the lowest priority so that it does not interfere with any other critical applications. I have found that this works more reliably.

(And I usually try to bribe the network engineers with chocolate to give traffic on TCP port 9387 high priority as this is the command and control port.)

A lot of large customers with extensive networks often deploy Riverbed appliances in order to optimise their WAN traffic. With almost every other protocol these appliances can save large amounts of bandwidth and improve network performance. I have never seen a Riverbed successfully compress a StoreOnce stream. Work with your network engineers to make sure that the StoreOnce data stream bypasses the Riverbed.

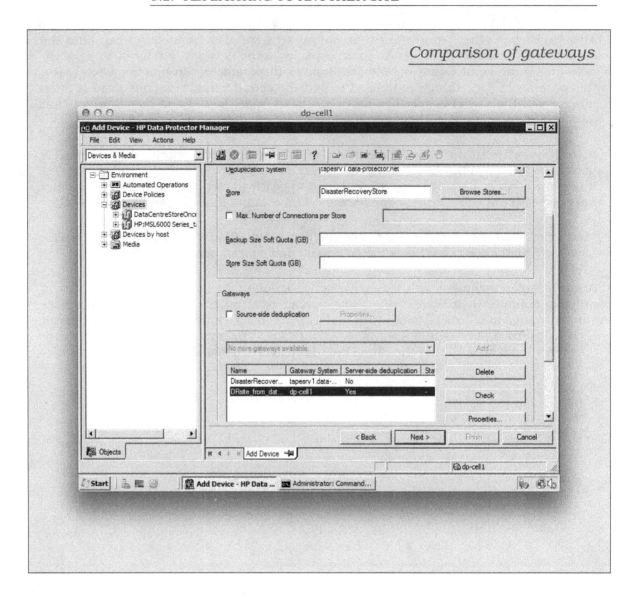

Reviewing the gateways in the summary it is very clear which gateways are local and which are remote based on the server side de-duplication column.

Low bandwidth replication

- Is just a copy job ...

- The destination device is a gateway for a remote StoreOnce system

- Does not guarantee identical de-duplication, but uncompressed stream will be the same

HP sell hardware StoreOnce systems and some of these have built-in replication mechanisms which DataProtector can control. Certain arrangements of this replication can guarantee that the deduplicated data at two sites is exactly identical. But this is rarely necessary. The goal is to have the *undeduplicated* data the same, which is guaranteed.

Statistically they stand a very good chance of being very similar but there is no guarantee (other than by sending exactly the same streams of data to them) that two StoreOnce devices will de-duplicate in the same way.

In practice you will often have a major StoreOnce system in the primary data centre which replicates data from small StoreOnce systems at remote offices. Much of the data at those small sites will be similar (for example Windows operating system binaries) which will de-duplicate more effectively in the primary data centre's StoreOnce as it is likely to have seen almost any chunk of data it receives from some other site before.

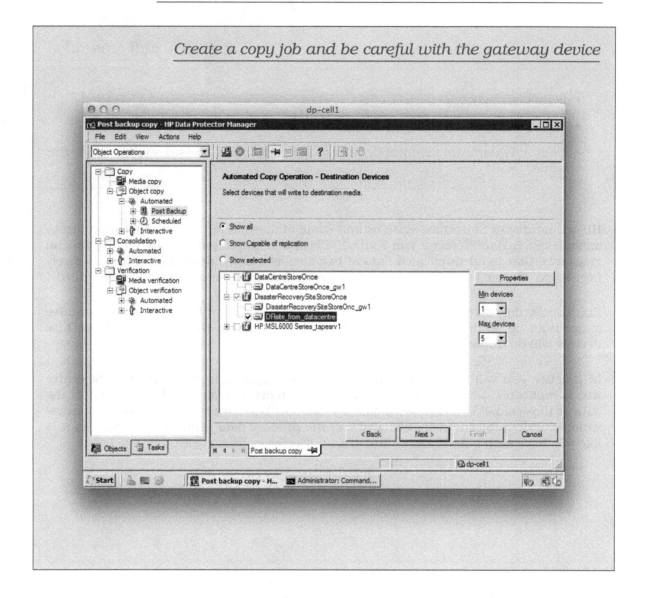

Be very careful to make sure that the device you choose has a high bandwidth link *from the library you will be copying from*. A good plan is to create a gateway to the secondary site on the computer that runs the primary site store: you can't get better bandwidth than localhost!

Secondly make sure that this device has the server-side de-duplication option turned on.

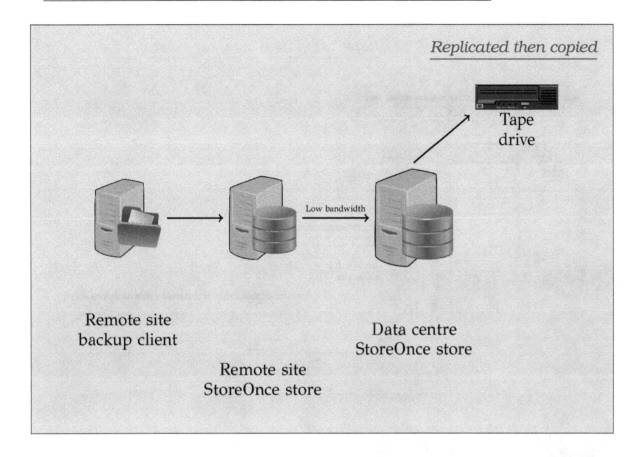

An architecture which a number of my customers are using happened spontaneously when they decided to replicate their remote office StoreOnce backups to the StoreOnce store in their primary data centre. It suddenly made more sense to use the tape drives in the primary data centre then it did to use tape drives in their remote offices.

Setting this up is not very difficult:

- You need a post-backup copy job which is triggered not after a backup but after the copy job which brings the data into the primary data centre.

- By default DataProtector will attempt to read the copy with the same device that was used to write it, which is obviously not what we want because that is the device in the remote site! So the source device needs to be changed.

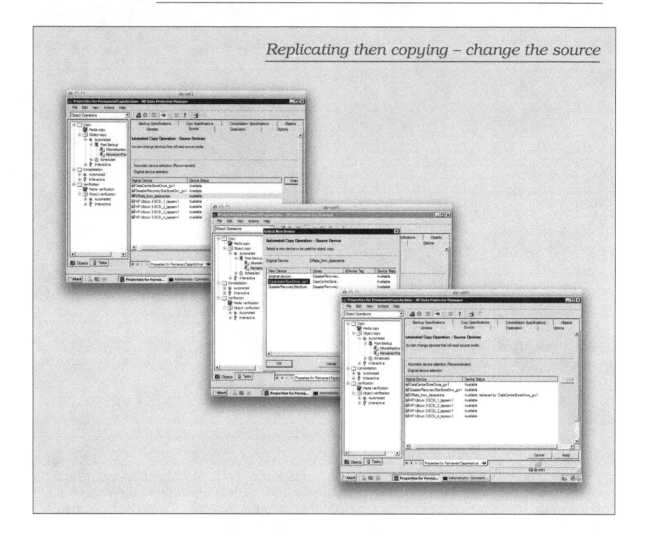

Replicating then copying – change the source

Create a post-backup copy job in exactly the same way as the other two examples in this book. Remember to replicate after the copy job, not after the backup job.

To tell DataProtector that you want to override what it should use for reading you make changes on the Source tab.

1. Select the device that was used – the device which you are wanting to change.

2. Hit the *Change* button at the right hand side of the screen.

3. You'll be presented with a list of alternate devices which you could use. Choose the gateway for the StoreOnce store which is on the computer that houses that store.

4. Hit OK

5. You will be presented with a summary screen showing that substitution.

9.3 Copying Lab

Copying Lab

1. Create a post-backup copy job to write your backup out to tape.

2. Test it, and also try running a backup to see the copy job appear.

3. Create a StoreOnce device on `tapesrvX.data-protector.net`. There is space for a StoreOnce library in the `/mnt` folder.

4. Create a low-bandwidth copy job to it.

5. (Bonus) Alter your backup to tape job so that it reads from the copy in the StoreOnce library on `tapesrvX`

10

Reporting

10.1 The Device Flow Report

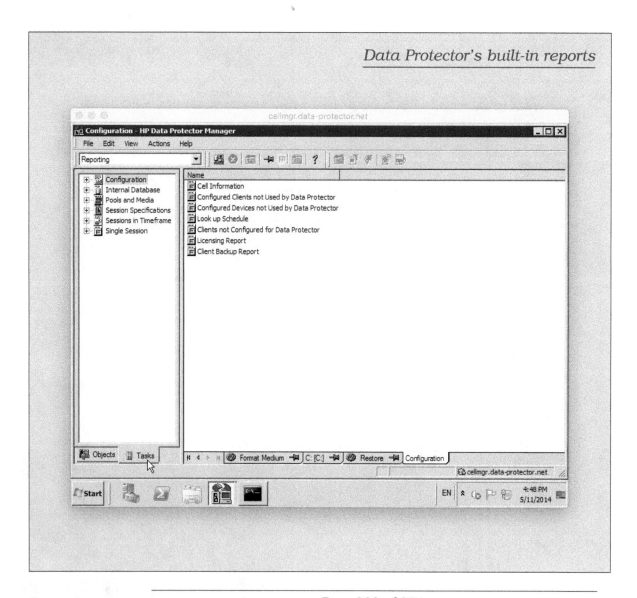

Data Protector's built-in reports

Data Protector comes with a wide variety of built-in reports. These can be scheduled to run automatically, triggered on certain events (such as the end of the backup session), initiated from the command line or run manually.

To run a report manually first go to the Reporting section and then click on the Tasks tab on the lower left hand corner of the Manager program.

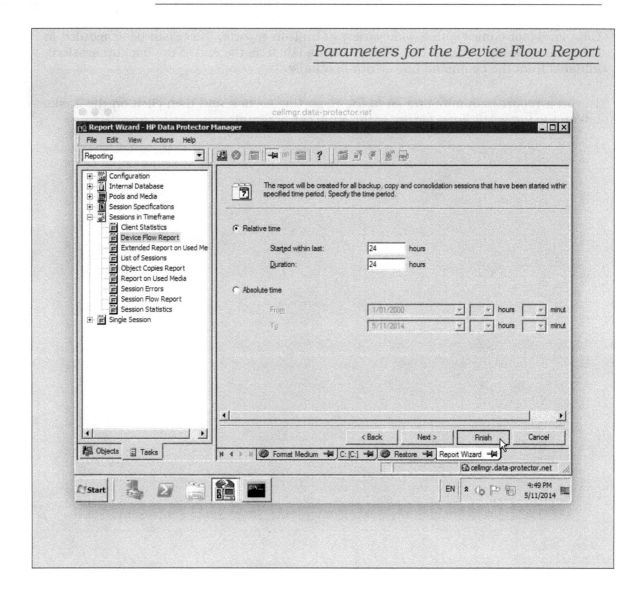

Parameters for the Device Flow Report

One of the most useful reports is the Device Flow Report. This report looks at a time period (the screenshot above shows how to do the last day's worth) and graphically displays which tape drives were in use and when.

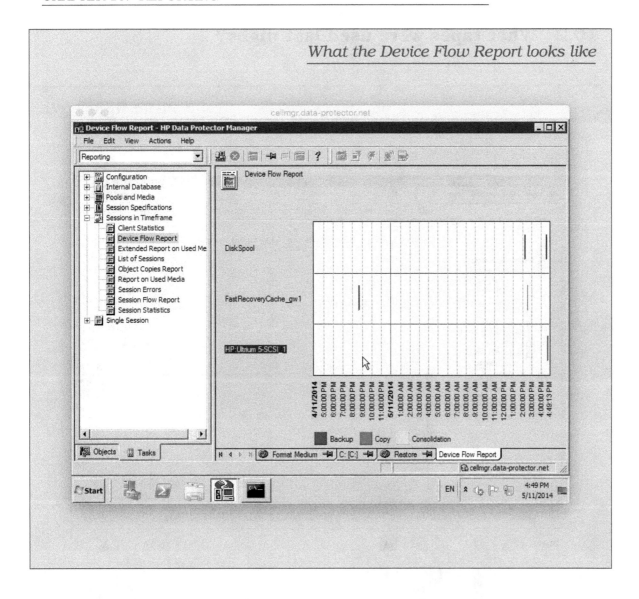

The report can be constrained just to show usage from a particular backup or backup group. It is somewhat interactive: as you move your mouse around the name of the drive gets highlighted.

In the screenshot above it is clear that there are plenty of windows of time in which we could schedule another backup.

This can be used in conjunction with the session flow report to identify backups which are held pending, waiting for a tape drive to become available. It becomes quite straight-forward to find a time to reschedule to.

10.2 What tapes were used last night?

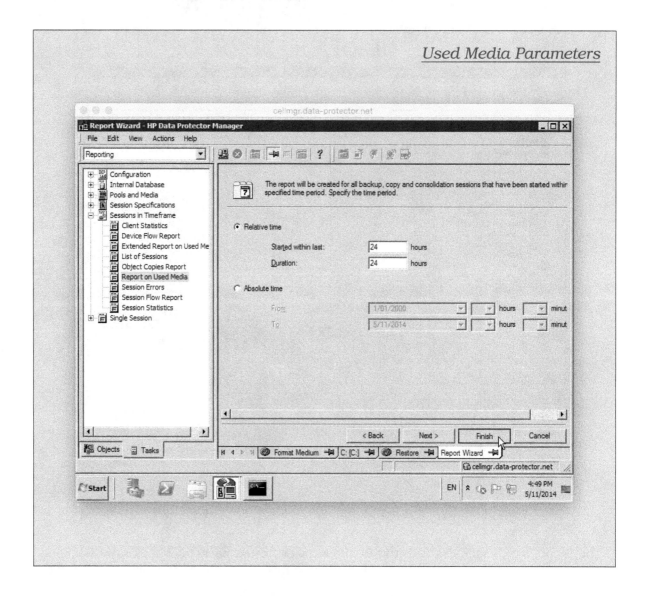

Another very useful report is the used media report, which can say what pieces of media were written to in a particular time window. Again this can be constrained further to show only media that were written by particular backups or backup groups.

Used Media Output

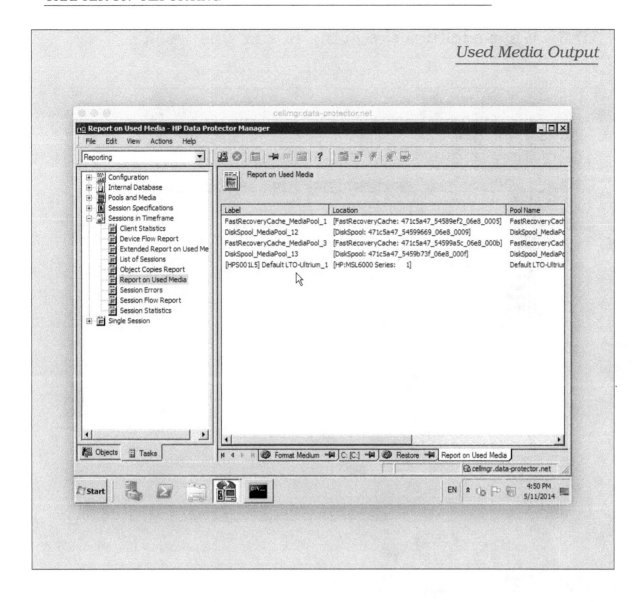

The media list can be sorted by the label, pool or current location. The location field can be updated through the GUI or through the command line (omnimm -modify_medium).

10.3   What backups are going to run this week?

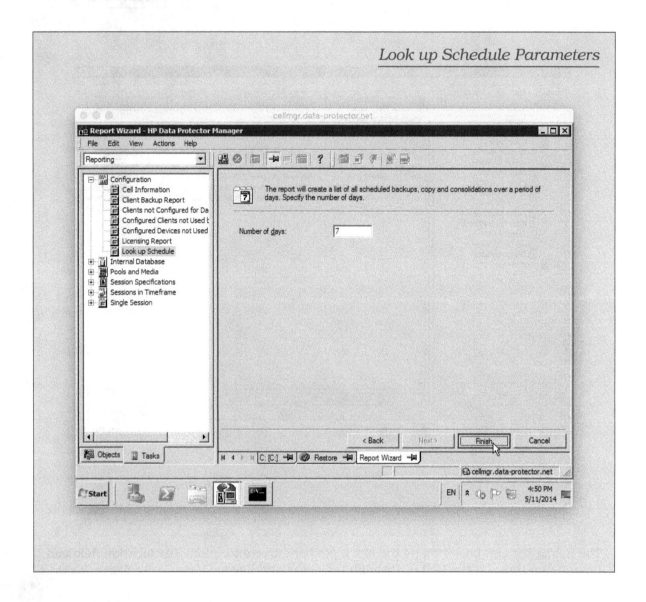

The schedule look up report only takes one parameter, and that is the number of days into the future to look at.

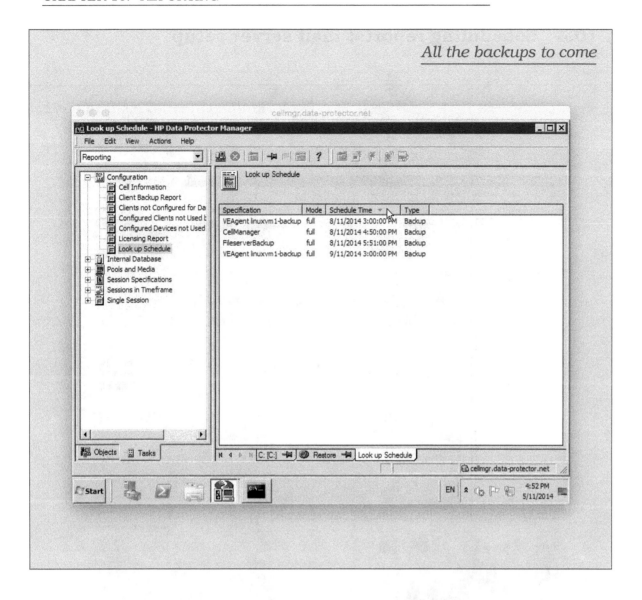

This very convenient report says operators the chore of maintaining a spreadsheet listing what jobs to expect will run. It only looks at backup jobs scheduled with the classic scheduler (not the advanced Scheduler) and of course cannot predict what backup jobs might be run interactively or triggered externally (e.g. via cron).

10.4   Scheduling reports: mail server setup

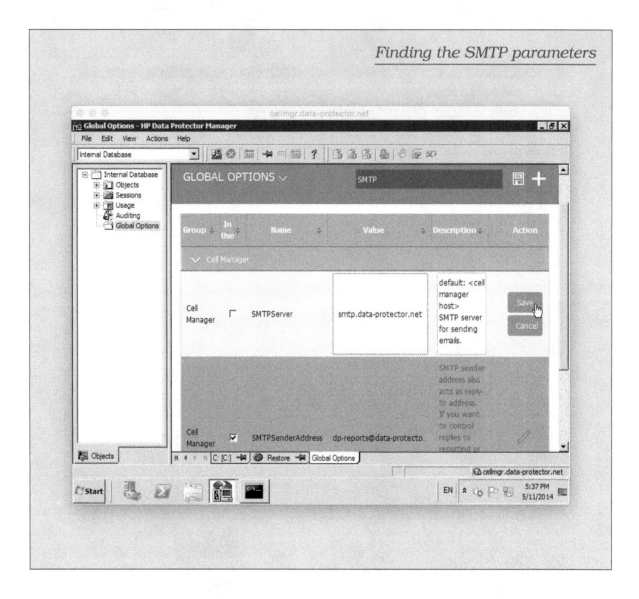

Finding the SMTP parameters

In most organisations, scheduled reports are emailed, although Data Protector can also push reports to an intranet and launch other programs.

There are two options for sending emails from Data Protector. If the cell manager is on Windows and MAPI has been set up, then this can be used.

Otherwise, Data Protector can send email by connecting directly to an SMTP server. This is by far the most common arrangement.

Go to the Internal Database section, and choose Global Options. This will bring up the very Web 2.0 looking user interface for modifying the global options file. In versions of Data Protector prior to 8.1, the only option was to edit the global options text file which was in:

Windows `C:\ProgramData\OmniBack\Config\Server\Options\Globals` (Or wherever Data Protector's database was installed)

Linux / HP-UX / Solaris "/etc/opt/omni/server/options/globals

Search for the parameters which include SMTP in their name.

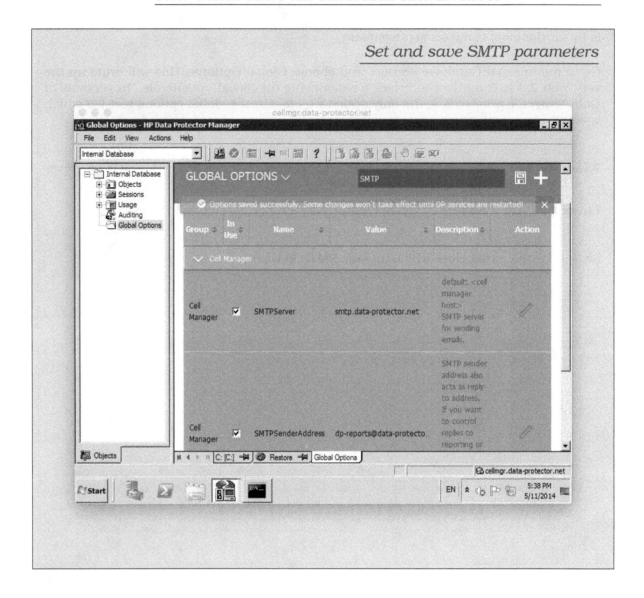

Set and save SMTP parameters

You will need to set the SMTP server parameter to the IP address or hostname of a mail server that listens on port 25 and accepts unauthenticated connections. (For customers running Google Apps for their email: you can't use `smtp.gmail.com`.)

If your cell manager is running on Linux or HP-UX, then you might be able to use the default value which is `localhost`.

You will also probably want to set the SMTP sender address. Depending on how your mail server is set up, this may or may not need to be a valid address. This is used as the "From" address and also the "Reply-To" address of any email which is sent from a notification or report from Data Protector.

10.5 Scheduling reports: daily media usage

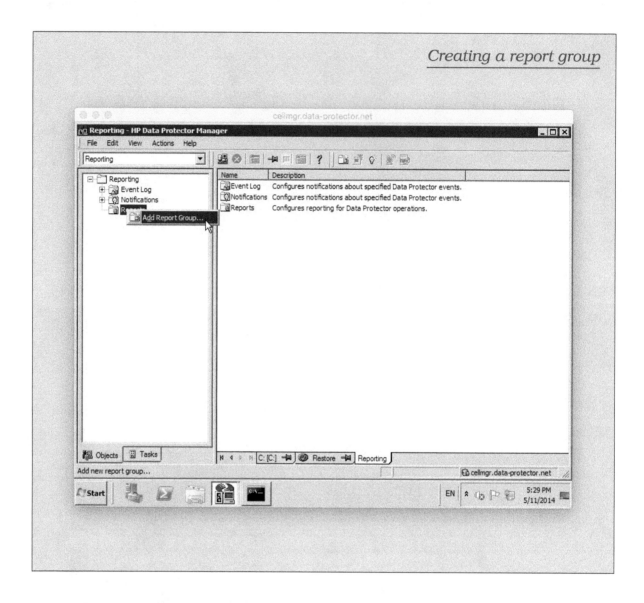

Creating a report group

Note that we are no longer on the Tasks tab, but back on the Objects tab (on the lower left-hand corner of the user interface).

Right clicking on the Reports container brings up a menu item: Add Report Group. Since reports can't be scheduled independently or directly, this is the first step towards getting a daily report of used media.

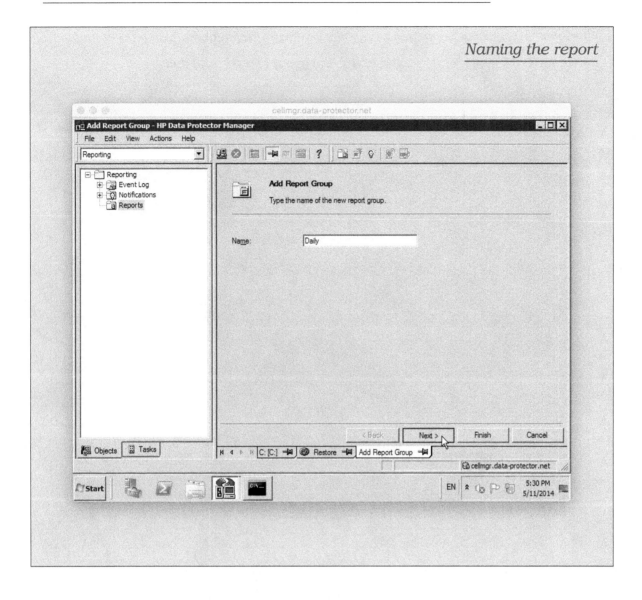

Naming the report

The name that you choose here will be used as a file name in two different locations. Firstly it will hold the details of the reports in this group:

Windows `C:\ProgramData\Omniback\Config\Server\rptgroups\`*reportname*

Linux / HP-UX `/etc/opt/omni/server/rptgroups/`*reportname*

Secondly, there will be a file of scheduling information.

Windows `C:\ProgramData\Omniback\Config\Server\rptschedules\`*reportname*

Linux / HP-UX `/etc/opt/omni/server/rptgroups/`*reportschedules*

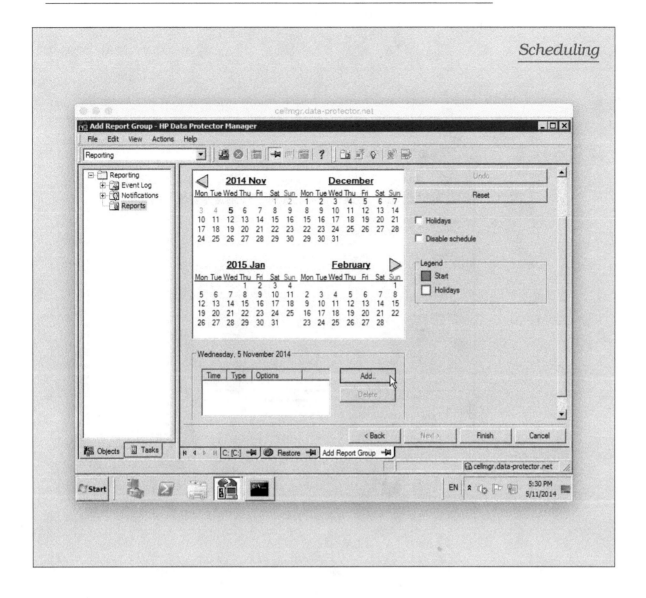

Scheduling works in exactly the same way as for backup and copy jobs. There is no advanced Scheduler for reports.

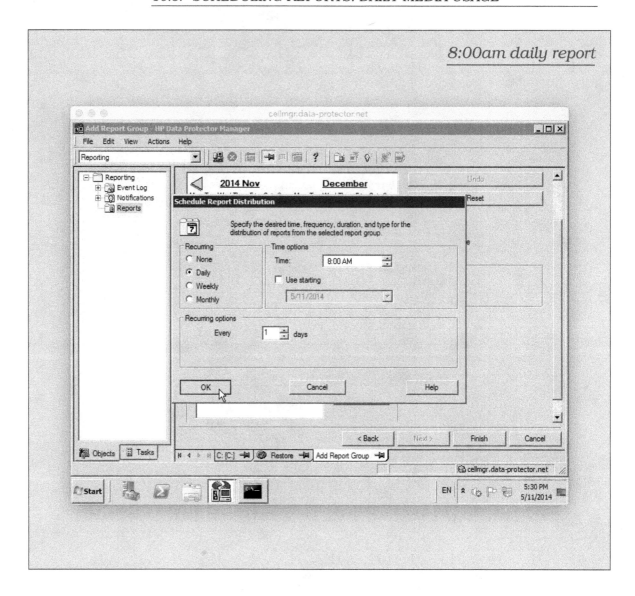

8:00am daily report

The goal here is to have a report ready for operators to take tapes out each morning, so an 8 o'clock in the morning schedule makes sense.

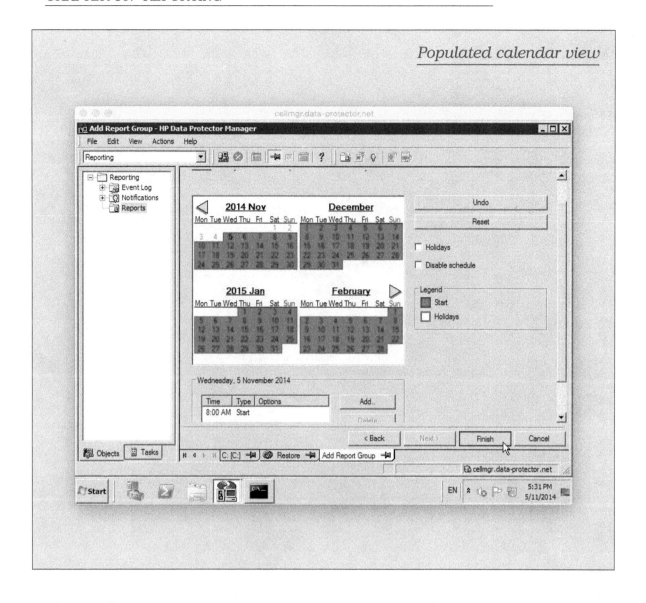

Populated calendar view

There is of course no such thing as an incremental running of the report, so the calendar tends to be a larger wash of red.

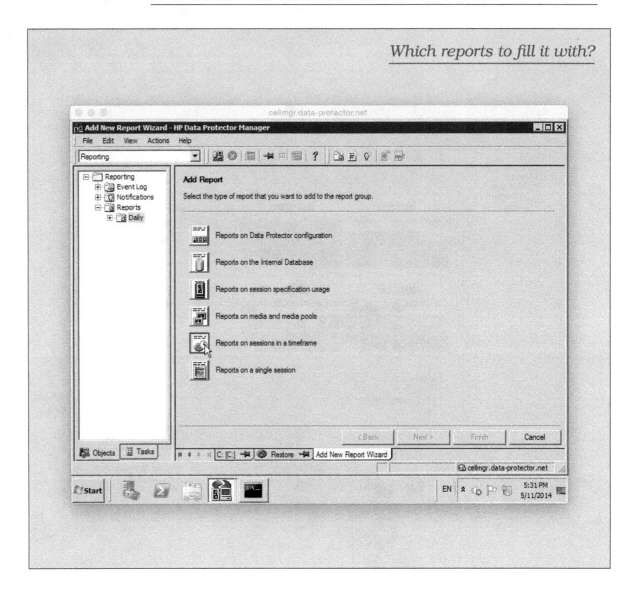

You will now be prompted for the reports to include in this report group. Choose a category first

Timeframe reports

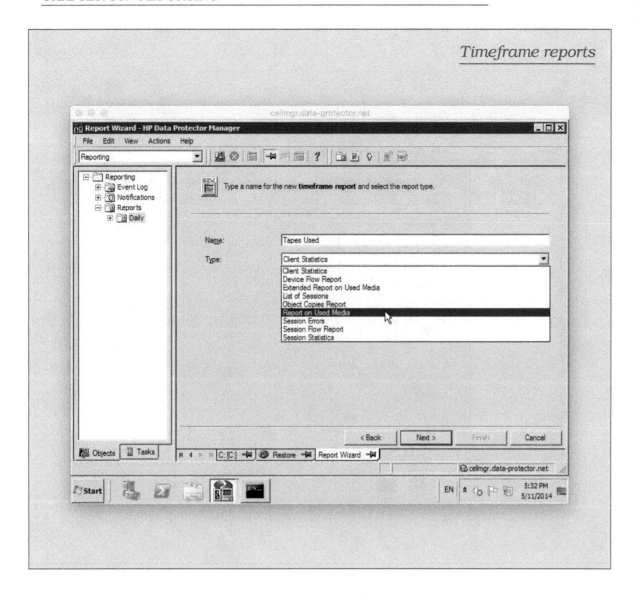

The reports available here are exactly the same as the reports available interactively.

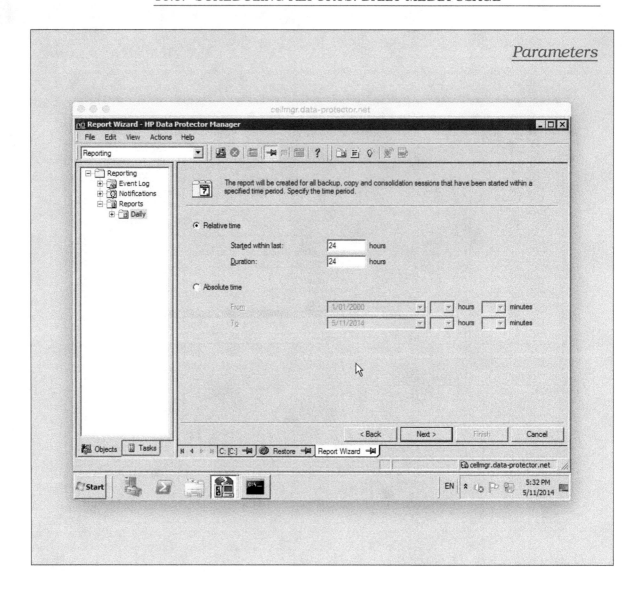

The parameters are also the same as for interactive reports. It would be very strange to have a scheduled report that always reported on the same absolute time interval, so this will almost always involve a relative time interval – this will be relative to the time when the report is running. So therefore in this example at 8 AM each morning we will get the list of tapes used since 8 AM the previous day.

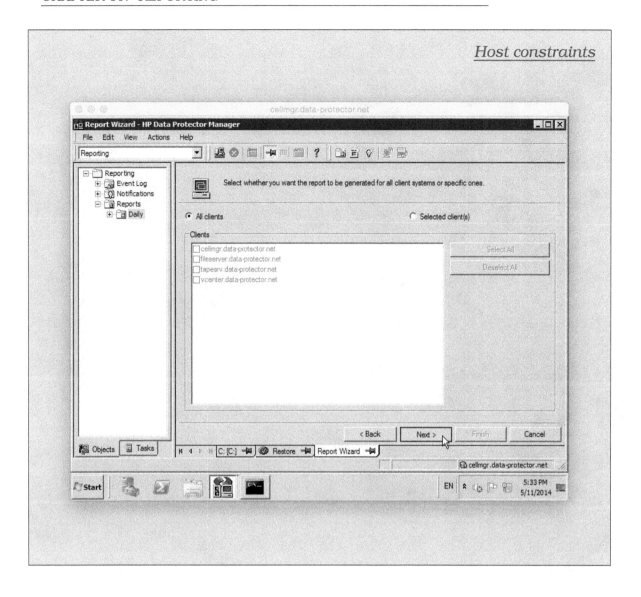

Organisations that have a single Data Protector cell spanning multiple sites (which is a very common setup) may not want to send reports to operators in London about tape usage in Beijing, so this report can be constrained by which clients were involved in the backup.

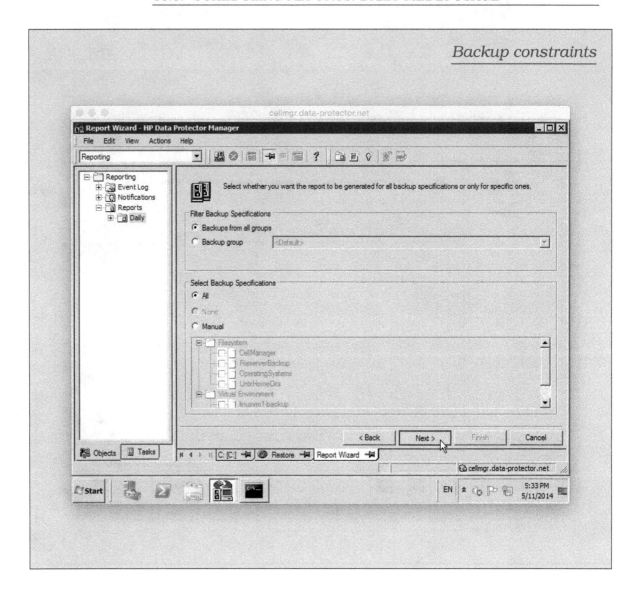

Here it is possible to constrain the report by backup group order to refer only to tapes that were written in a particular backup specification.

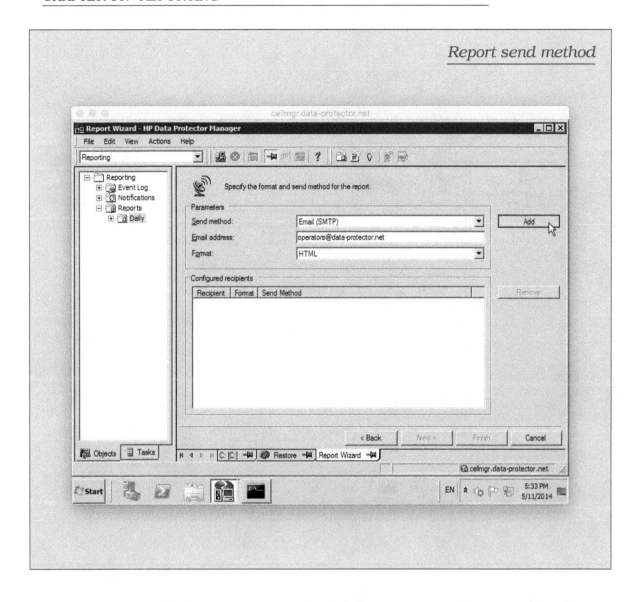

Each report can be sent to many different email addresses. Reports can also be generated in other formats (such as plain text or tab delimited files) which are easier to process with programs. They can also be sent by methods other than email (such as launching a program, writing to a log file, displaying a pop-up dialogue box and several others).

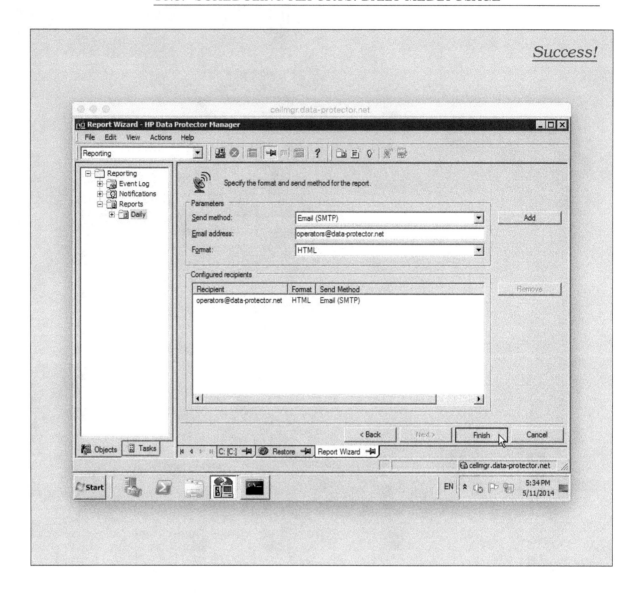

Now that the recipient is displayed in the "configured recipients" pane, all the setup work has now been done.

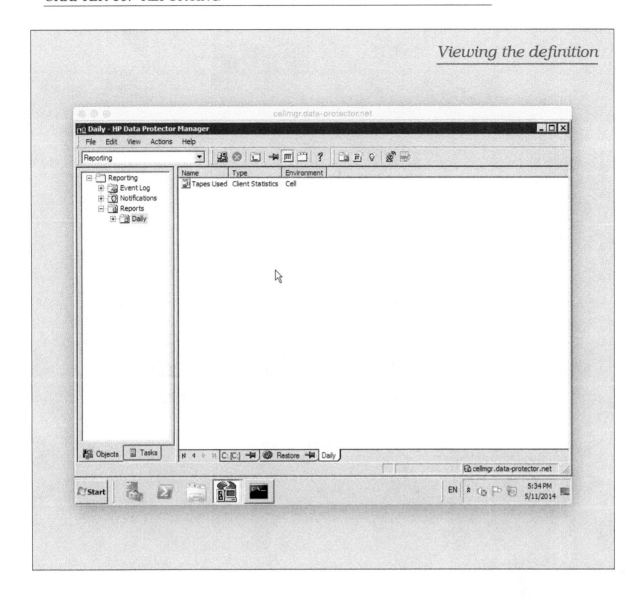

This is how the report definition and report group are displayed. For testing, it is possible to right click on the report group and run it. This won't necessarily display anything, but it will trigger the emails to be sent.

Part V

The Internal Database

11

Restoring the Internal Database

11.1 Being prepared

What you want to have around before a disaster
<hr>

- IDB backup on **tape**

- media.log

- omnidownload output (very useful)

- mcf files (optional but useful)

- DR-recovery images (convenient)

One of the common requirements before a Data Protector deployment project can be signed-off as complete is to demonstrate that you can recover from a disaster on the cell manager.

You probably want to email, `rsync` or `robocopy` these on a regular basis to somewhere safe.

IDB backup on tape Tapes are self-contained. It is much, much easier to recover a database from tape than any other media.

229

media.log The `media.log` file contains a list of all media used in backups. It tells you which tapes you should look at for the most recent database backup.

mcf files From the tape on which you put the most recent internal database backup. This will speed up the import process.

omnidownload output For every device and library; at the very least you want the ones you will use in recovering the cell manager.

Ignite-UX of the cell manager If your cell manager is on HP-UX.

EADR ISO of the cell manager If your cell manager is on Windows or Linux

```
                                                        media.log


9/12/2013 7:18:35 AM c8c7cbef:52316aca:07e8:0008
   "DataCentreStoreOnce_MediaPool_7" [2013/09/12-10]
9/12/2013 7:18:36 AM c8c7cbef:52316aca:07e8:0008
   "DataCentreStoreOnce_MediaPool_7" [2013/09/12-10]
9/12/2013 7:53:20 AM 1cc3040a:523159fe:0b20:0001
   "[HPS001L3] Datacentre LTO-3 Pool_1" [2013/09/12-12] OmniDB
```

The media log is written to whenever a tape is selected to be used in a backup, copy or media session.

Windows cell managers `C:\ProgramData\OmniBack\log\Server\media.log` (unless installed elsewhere)

Linux / HP-UX cell managers `/var/opt/omni/log/server/media.log`

Line breaks were added in the sample displayed for readability.

You really want to keep a copy of this file as it is a last resort for finding an IDB backup if you need it. It's not a large file, so `robocopy` or `rsync` it to another server several times per day.

You will also often find lines like this in the media log (line breaks inserted again):

```
23/01/2015 9:26:55 AM 471c5a47:5459b92c:0598:0001
   "[HPS001L5] Default LTO-Ultrium_1" [TAPE WRITE STATISTICS]
   Logical drive: Drive 3:
Errors corrected with no delay: 0
Errors corrected with delay: 0
Total: 0
Total errors corrected: 0
Total correction algorithm processed: 0
Total bytes processed: 0
Total uncorrected errors: 0
```

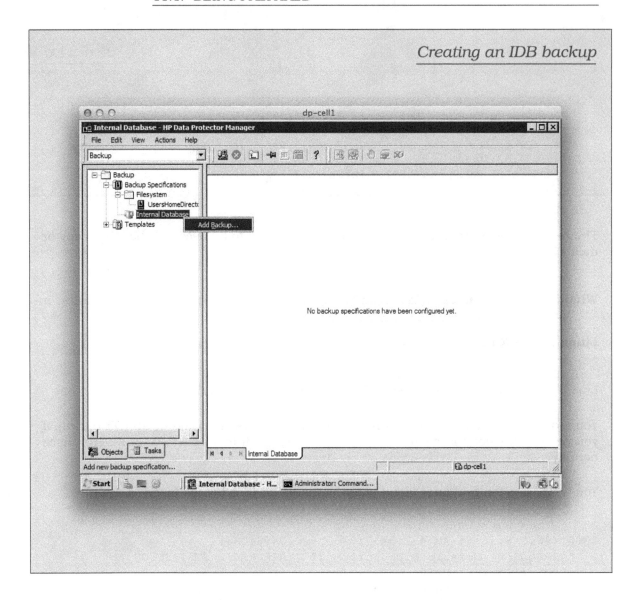

Creating an IDB backup

It is possible to have more than one internal database backup configured. You might do this because you want to restore configuration files from a low latency StoreOnce backup but still want to have a tape backup of the internal database.

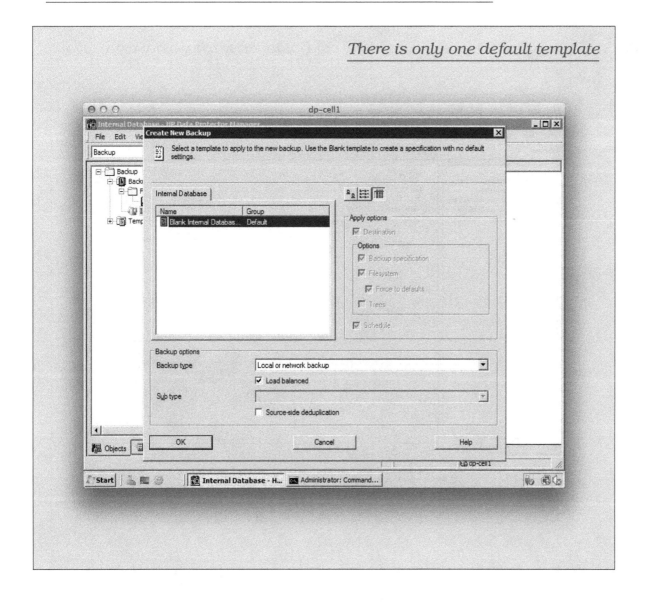

In fact the only choice available in the screenshot above is whether or not to load balance the backup (and since you definitely want the backup to fit onto a single piece of media, it's irrelevant whether you load balance or not) and whether you want to backup using source side de-duplication (and you are unlikely to want to backup to a StoreOnce device anyway).

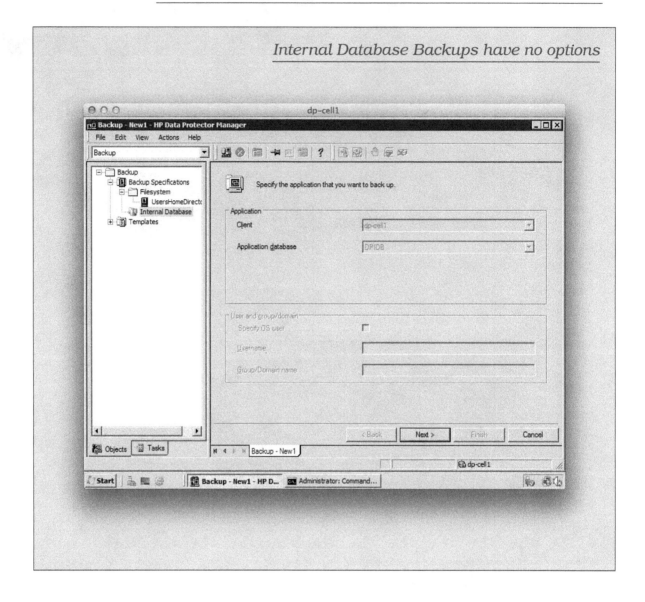

Internal Database Backups have no options

There are no options to choose on this screen either.

Customers who upgraded from DataProtector 7 or earlier to version 8 will find that their old internal database backups have been upgraded to version 8 style internal database backup. As of the release to market of version of v8 there were three major issues:

- If the previous backup configuration had had an owner, then the upgraded version would have an owner as well, and as can be seen in the screenshot it is invalid to set ownership on internal database backups in version 8.

- There was often corruption in the database after the upgrade (perhaps because of the migration from Raima Velocis to PostgreSQL) which would prevent the internal database check from working, and therefore prevent the internal database backup from running.

- A hot backup licence was required on the cell manager. Because this is no longer a file system backup, the internal licensing logic for DataProtector wants to see an online integration licence for this backup. In the future HP may choose to bundle an extra online extension license to solve this problem, or they may correct the logic in the code. Customers who have upgraded are encouraged to contact the response centre to get a temporary resolution.

These have all been resolved in upgrades to 8.1 and 9.0.

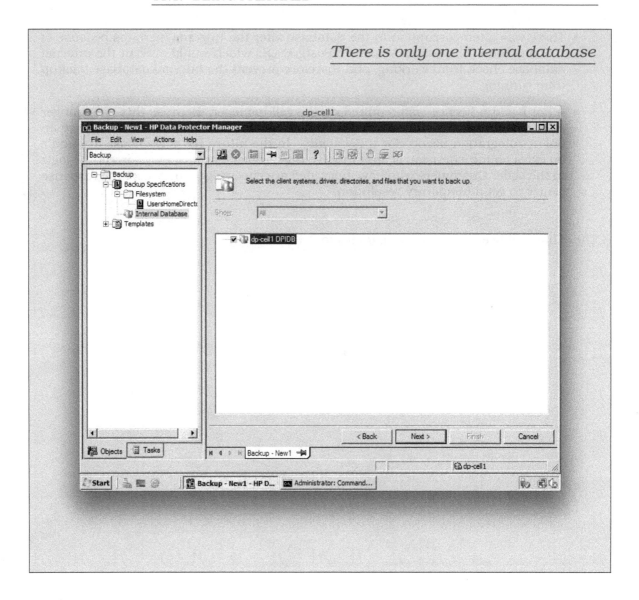

There is also nothing to choose on this screen either as there is only one internal database.

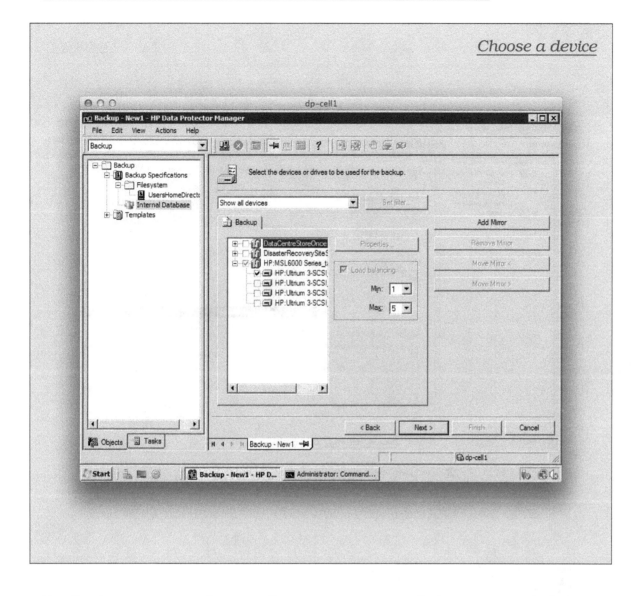

Finally, there is a screen that actually requires some sort of administrator response!

In the screenshot above I have chosen one tape drive to perform the backup. I could have chosen more: if I had selected all 4 tape drives and reduced the maximum load balancing concurrency down to 1 (to be absolutely sure that only one type drivers used), then the backup would use whichever tape drive became available first.

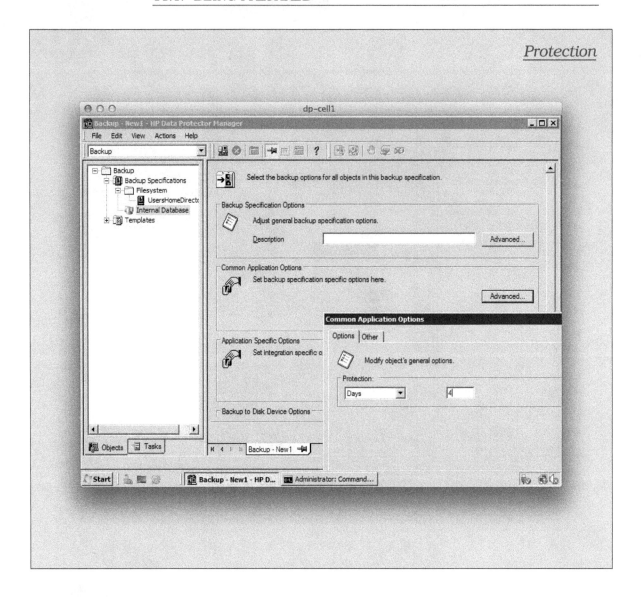

The default protection (from `Common Application Options`) is permanent. This doesn't make much sense; it is very rare that you would want to wind your database back very far. For example, if you have a protection for 3 months on a IDB database, you are proposing that you might fail to notice a corrupted database for three months.

So I set this to a smaller value.

Scheduling

- Schedule IDB backup at a time when few backups are running

- Mid-morning (9am or 10am) is quite common

If possible, find a time when no backups are running. If you can, this is a perfect time for an IDB backup. IDB backups won't take long: you need to have a very large cell to have a 200GB internal database backup.

If you can't find a completely idle time – for example, because you have a database which has transaction logs backed up every 15 minutes – then just look for a time of low utilisation. In theory the internal database can be recovered with transaction logs to almost any time, but in practice it isn't always possible, particularly if the whole computer failed taking the transaction logs with it. Backing up when not much is happening means that in the worst case (when you have to restore back to a point-in-time) you might only lose a couple of small sessions.

11.2 IDB Backup Lab

Backup your internal database

1. Create an IDB backup which writes to your tape drive

2. Run the IDB backup

11.3 Restoring

> *Here be bugs*
>
> - Numerous bugs
> - Not much documentation

There are quite a few problems with the capabilities of DataProtector's IDB restore. Very few options actually work.

The documentation assumes everything will work perfectly when quite often it doesn't.

What if my database is completely corrupted?

1. Can you run `omnidbinit` to re-initialise?

2. Otherwise, re-install DataProtector if necessary

If the database is simply corrupted, then you can use `omnidbinit` to put things back into a reasonable shape. If it is slightly corrupted (e.g. perhaps just a portion of the database, such as the DCBF) then it might be possible to reinitialise that portion. For example, there is a fresh copy of the DCBF portion of the database in:

Windows cell managers `C:\ProgramData\OmniBack\NewConfig\db80\dcbf` (unless installed elsewhere)

Linux / HP-UX cell managers `/var/opt/omni/newconfig/db80/dcbf`

However, this is not sufficient to recreate the PostgreSQL portion of the database. While it might be possible to recreate these with `initdb` it is faster and safer to reinstall the DataProtector software.

Re-create one device (and its library)

- `omniupload`
- Auto-configure

If you followed the instructions at the start of this chapter, you would have run `omnidownload` `-library` for every tape library in your system, and you would have run `omnidownload` `-device` for every device as well. The output from these are text files, quite small (rarely more than a few kilobytes) and can be saved offline somewhere.

If you have this on hand, you can use `omniupload -create_library` and `omniupload` `-create_device`. These will re-create your device definitions.

On the other hand, as you only need to get one tape drive defined again, if you know which machine it is connected to, you can simply auto-configure to recreate a device definition.

When the database is restored, it will be restored including the database tables with the device definitions in them. These are `dp_medmng_tape_drive` and `dp_medmng_device` but the view `dp_devices` seems easier to work with. It looks like HP had one schema for Data Protector 8.0 and then wrapped it with various SQL views for later versions.

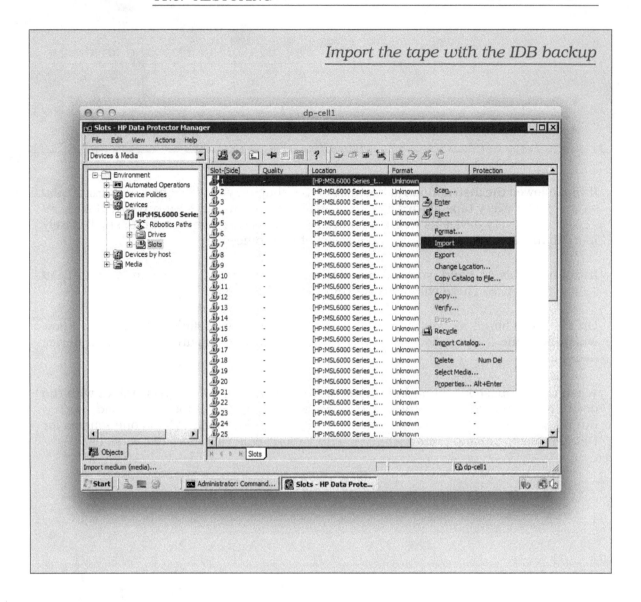

Import the tape with the IDB backup

The goal here is to have the new database have a record of the backup session of the old database.

If you're fortunate enough to have MCF files around then you can import from these and that will obviously be much faster. Worst case, you have to import from the backup media as we are doing here.

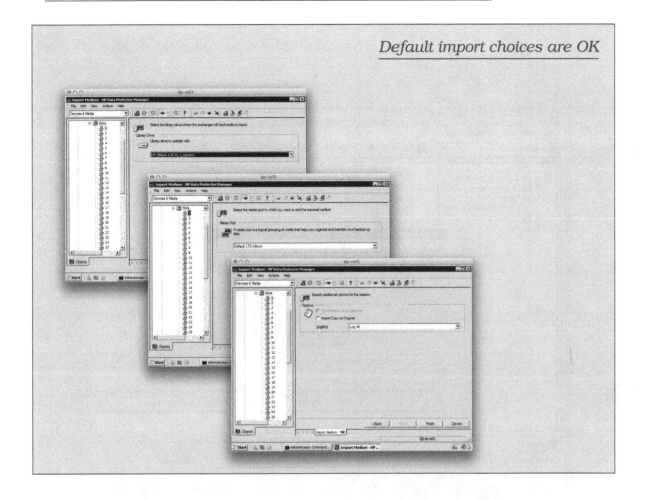

You will only have one device to use, and the media pool will be the default media pool for the device type, but when you have restored database all this will be replaced.

It also does not particularly matter what level of logging you use and the database will not have any original copies so the *Import Copy As Original* option is irrelevant as well.

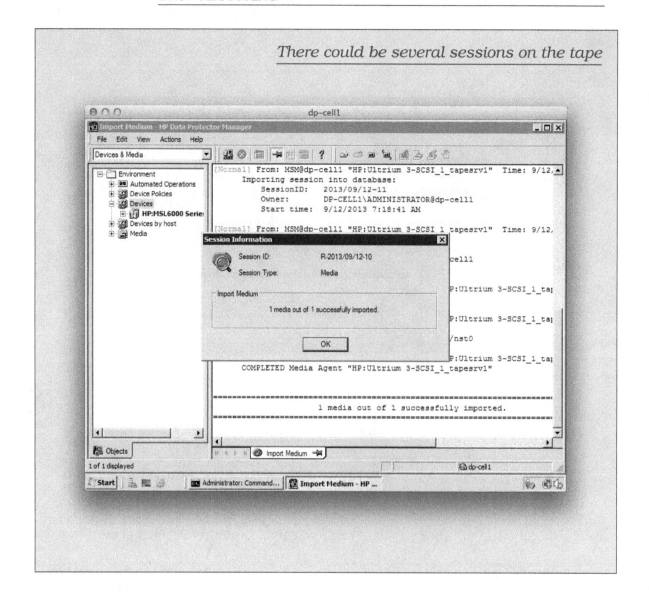

Do not be surprised if there are many sessions imported: after all there may have been many sessions on that media. As long as the most recent internal database backup is in there somewhere, all should be good.

Check the sessions that were imported

- Is the latest IDB session in the session list?

- If not, double check the `media.log` file

Your session history will now show a very brief list: it will just show sessions which were on the media that you have just imported.

If you do not see an internal database backup session in the session history now then something went wrong in the previous steps.

Also, when you switch to the restore context there should be an option to restore the Internal Database.

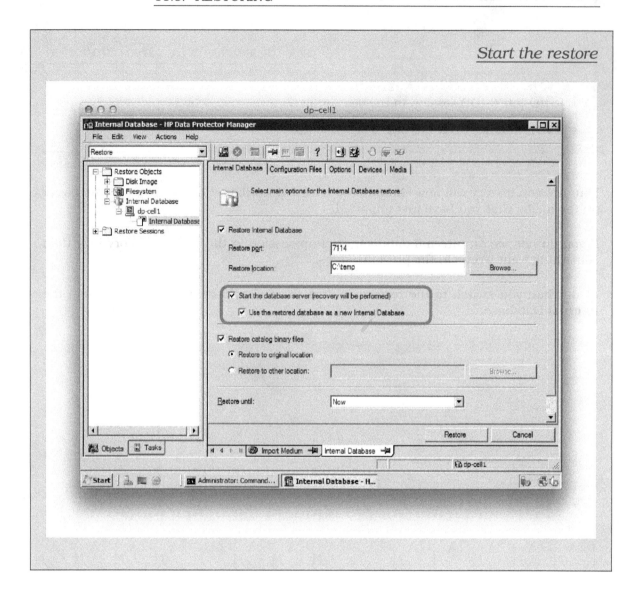

Uncheck the 2 options:

- Start the database server (recovery will be performed)
- Use the restored database as a new Internal Database

These two options do not appear to work in an out-of-the-box version 8 system. You will need to provide two empty directories: one for the PostgreSQL data and one for the DCBF files.

After the restore is complete

1. Stop DataProtector

2. Move the temporary database out of the way

3. Move the restored folders in place

4. Re-create junction points / symlinks (if necessary)

5. Start Dataprotector

Step 1: Run the command `omnisv stop`.

Step 2

There are 3 PostgreSQL folders restored:

pg This is the configuration and bootstrap information for the PostgreSQL server.
idb This is the table space for the core internal database.
jce This is the table space for the non-core data.

By default the original paths for where the database lived are:

Windows cell managers `C:\Program Files\OmniBack\server\db80` (unless DataProtector was installed in a different directory)

UNIX / Linux cell managers "/var/opt/omni/server/db80 "

Hopefully you'll never need to use the temporary database again, but if something goes wrong in the next few steps and you want to restore again, the quickest and easiest thing to do will be just to replace these folders back when they were. So move the 3 folders (pg, idb, and jce) out of this database directory and put them somewhere safe.

Likewise, the DCBF directory in the same location should be moved somewhere else as well.

Step 3: In the first of the folder locations you specified when you ran the restore you will find the 3 IDB folders. Move these into the location that you just freed up in the previous step.

The second of the folder locations will contain the DCBF files; this can be moved in place as well.

Step 4: There is a folder inside the `pg` folder called `pg_tblspc`. On Windows it has 2 junction points inside it, and on Linux these are symbolic links. They point to the `idb` and `jce` folders. The tricky part about this is that if you restore the internal database into `C:\temp` (or `/tmp`) then the junction points inside the `pg_tblspc` folder will point to `C:\temp\idb` and `C:\temp\jce` (or `/tmp/idb` and `/tmp/jce`). This is obviously not a good place for them to live permanently, and in any case, you have just moved the data from that location.

The Windows command-line commands to resolve this issue look like this:

```
C:
cd
\ProgramData\Omniback\Server\db80\pg\pg_tblspc
rmdir 16387
rmdir 16445
mklink /j 16387 C:\ProgramData\Omniback\Server\db80\idb
mklink /j 16445 C:\ProgramData\Omniback\Server\db80\jce
```

But change these commands as appropriate, depending on where you installed DataProtector and changing the numbers in the last 4 lines as appropriate to match what was restored.

Step 5: `omnisv start`

11.4   IDB Lab

IDB Recovery Lab

1. Uninstall DataProtector

2. Re-install DataProtector

3. Recover your old database

Did it work?

```
$ omnidbcheck

Check Level              Mode                       Status
==============================================================
Database connection      -connection                OK
Schema consistency       -schema_consistency        OK
Datafiles consistency    -verify_db_files           OK
DCBF(presence and size)  -bf                        OK
DONE!
```

If `omnidbcheck -extended` reports OK on every area, then it is very likely that the database is working.

Authentication problems?

```
$OMNICONF/config/server/idb/idb.config

PGIDBNAME='hpdpidb';
PGUSER='hpdpidb_app';
PGPASSWORD='OXByeXNzdmY5Z3Btdw==';
PGSUPERUSER='hpdp';
PGSUPERPASSWORD='NHElbGtpczlycGZ3bw==';
```

It is possible that when you recreated the database and restored over it, that the user authentication information in the `idb.config` file might not match what PostgreSQL is expecting. All the commands which interact with the internal database – such as `omnidbcheck` – use the contents of the `idb.config` file to find the right credentials to use.

The passwords are not heavily encrypted: in fact they are not encrypted at all and just stored in base64 encoded format. There are many tools for decoding base64 content. If you are not worried about security there is a website http://www.base64decode.org/ that you can just copy and paste these into to get a decoding.

The two passwords above decode to:

- 9pryssvf9gpmw
- 4q5lkis9rpfwo

We can do one of two actions. We can update the `idb.config` file to match whatever the database is expecting (if you know what this is), or update the database to reflect what is in the `idb.config` file.

```
host all all 127.0.0.1/32 trust
host all all ::1/128 trust
```

The access control file for PostGreSQL is in:

Linux / HP-UX `/var/opt/omni/server/db80/pg/pg_hba.conf`

Windows `C:\programData\Omniback\server\db80\pg\pg_hba.conf` (unless installed elsewhere).

It contains two lines:

```
host postgres hpdp 127.0.0.1/32 sspi map=hpdpidb
host postgres hpdp ::1/128 sspi map=hpdpidb
```

Comment these out, and add the following lines to unlock all security:

```
host all all 127.0.0.1/32 trust
host all all ::1/128 trust
```

You can either restart Data Protector altogether, or just reconfigure PostgreSQL:

```
C:\Program Files\Omniback\idb\bin\pg ctl reload \
 -D C:\ProgramData\OmniBack\server\db80\pg
```

Running SQL against the database

- `omnidbutil -run_script` *filename.sql* `-detail`

- `psql -U hpdp --port 7112 --host=127.0.0.1 -d hpdpidb`

Obviously `omnidbutil` is the easier option, but it does not run as a superuser (it runs commands as `hpdpidb_app`) so it cannot be used to reset the `hpdp` user.

The `psql` program is found in:

Windows C:\Program Files\Omniback\idb\bin\psql.exe
Linux / HP-UX /opt/omni/idb/bin/psql

Altering a user's password

ALTER ROLE hpdpidb'app WITH PASSWORD '9pryssvf9gpmw';
ALTER ROLE hpdp WITH PASSWORD '4q5lkis9rpfwo';

After you have run this, you can revert the `pg_hba.conf` file back to its original.

## 12

IDB Schema

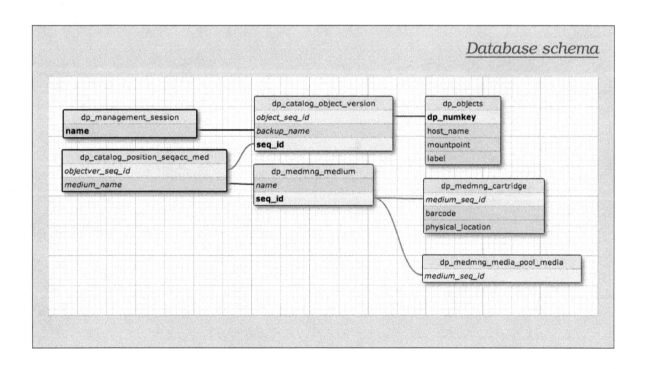

Database schema

As far as I can tell, HP don't document the schema of the PostgreSQL internal database. What follows is my investigations as I was chasing up a customer for whom thousands of sessions were giving strange results. (When they *looked* at a medium and went to the Objects tab to find, the GUI responded with "in order to delete this medium, export it first".)

To find out what tables exist, PostgreSQL has a command \d to display all tables. That was the starting point, as well as using `pgdump` before and after a backup to compare the differences.

There are seven important database tables which are affected in the normal operations of running a backup.

---

dp_management_session

- name ("2014/07/14 0007")
- application˙uuid

`dp_management_session` has a column **"name"** which looks like this: "2014/07/14 0007". In other words, the session name as it appears in every command, except that it has a space instead of a dash.

The name is used as a unique key (as it should be unique!) in conjunction with the column 'application_uuid'. I haven't figured out exactly what that's doing, but I'm presuming it's something to do with the manager-of-managers product, where you might have centralised all your media into one cell. In this case you could have two or identical session names referred to in the database, one from each of the client cells and one from the manager cell. To simplify things, I've ignored the `application_uuid` column(s) in the diagram on the previous page.

- hostname
- mountpoint
- label
- uuid
- dp_numkey

Obviously, the backup should write something. If this is the first time this filesystem (or database or Exchange server, etc.) has been backed up, then the `dp_objects` table will have a new row added to it, with the hostname, mountpoint and label of the object being backed up. The columns `uuid` and `dp_numkey` act like the primary key for this table, which means that if you aren't running manager-of-managers, the `dp_numkey` will be unique.

dp_catalog_object_version

- `backup_name` (generally referencing `dp_management_session.name`)
- `object_seq_id` references `dp_objects`
- `seq_id`

Each time a backup of a filesystem runs, a row is added to `dp_catalog_object_version`. If there are several filesystems being backed up in one job, this table may have many rows added for each backup run.

There is a column `backup_name` which partly references `dp_management_session.name`. I say partly, because there is no foreign key between them, and in fact, sometimes backup'name is null. Presumably what's going on is that a backup could have a copy made, and then the original expires, delete the original session, leaving a catalog object version which doesn't correspond to a session.

The column `object_seq_id` references `dp_objects` (together with the usual uuid story).

The primary key is the combination of application'uuid (as usual) and a field called `seq_id`.

- dp_catalog_object_datastream
- dp_catalog_object_versession

There is a row created in the dp_catalog_object_datastream table and also one in the table dp_catalog_object_versession – one for each row added to the database table dp_catalog_object_version.

These don't seem very interesting: the former looks like it's something to do with enforcing device policies, and the latter a record of a post-backup verification.

---

dp_catalog_position_seqacc_med

- `objver_seq_id` → `dp_catalog_object_version.seq_id`
- `medium_name` (tape header)

The oddly and painfully named `dp_catalog_position_seqacc_med` maps backup objects to positions on tapes. This is obviously a very large table!

The column `objver_seq_id` references the dp`catalog`object`version's seq`id column, essentially "what is backed up here?"

The column `medium_name` references the unique header ID of the tape, for example '7b5ba8c0:53c3ae35:07eb:0014'.

There is another table called `dp_positions` which is a little bit more accessible, but inserts, updates and deletions from this table trigger a function instead (presumably to update `dp_catalog_position_seqacc_med`). In a few tests this table got populated and `dp_positions` did not.

If you are backing up to a StoreOnce device, or to a file library then there's a good chance that this backup will cause a new medium to be created. This will also happen when you format a new tape in either a physical tape library of a virtual tape library.

- `medium_seq_id` → `dp_medmng_medium`

The tapes are all listed in `dp_medmng_media_pool_media`. The column `medium_seq_id` (which is not the medium header, it's just an ID) is the key into the dp`medmng`medium tape.

---

dp_medmng_cartridge / dp_medmng_medium

dp_medmng_cartridge

- barcode
- physical_location
- medium_seq_id

dp_medmng_medium

- seq_id
- name (tape header)

There seems to be a distinction made between the medium itself, and the cartridge holding it. The dp_medmng_cartridge table has a barcode, a physical_location and a contained medium_seq_id. The dp_medmng_medium table has a unique seq_id and a name. The name is the header on the tape.

Part VI

Protecting Applications

13

VMware

13.1   Installing the VEAgent Component

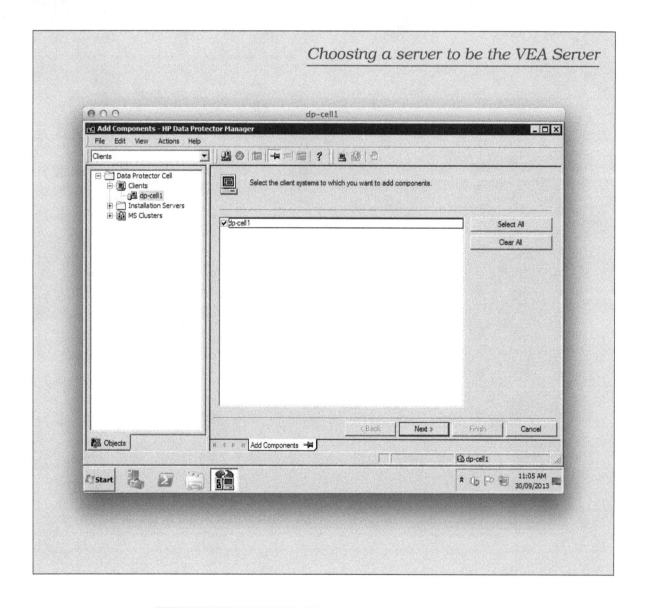

Unlike most other integration components, the server that controls the VMware backups does not have to be the same server as the one with the data in it.

The decision process for choosing which server to use goes something like this:

- Do you want to backup to tape drive directly, and do you need that to be a supported configuration? If so, then you need the machine zoned into the SAN infrastructure. The vCenter server might be an appropriate choice if you don't care about load on it, as would some other server that happened to have high-speed access to the disk storage holding the VMDK files to which the tape drive could be attached.

- Do you want to backup to a tape drive directly, but being a supported configuration is not important? (For example, if this were a test/development environment of some kind.) You can configure a SCSI passthrough device for a virtual machine to access the tape drive. VMware do not support this, but the underlying technology is irrelevant for DataProtector

- if you are backing up to a StoreOnce device, then it does not particularly matter where you put the VEAgent. A virtual machine is the most convenient if you have sufficient CPU in your VMware cluster, but a physical machine zoned into the SAN infrastructure will work as well.

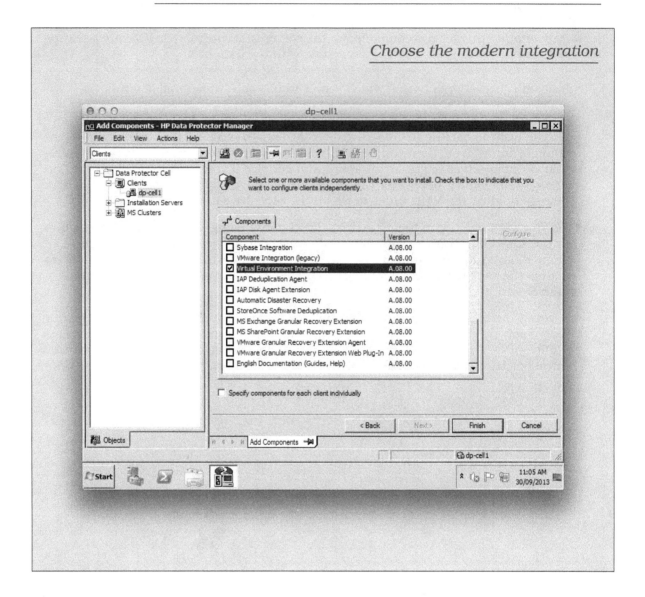

The legacy integration is only relevant for VMware infrastructure older than version 4. For any recent servers use the Virtual Environment Integration.

This same Virtual Environment Integration supports VMware and Hyper-V backups. The backup specification determines what technology is used for the backup.

You do not need the VMware Granular Recovery Extension in order to perform a VMware backup or restore. It is only used if you want to initiate file level recovery from virtual disk images in the vCenter console.

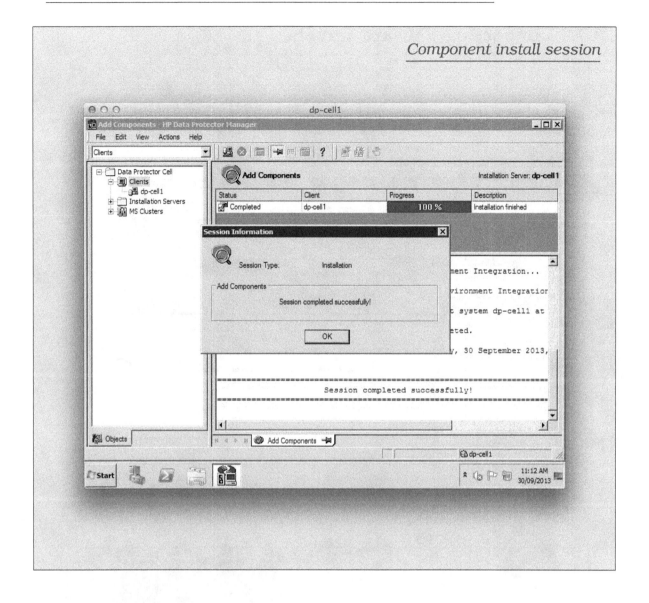

The component installation session for the VEAgent is no different to any other component installation.

13.2 Importing VMware servers

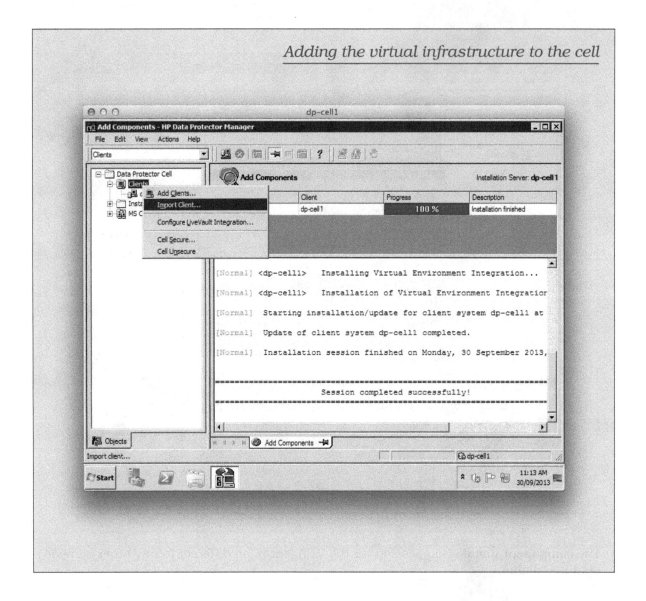

Before we can configure a backup of a virtual machine we need to import the infrastructure on which that virtual machine is running.

As before, right click on Clients in the GUI and choose Import Client.

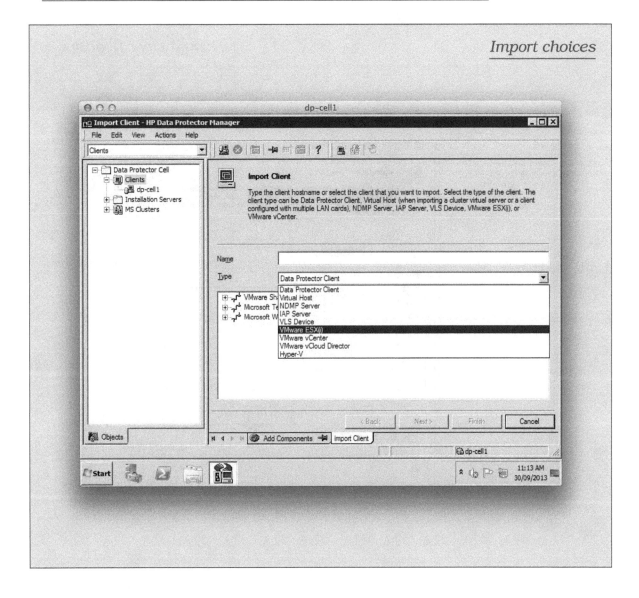

The screenshot above shows importing an ESX server, but the procedure is the same for a vCenter server. You do not need to import ESX hosts which are under the control of a vCenter server. Thus even quite large organisations might only have one imported VMware cell member.

If you are planning to use the VMware Granular Recovery Extension, note that you need to install the vCenter server as an ordinary member of the cell first (by installing a disk agent on it, for example) before then importing it again as a vCenter server.

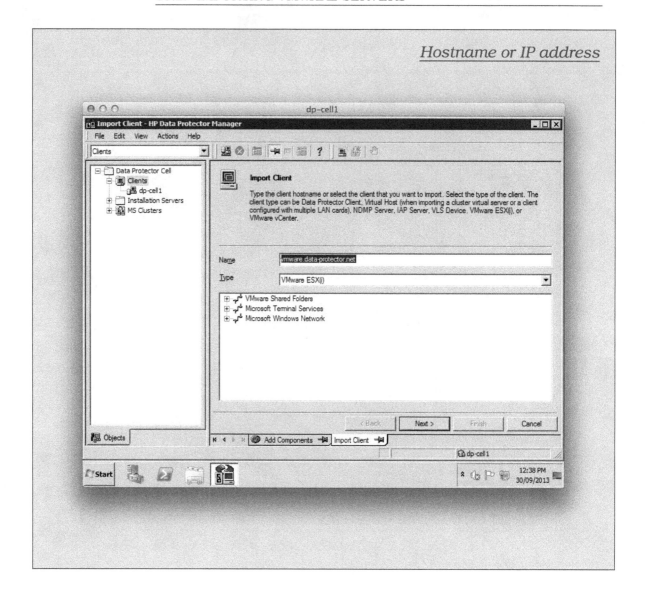

It is possible to import a server just using its IP address if DNS is not available.

(Note again: the screenshot shows this for an ESXi server, but the same is true for a vCenter server).

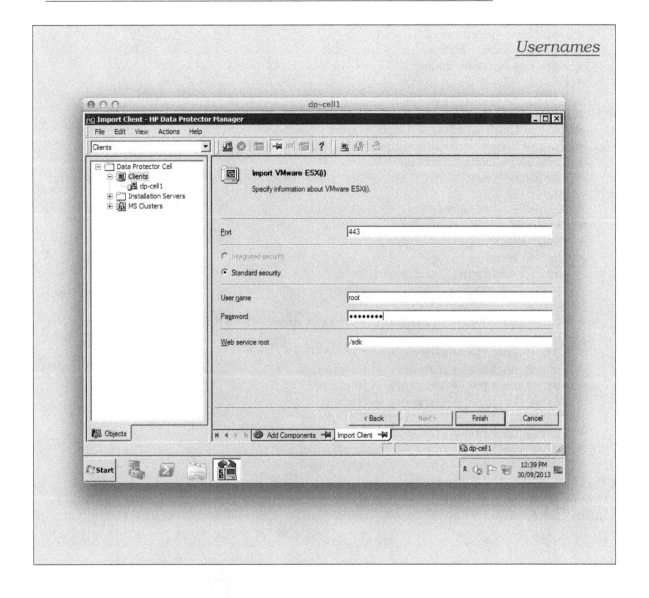

For an ESXi server, you will probably use the `root` user because your environment is quite small.

If you are importing a vCenter server, you will probably create another user in the vCenter console with the following rights:

- Datastore → Allocate space
- Datastore → Browse datastore
- Datastore → Low level file operations
- Datastore → Remove file

- Datastore → Rename datastore
- Folder → Delete folder
- Folder → Rename folder
- Global → Disable methods
- Global → Enable methods
- Global → Licenses
- Host → Configuration → Maintenance
- Host → Inventory → Add standalone host
- Network → Assign network
- Resource → Assign virtual machine to resource pool Resource → Remove resource pool
- Resource → Rename resource pool
- Sessions → Validate session
- vApp → Delete
- vApp → Rename
- vApp → Add virtual machine
- Virtual machine → State → Revert to snapshot Virtual machine → Configuration (*everything under this*)
- Virtual machine → Interaction → Answer question Virtual machine → Interaction → Power Off
- Virtual machine → Interaction → Power On
- Virtual machine → Inventory → Create new
- Virtual machine → Inventory → Register
- Virtual machine → Inventory → Remove
- Virtual machine → Inventory → Unregister
- Virtual machine → Provisioning (*everything under this*)
- Virtual machine → State → Create snapshot
- Virtual machine → State → Remove snapshot

Note that these rights can't be done at the datacenter or cluster level – they have to be at the top level.

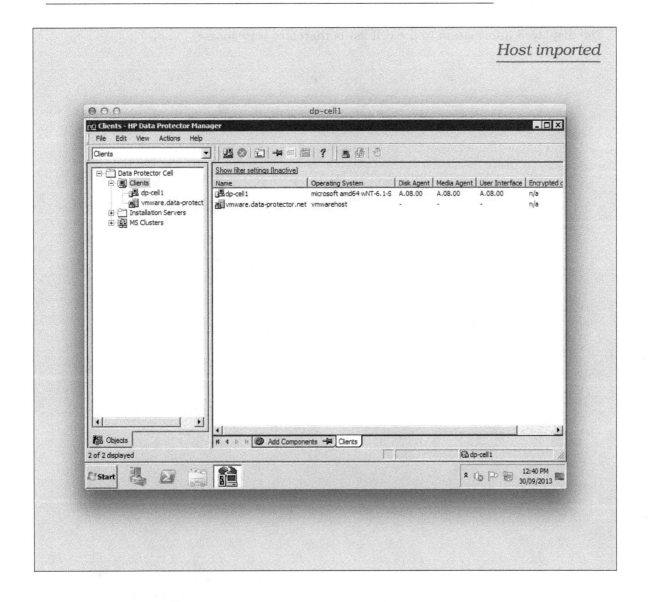

DataProtector does not verify whether the parameters you set on the previous screen actually work. That will only become obvious during backup and restore.

The `cell_info` file contains no extra information other than what was entered – no discovery has taken place. The password is encrypted.

```
-host "vmware.data-protector.net" -os "vmwarehost" -appserver_type "vmwarehost"
-appserver_subtype "esx" -appserver_port 443 -appserver_user "root" -appserver_pass
"[<GB+z2<" -appserver_cert "" -appserver_web_root "/sdk" -appserver_organization
"" -appserver_integrated_security "0"
```

The displayed information in the cell list is therefore very sparse.

13.3 VMware Preparation Lab

VM Preparation Lab

1. If you do not have a server in your cell with the VEAgent installed, install it now.

2. Import the ESXi host `vmware.data-protector.net` into your cell.

13.4 Backing up VMware images

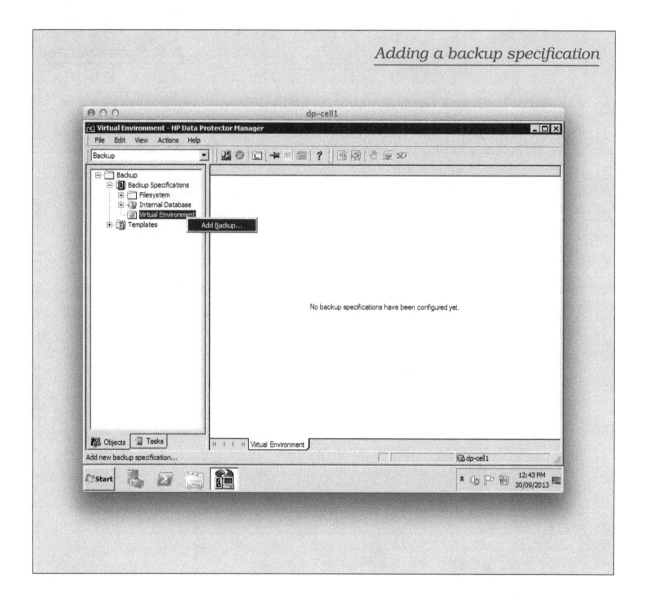

Because we have installed the Virtual Environment Integration agent on a computer in the cell, the Virtual Environment backup type becomes visible in the Backup Specifications folder.

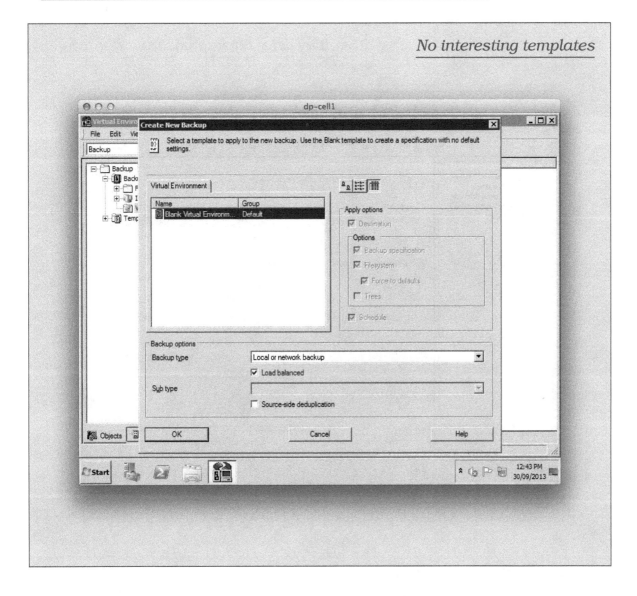

Out-of-the-box there are no interesting templates. There is no alternative Backup type. Load balancing and source deduplication function the same as they do in file system backups.

The location for the templates if you want to create additional ones:

Windows cell managers `C:\ProgramData\OmniBack\Config\Server\dltemplates\lists\VEAgent`

HP-UX/Linux cell managers `/etc/opt/omni/server/dltemplates/lists/VEAgent`

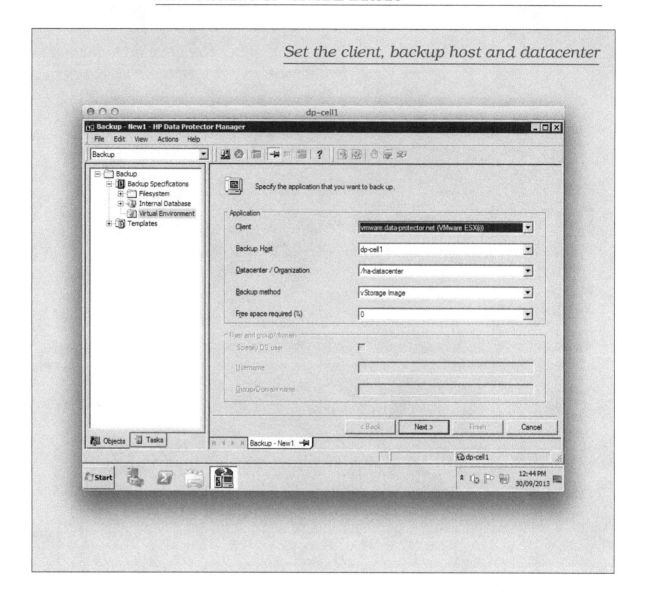

The client is the name of the vCenter server or ESXi server in which the target virtual machines or virtual disks can be found.

The Backup Host is the server on which the Virtual Environment Integration agent is installed, which might be a virtual machine inside the VMware environment, or might be a physical machine.

DataProtector will connect to the vCenter server from the backup host using the credentials that were stored to get a list of data centres. It is not possible to backup more than one datacentre at a time in a single job. However is possible to run several backups concurrently.

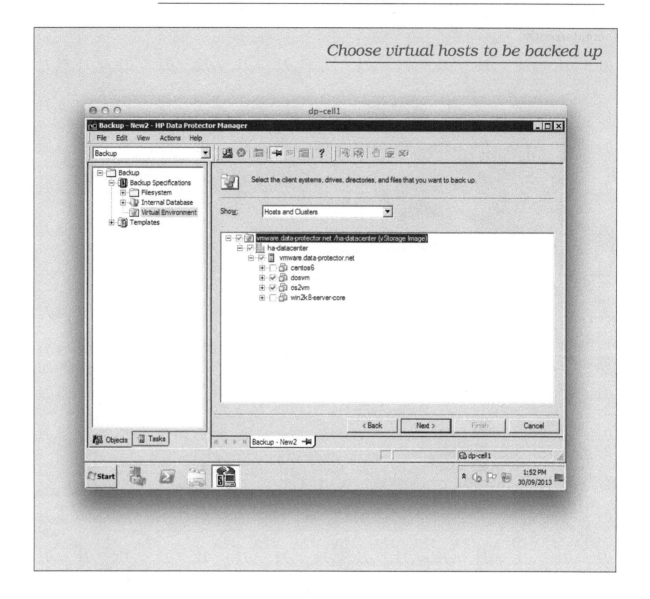

Choose virtual hosts to be backed up

It is possible to backup whole groups of virtual machines by clicking on a folder (such as the `ha-datacenter` in the above screenshot), or at a VMware resource group level. This is the best way of guaranteeing that all virtual servers in your environment are backed up.

The alternative (which is what is done in the screenshot above) is to select individually each virtual machine for protection.

It is possible to expand the virtual machine view in order to back up individual virtual disks. However, if the virtual machine only has one virtual disk then selecting the disk will automatically select the whole virtual machine.

If a virtual machine is selected (either directly, or because it is a member of a group that has been selected) then DataProtector will back up the VMDK files for all disks attached to the virtual machine and also the VMX file defining the virtual machine itself.

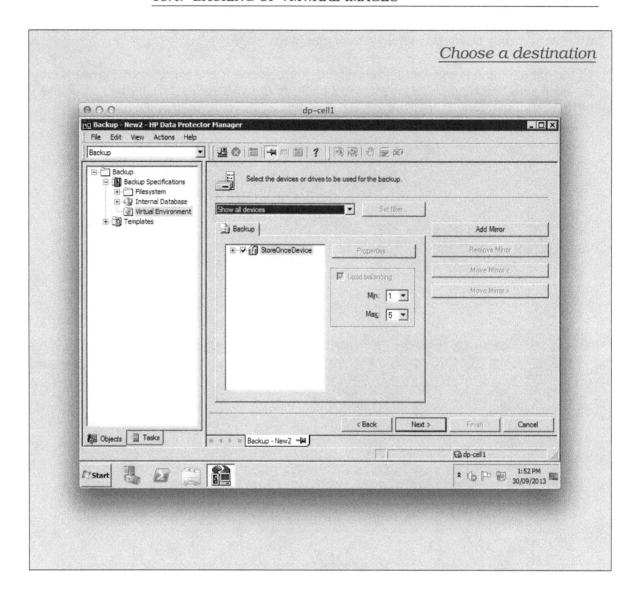

Virtual Environment backups can write to any device supported for file system backups.

A de-duplication store which backs up the C drive of a Windows server as a file system and which also backs up the equivalent virtual disk as a Virtual Environment backup will not deliver perfect de-duplication, but it will usually find large chunks of data in common.

If the virtual machines are created from VM templates then StoreOnce will be extremely successful in finding duplicate chunks between backups. Again, remember that Store-Once is a global de-duplication so that it will find a chunk even if it was part of a backup of a different virtual machine on a different datacentre that occurred several weeks ago.

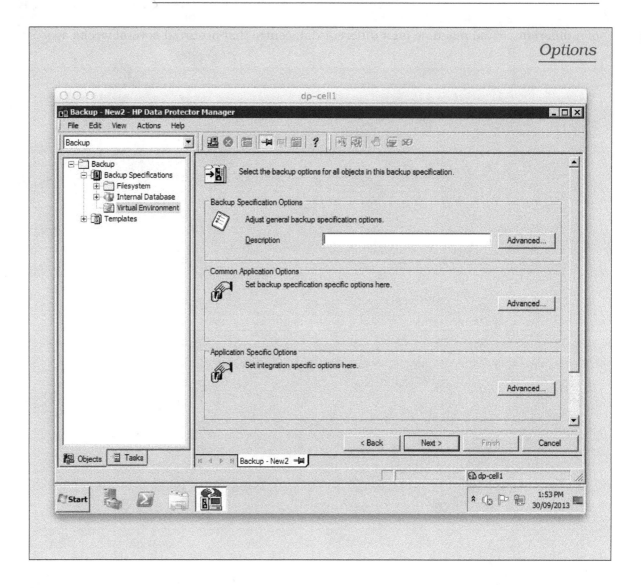

The options screen is similar to the equivalent screen for a file system backup, with the exception that there are now Common Application Options and Application-Specific Options.

The Backup Specification Options (description, pre-exec, post-exec, ownership) are exactly the same.

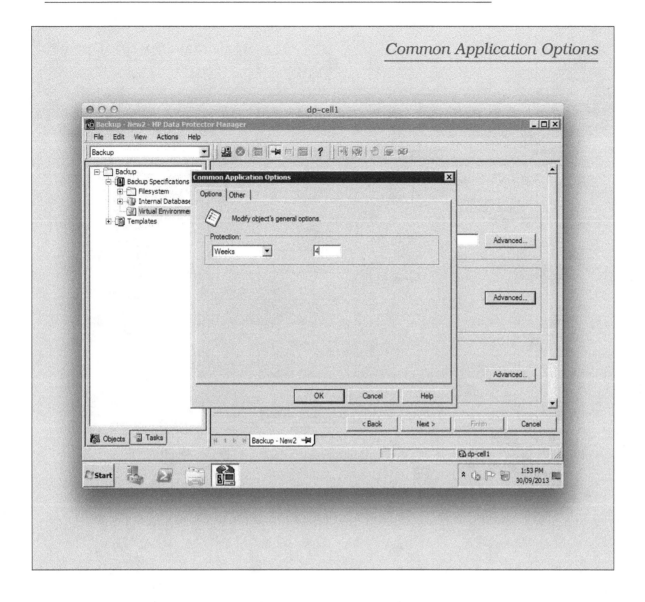

Hitting the Advanced button for Common Application Options shows a screen that has far fewer choices compared to file system backups. The default protection is permanent, which is probably the most important parameter to change.

The Other tab has options for displaying statistical information (which is not very informative except for very large environments), whether the backup is public or private (to be used in conjunction with ownership) and whether to ignore low severity messages. They are very rarely used.

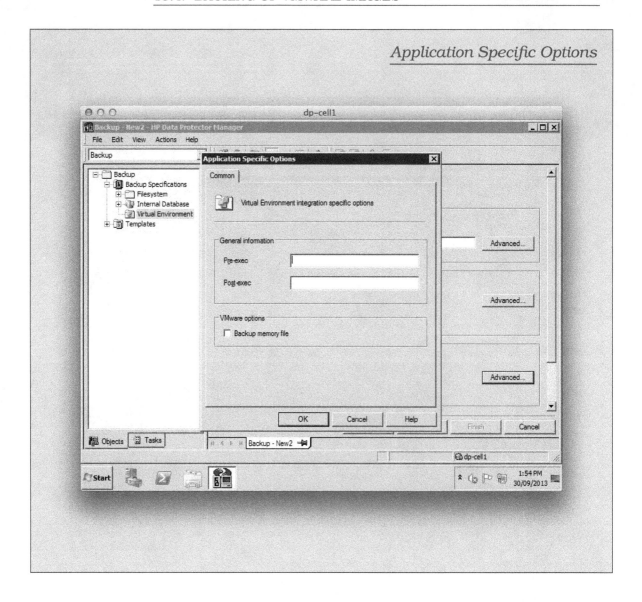

Backing up the memory file means that it is possible to restore the virtual machine to the state had at a particular moment in time. This is very rarely used, as most virtual machines are used for applications that span across the network and where the state of one individual machine is irrelevant.

The default is not to backup the memory file which is essentially equivalent to creating a crash consistent backup of the virtual machine. This of course saves several gigabytes of backup data.

Scheduling

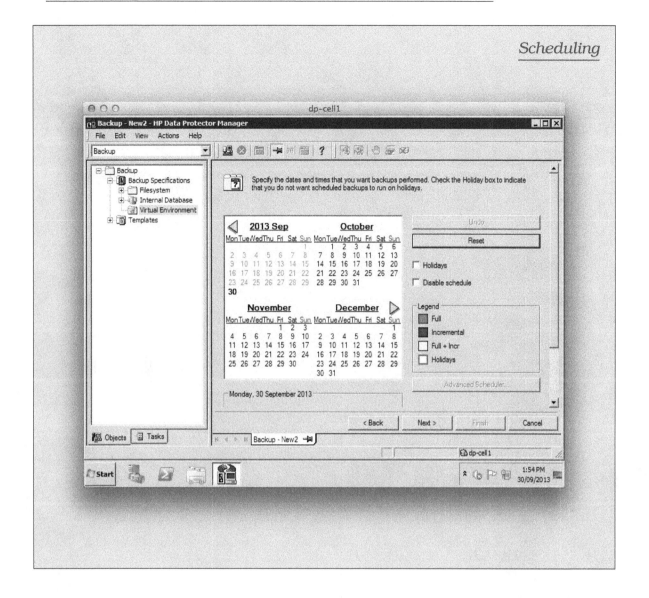

Backup scheduling is the same for Virtual Environment backups as it is for file system backups, except that instead of numerous alternative incremental backup options, there are three: full, differential and incremental.

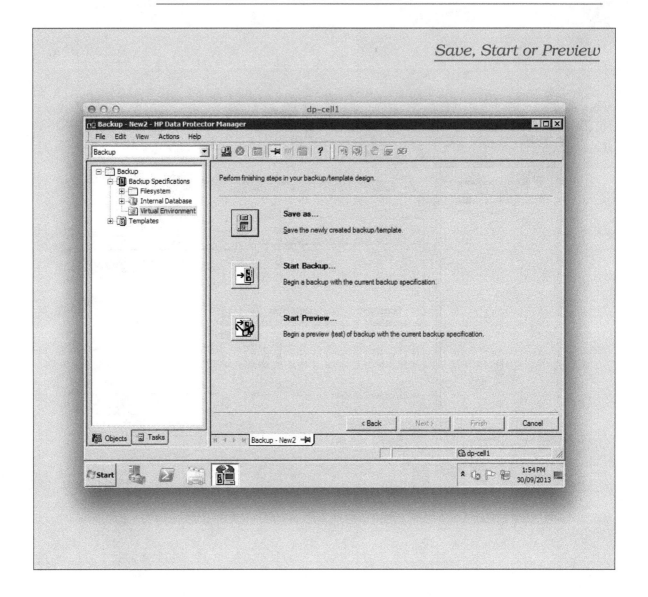

The name used for the specification becomes the name of the file on the cell manager defining the job:

Windows cell manager "C:\ProgramData\OmniBack\Config\Server\BarLists\VEAgent

HP-UX/Linux cell manager /etc/opt/omni/server/BarLists/VEAgent

There is also a corresponding file with the same name in the BarSchedules folder.

13.5 Important VMware Backup Parameters

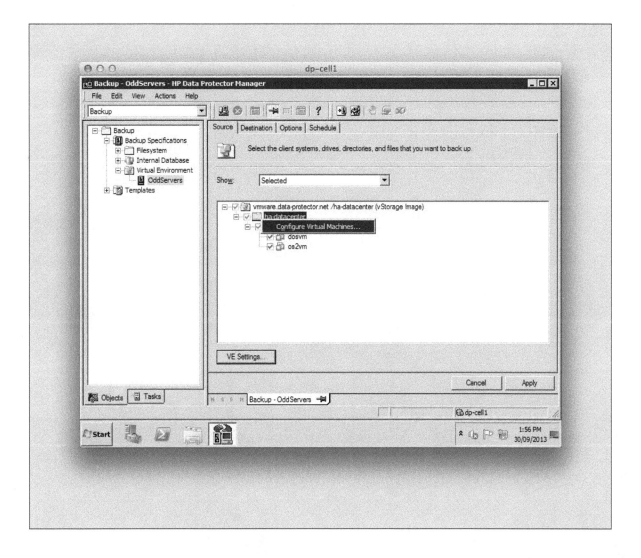

The next few screenshots show the parameters that you will want to set in order for differential and incremental backups to work, and also in order to use change block tracking.

These parameters are actually independent of any backup job: if a virtual machine or group appears in two different specifications, then you only need to set this once. But bizarrely, these can only be set from inside an already-saved specification.

These parameters can be set individually for each virtual machine, or as a group. Right click on the virtual machine or group as appropriate.

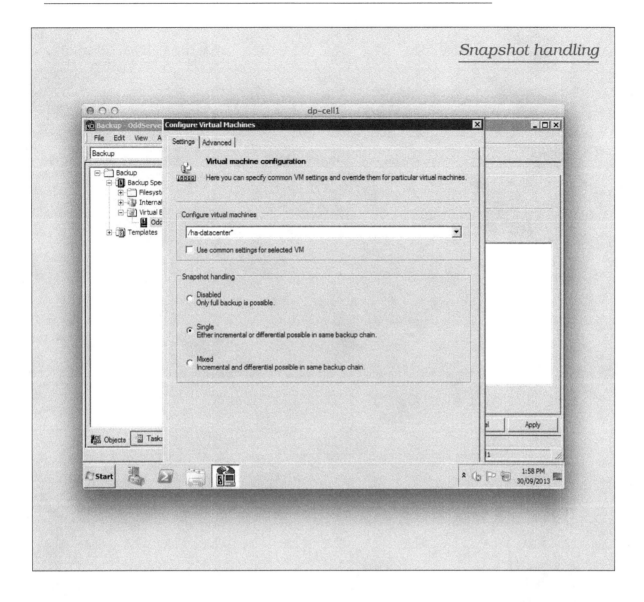

The default for the *Use common settings for selected VM* checkbox is on, and the default for snapshot handling is **disabled**. This means that incremental and differential backups will not happen, but that there will be no wasted space on the data store outside of backup windows.

Single is usually the appropriate choice.

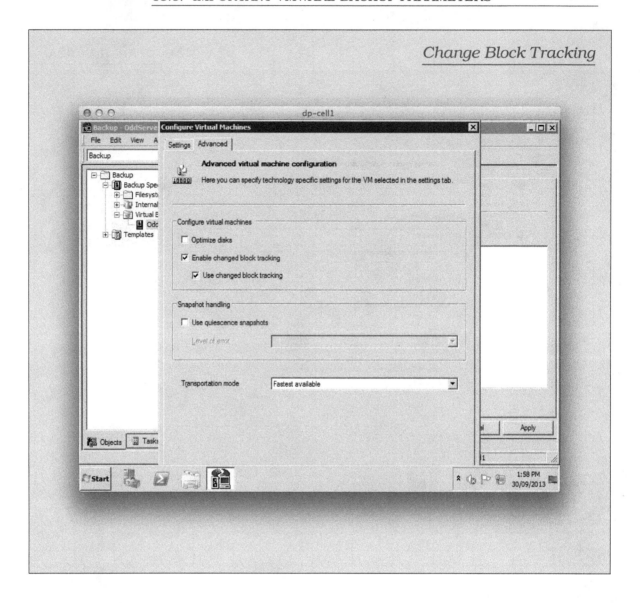

Change Block Tracking

There are two ways of taking an incremental or differential backup of a virtual machine: by creating snapshots which take up a lot of space on the data store, or by backing up changed blocks as reported by VMware.

In general, the most efficient way of taking a VMware virtual machine backup is to use incremental backups in conjunction with change block tracking.

Data Protector will connect to the Vsphere server and //alter the .vmx file// for each virtual machine it is backing up to enable change block tracking. You will see `ctkEnabled = "TRUE"` for the virtual machine, and also for each virtual disk.

In version 8.1, HP added another checkbox to allow fallback (to a full backup) if change block tracking does not work.

In vSphere 5.x, Storage vMotion will reset CBT. This will cause the next incremental backup to fail or promote itself to being a full backup.

Note also that change block tracking does not work for raw device mappings in physical compatibility mode (RDM / pRDM).

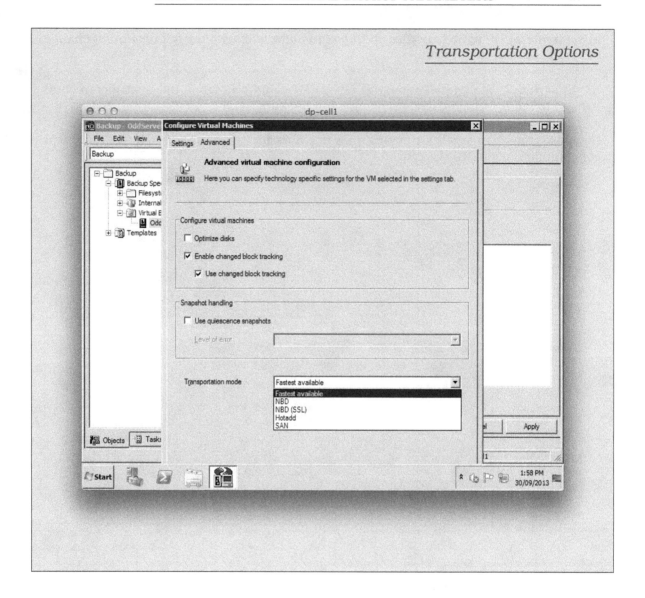

Transportation Options

The best transportation options are Hotadd and SAN, which are roughly equivalent in server load and throughput.

The worst option is NBD, with the SSL version of NBD even worse still. You are doing really well if you can get 60MB/s with an NBDSSL backup. The customer I saw this at (in 2014) used a very high-end dedicated x64 media server writing to a B6200 virtual tape library.

Hotadd is used when the VEAgent is running the backup from a virtual machine inside the VMware environment that is being backed up. When there is disk storage from another virtual machine that needs to be read, the VEAgent simply requests that the snapshot be made accessible to the VEAgent's virtual machine.

Hotadd doesn't perform very well either, because VMware don't allow direct access to a tape drive from inside a virtual machine. But if you are doing source-side deduplication of very similar large backups, the network traffic sent may be quite small, and the overhead of doing this might not be too dreadful.

SAN is used when the VEAgent is running on a server zoned in to have visibility of the data store which has the VMDK files (or RDMs) of the virtual machines to be backed up. The VEAgent extracts out the unique identifier number from the database and is then able to map that into a path which it can mount and read.

SAN based backups can sometimes run faster than 100MB/s when the infrastructure can support that sort of throughput.

If no other option is available, NBD can be used. The problem with that is that all data is going to be sent over the ethernet network, which in general will be many times slower than SCSI or fibre channel access.

Look in the session log for a message that describes the method being used for each backup.

13.6 VEAgent Backup Session

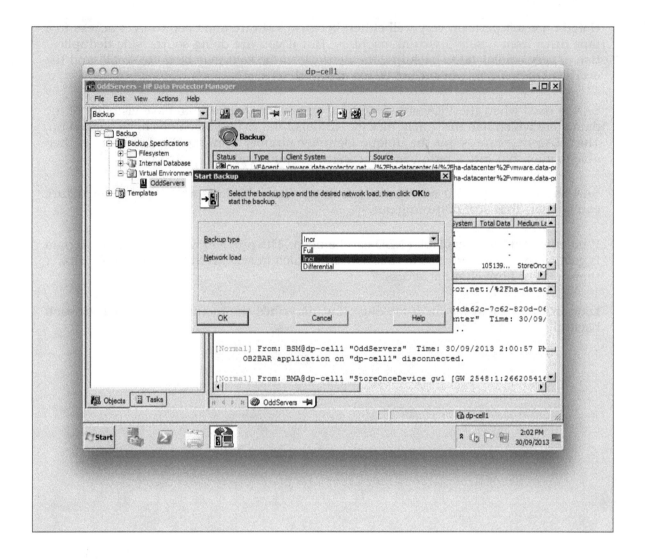

There are only 3 alternatives:

Full Backup the whole of the VMX file (if selected) and every block from any selected VMDK and RDM files.

Incr Back up the whole of the VMX file (if selected) and any blocks changed since the previous backup.

Differential Back up the whole of the VMX file (if selected) and any blocks changed since the previous *full* backup.

The last two will only work if the snapshot handling option for every virtual machine is set to *Single* or *Mixed*.

There are a few notes to be aware of for RDM files.

- **Physical RDMs** (pRDM storage) cannot be backed up by Data Protector through a VMware backup. This is by design: pRDMs get used when you want to bypass VMware altogether for I/O to a device. You would back these up through the application that is using the pRDM.

- **Virtual RDMs** (vRDM storage) are only backed up if they are less than 2TB in size.

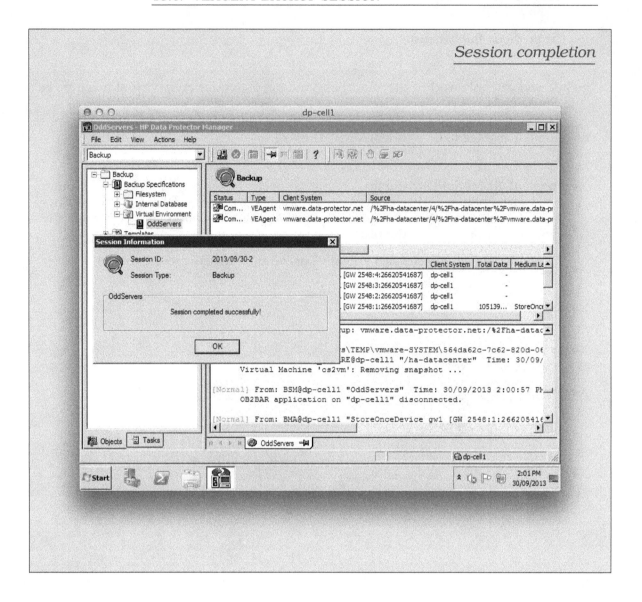

Session completion

The session will record the source objects as long URL-encoded paths.

One of the most common problems to occur in VMware environments is for the backup to be unable to remove the snapshot that was created. This come up as warnings: the backup will be considered successful even though this may be indicative of significant problems in the VMware infrastructure.

13.7   VMware Backup Specification Lab

VMware Backup Specification Lab

1. Create a backup specification to back up a few virtual machines on `vmware.data-protector.net`

2. Confirm that this has been created by looking in the BarLists folder and the BarSchedules folder.

3. Configure the VM settings to allow incremental backups and to use changed block tracking.

4. Run a full backup and an incremental backup using the specification you created.

13.8 Backing up virtual disks

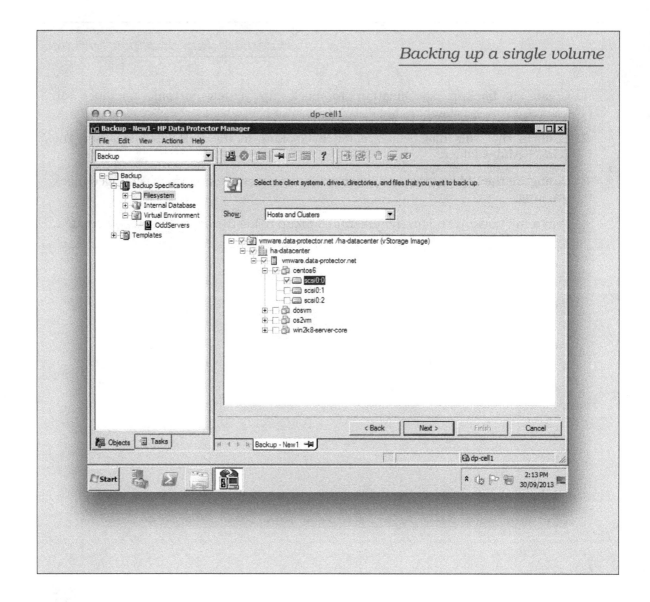

It is possible to select individual virtual disks to be backed up. This is quite common in environments where the C drive (or root filesystems) are created by cloning templates and stay almost completely unchanged over time, while all mutable data is stored on other drives. In such environments, the primary disk may be backed up using the Virtual Environment agents and the data may be backed up using traditional file system backups or other integration agents.

This is done simply by expanding the virtual machine to show the disks, and then selecting the appropriate disks.

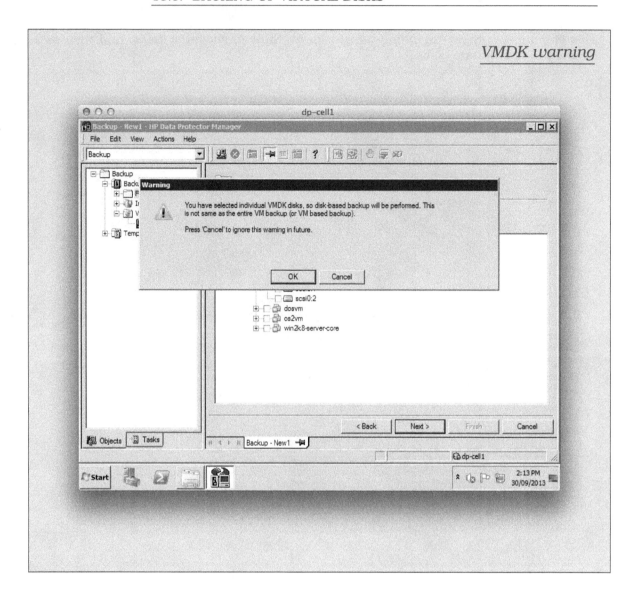

Backing up an individual disk does not back up the VMX file that defines the virtual machine. So in the event of a disaster where the virtual machine has been accidentally deleted or otherwise destroyed, the VMware administrator would have to create a new virtual machine from scratch or from memory and then restore the drive back from DataProtector.

13.9 Installing the Granular Recovery Extension

What is the GRE?

	File backup	**VM backup**
File restore	omnir	GRE
System restore	autodr	omnir

If you have taken a file system backup, then it is very easy to restore individual files. Restoring a whole system from bare metal is a little bit more complicated and requires the automated disaster recovery module.

If you have taken a VM level backup, then restoring the whole system back is very simple. But if you've taken a VM level backup and want to restore an individual file, then the process is a little bit more complicated.

Without the Granular Recovery Extension, you would restore a virtual disk and attach that to the computer that you want to restore the file to, mount the virtual disk and then select the file out by hand.

The Granular Recovery Extension automates the process. Depending on how you backed up the virtual machine, it can be nearly as quick as restoring a file from a file system level backup.

The Granular Recovery Extension is licensed separately to the VMware backup. Thus you will need an online extension license for each ESX server which you will be backing up or restoring to and also a GRE license for each ESX server. Fortunately the GRE licences are relatively cheap.

Of course if you are using capacity-based licences, then you are automatically licensed for everything including the GRE.

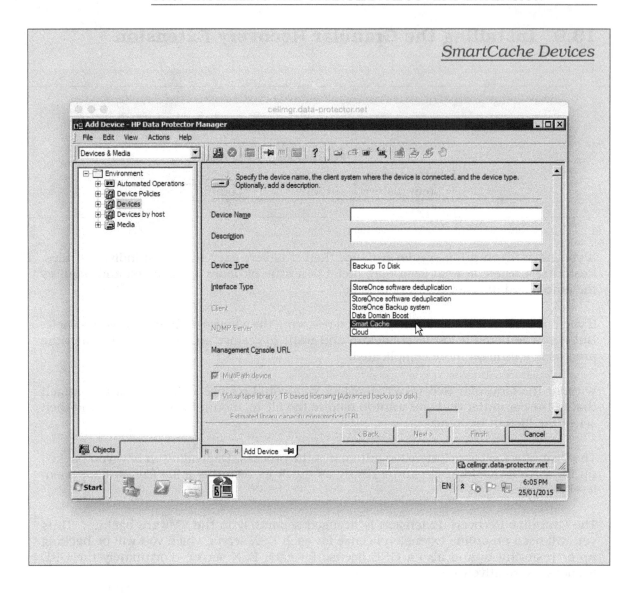

HP added a new device type in Data Protector version 9. It is called a **SmartCache**.

You can use any device when you backup VMware images, but there are some advantages if you use SmartCache.

<u>*SmartCache Distinctives*</u>

- Disk-based backup

- No compression, no deduplication

- Ideally: a 1-2 day staging point before copying to StoreOnce

- Instantaneous mount for GRE restore

Backing up to a SmartCache devices very fast, as you would expect for a disk-based backup device. Unfortunately it does no compression or de-duplication so if you are backing up a 40 GB virtual machine, you will need 40 GB for the backup. So it is not really practical storage format for long-term archiving!

SmartCache devices are the fastest way of performing a Granular Recovery restore. With a SmartCache device the mount operation completes immediately. With non-SmartCache devices, the virtual machine disk is restored into a staging directory first. Since it can take some time to restore a few hundred gigabytes of virtual disk (compared to the length of time it takes to restore one file out of that virtual disk) they can be significant time savings by using a SmartCache device.

A typical VMware backup for an important virtual machine will use a SmartCache device as its destination. 1 to 2 days later there will be a copy job to put it into StoreOnce storage (while recycling the protection on the SmartCache storage). Perhaps at the weekend, or perhaps after a week or two there will be copy job to take it from StoreOnce and put it on tape.

Less important virtual machines - where it is okay to recover files in a few hours instead of instantly - would probably be backed up to StoreOnce initially, and then copied off to tape without ever using a SmartCache device.

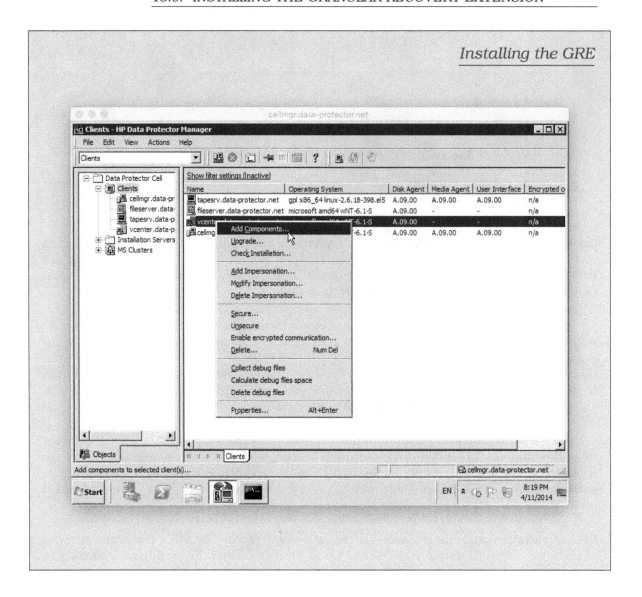

The Granular Recovery Extension is installed in the same way as any other Data Protector component.

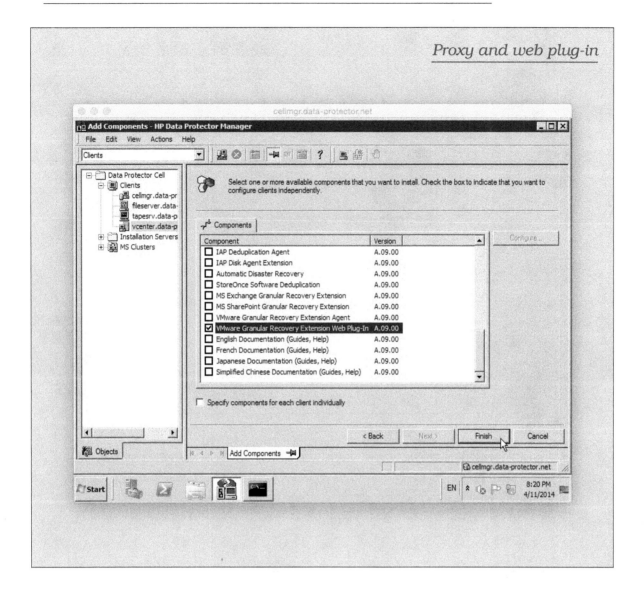

There are two components to install:

VMware GRE Web Plug-In This needs to be installed on the Vsphere server

VMware GRE Agent You want to install this agent on a Windows system and on a Linux system which have at least one large file system with a lot of spare disk space, as this is where a staging recovery will be restored to.

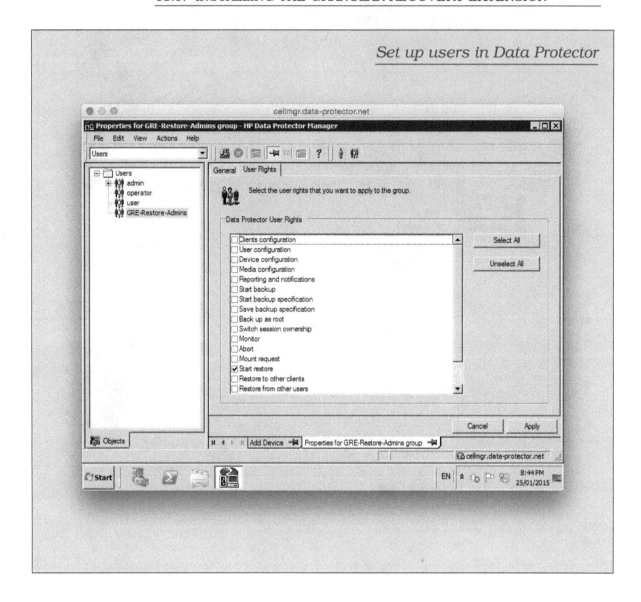

You do not have to authorise every VMware administrator to be able to initiate restores. You can have operators whose only right is the ability to request a restore.

I have not seen any site where such operators have been set up. In reality I see that every VMware administrator gets given the right to `start a restore`. But because they are not always Data Protector Administrators as well (and won't ever use the Data Protector GUI) there's no need to give them full admin rights.

Configuring the GRE

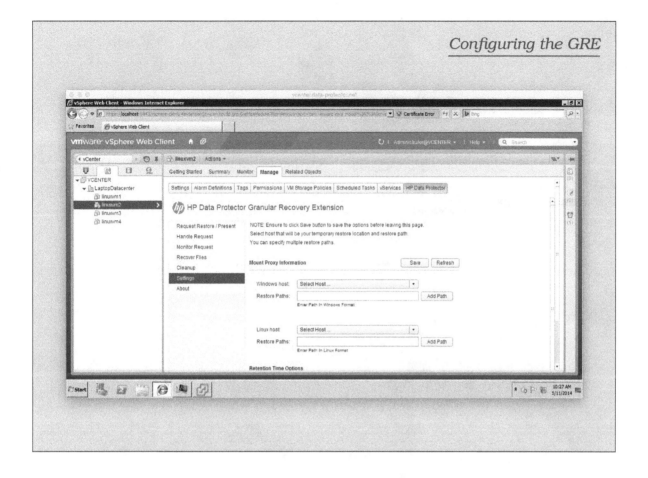

Once the agents are all installed and the users are in place, going to the Vsphere web console and find a virtual machine. There will be a new tab under `Manage` called `HP Data Protector`.

The settings that you give here apply to all virtual machines on this Vsphere server, not just the virtual machine that is selected in the left-hand pane.

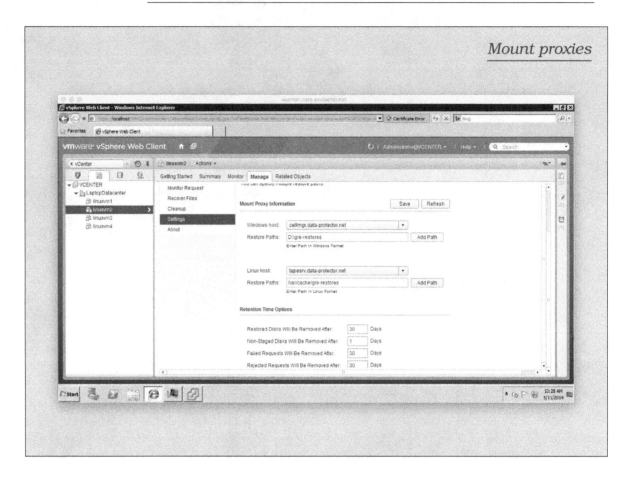

Files that were in a Windows virtual machines can only be restored from other Windows systems. This is because the Windows disk layout (MBR / GPT, NTFS filesystems, etc.) is designed only to be read by other Windows systems.

Files that were in a Linux virtual machine can only be restored from other Linux systems, but there are a number of strange design decisions that mean that in practice it can be very hard to use the GRE with Linux. For example, it can only restore using the SMB protocol, which means that the Linux mount proxy host listed here must have the `smbclient` program installed and that the system that you are wanting to restore to must have `samba` installed and have a share visible.

Using the GRE

Now test it!

The granular recovery extension is hard to get installed and working correctly. You will need to test this extensively, by running through the process of attempting to restore individual files on Windows and Linux systems repeatedly until all the issues have been resolved.

Details and screenshots on performing restores with the GRE is in the book *Operating, Running and Supporting HP Data Protector 9*.

Part VII

Cloud

14

A new device

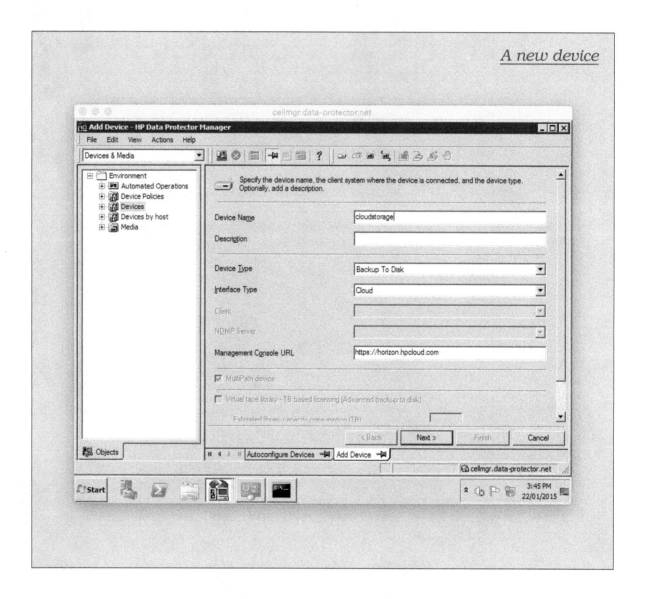

In Data Protector version 9.02, HP introduced a new interface type for backing up to disk. The **Cloud** interface type lets you treat HP public cloud object storage as a backup destination.

Object storage (in Open Stack) is like a filesystem in the cloud. In the Amazon cloud, object storage is known as S3.

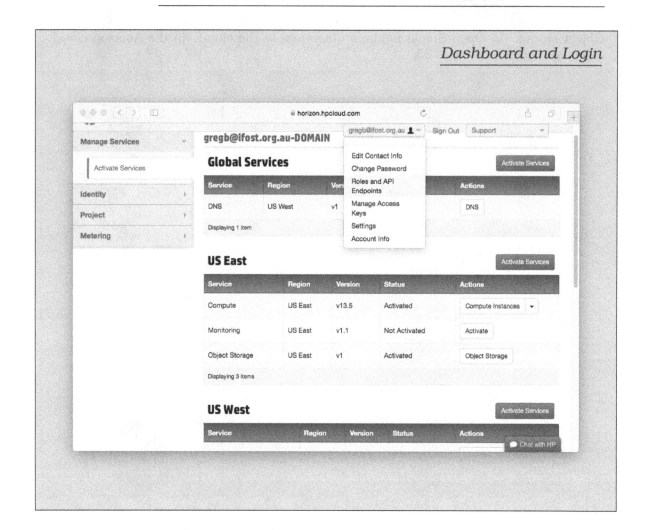

If you don't already have an account with the HP public cloud, take the opportunity to sign up as there are many free credits available for introductory use.

You will need to activate object storage in the location where you intend to keep your backups. As I'm writing this in 2015, the only options are US East and US West.

It is not necessary to use HP's infrastructure here, as any Open Stack environment will have the same capabilities. However the Helion cloud provides everything you need. In order to access the object storage, you'll need to configure Data Protector with the endpoint URL and parameters. These can be found in the menu item `Roles and API Endpoints`.

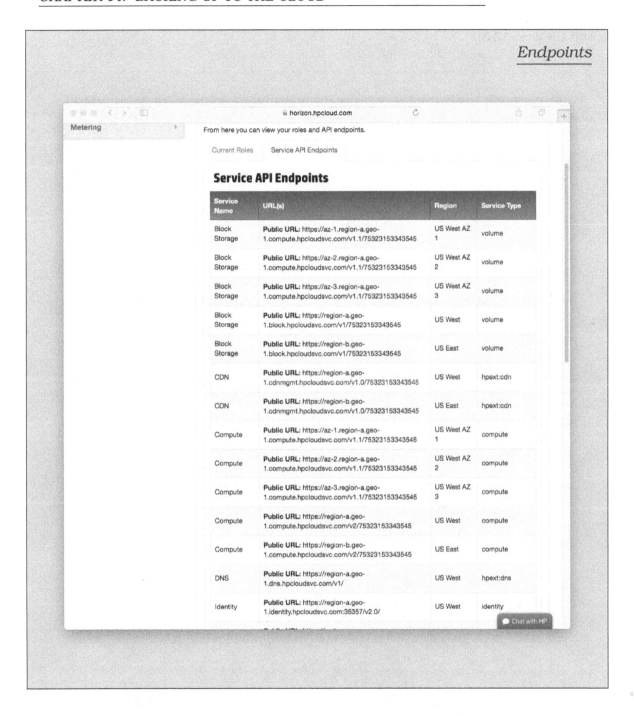

There is a very long list of endpoints, one for each service, and one for each location, and there can be more than one version of the API. Look for the newest and keep in mind that each region can have multiple availability zones (e.g. US West AZ 1, US West AZ 2

and US West AZ 3).

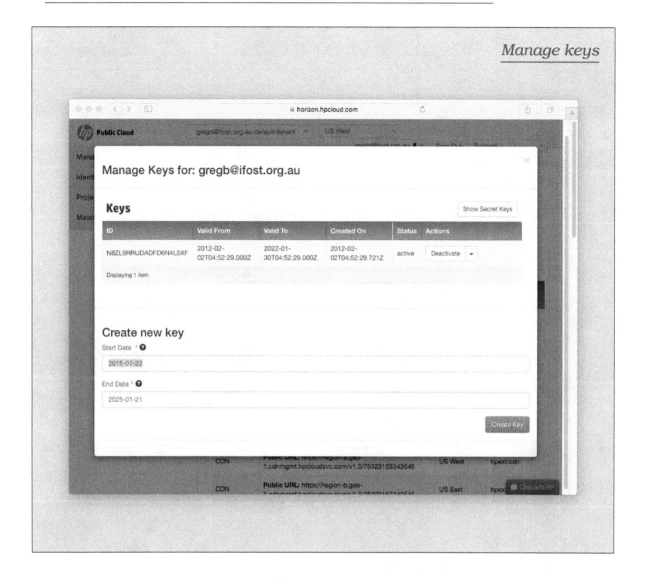

You may wish to create a new set of keys for accessing the service. There is one created by default when you sign up to the HP Cloud. You will need both the ID and the secret key.

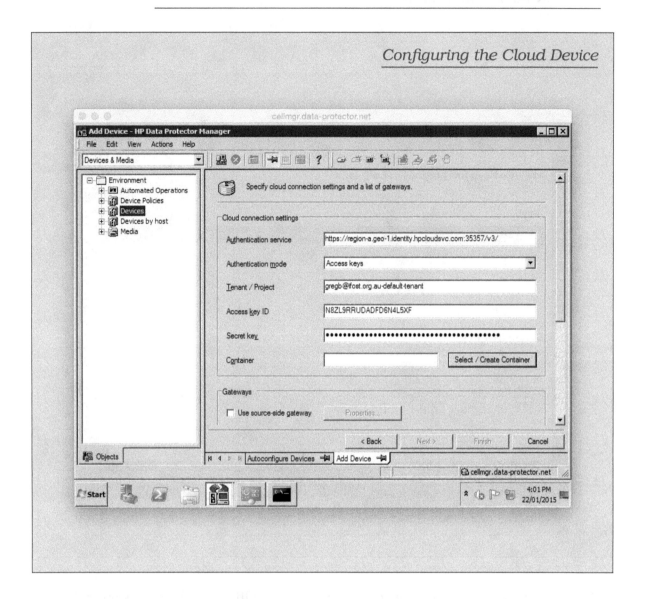

This is the next screen for configuring a Cloud backup device. You need to provide the authentication service (from the long list), the tenant or project (which you can see at the top of the HP Cloud dashboard), and the access key and secret key (which you saw on the previous page).

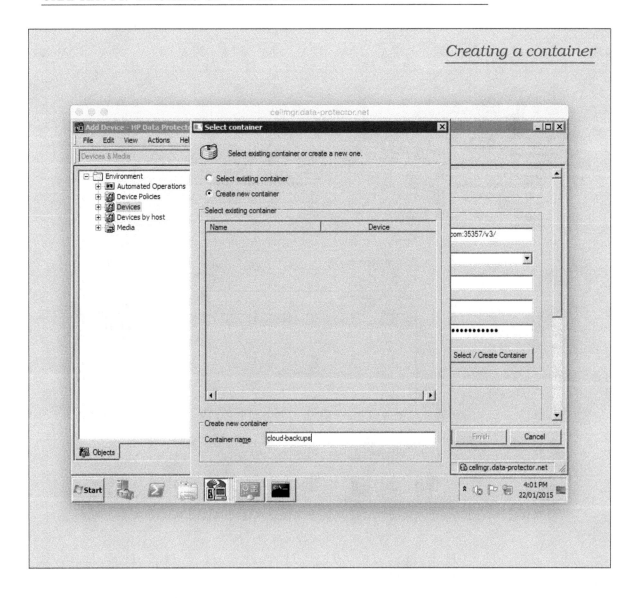

A container is simply a pseudo-folder in the cloud object storage. You won't have any initially if you have not previously used the HP cloud storage service.

Almost any file name characters are valid here, although delimiters such as slash (/) cause problems.

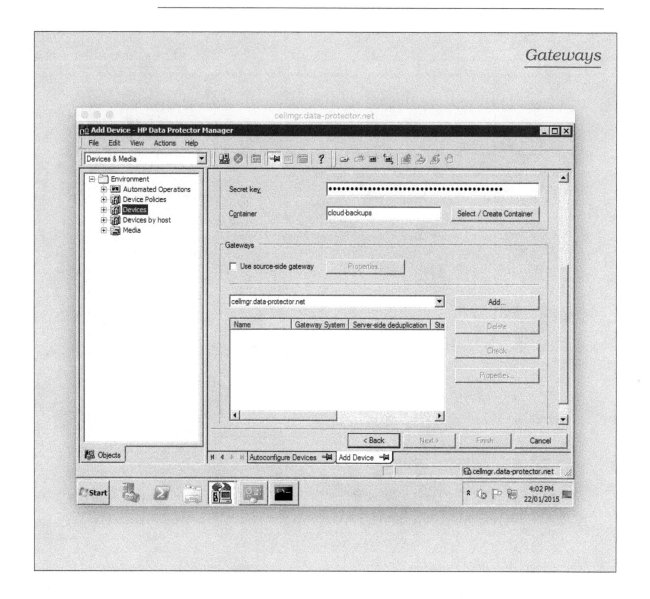

Cloud devices are similar to StoreOnce devices. The StoreOnce device has its storage separate to the gateway for writing to that storage, and a Cloud device has its storage far, far away from the computers it is going to back up. So it is necessary to create a gateway to access the cloud storage.

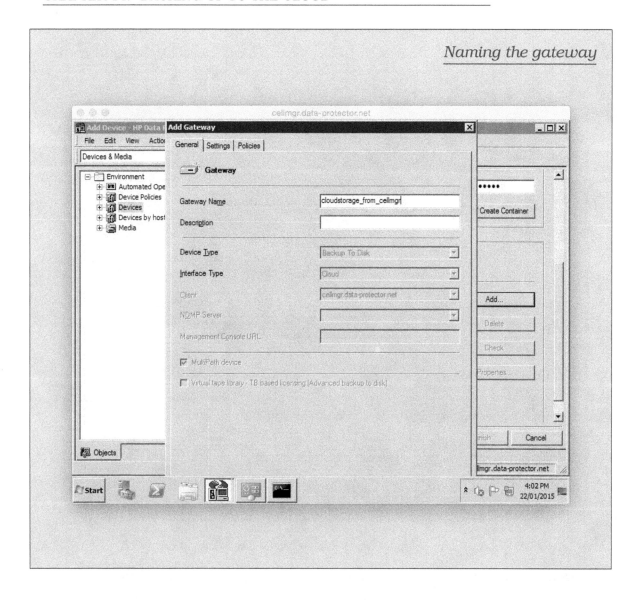

Naming the gateway

The default is of course to call it the name of the device followed by _gw1 which is not the clearest for later administration. It is better to change the name now to reflect where the data will be tunnelled in from.

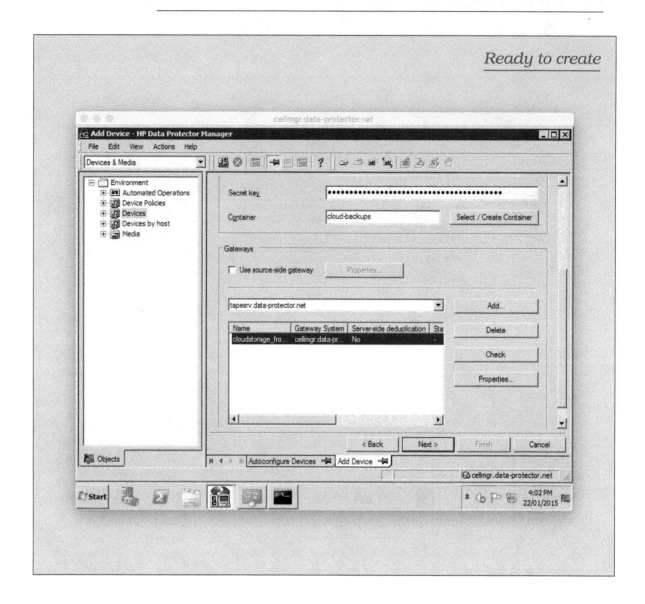

We have now supplied all the information necessary in order to create this device. Notice that the `Next` button is now available.

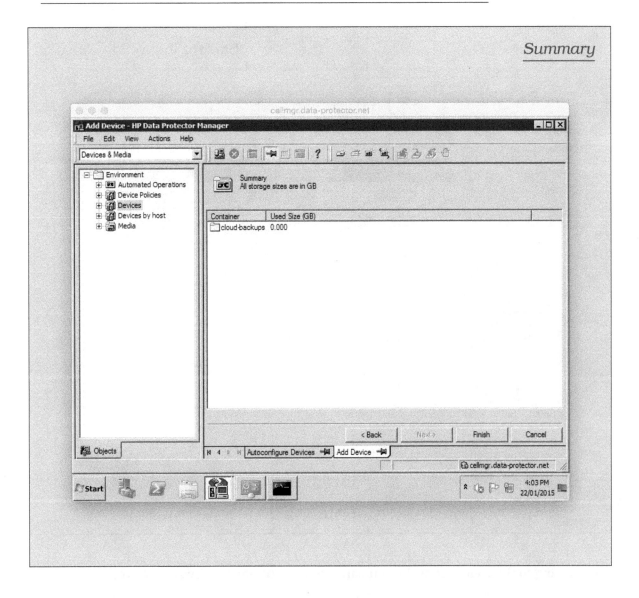

The device is not actually created until you hit the Finish button.

You can now use this device in any backup job. Remember that the initial backup will require a great deal of outgoing bandwidth.

Returning to the Helion console, you can see the container that was just created.

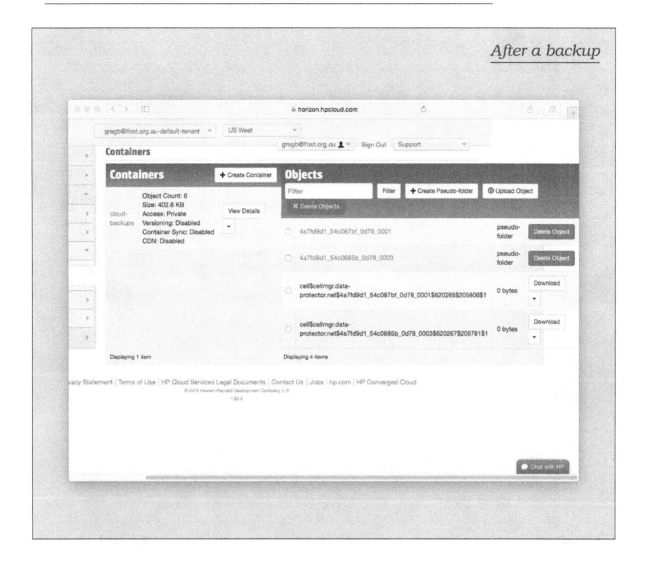

Each backup stream is a new pseudo-folder, so you should see at least one of these for every backup session. Do not delete the objects from the Helion console: Data Protector will take care of freeing up space once the backup session has had its protection expire.

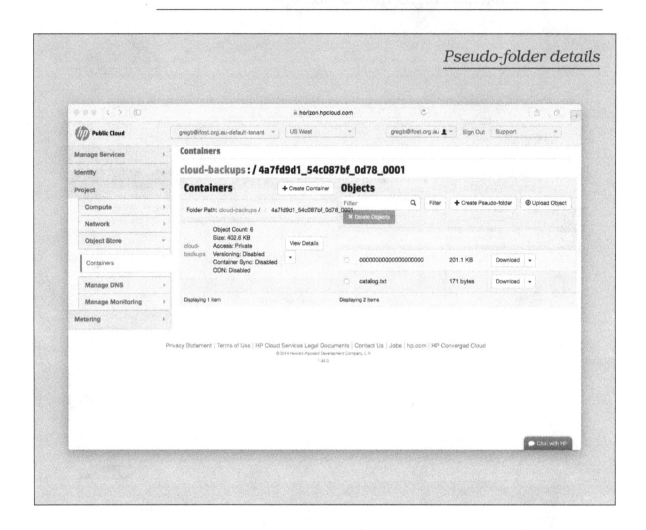

The screenshot shows the structure of the files in the pseudo-folder after a backup.

15

Backing up cloud-hosted servers

15.1 StoreOnce in the cloud

> *Pets vs Cattle*
>
> **Cattle**
> - Built from scripts
> - Have no unique data
> - Reboot / terminate when faulty
>
> **Pets**
> - Built by hand
> - May contain valuable data
> - Sysadmins troubleshoot problems

Your cloud-hosted infrastructure (whether it is on Azure, AWS, Google App Engine, IBM Rackspace or HP Cloud) is going to consist of two kinds of system.

There are **cattle**, which are machines that you have automatically created and which contain no state that can be lost. They might have a replica of some data, but there will be other copies. If these machines fail, you just restart them or create a new instance. Hopefully you have this process automated.

There is simply no point in backing up **cattle** because you will never restore from them.

333

You might want to back up a replica of their data; perhaps you would install a copy of the cell console software and trigger `omnib` as part of the cluster-wide scheduling.

Pets on the other hand, are machines that you administer and are installed manually. When these fail, you want to restore from a backup.

- Create images with DP pre-installed

- Have the cell-manager pre-defined

- Script appending to the `cell_info` file

- Automate creation of datalists

Note that it is very easy to "discover" what instances you have running in the cloud. For example with Amazon you can run `ec2-describe-instances`. You can parse the output from this to generate text that you can append onto the `cell_info` file on the cell manager.

You can also use this output to create or modify existing datalists. In general I create one or two by hand and then make sure that I can automate creating similar such datalists for every other virtual machine that gets run up in the cloud.

Virtual machines (cloud hosted server instances) are created from machine image files. Amazon calls these AMIs. In most organisations the machine image files are customised somewhat for the tasks at hand. It saves a lot of time and bandwidth to create these machine images with the Data Protector software already installed, and the cell server predefined.

The simplest way to arrange this is to take a fresh machine image, run up an instance from it, push the installation from an installation server and then create a machine image from that instance.

The cell server file on Linux clients is:

```
/etc/opt/omni/client/cell_server
```

Why not a dedicated cloud backup solution?

- Already have DP

- Cost

If you are a completely green-field site, then you won't have any backup infrastructure in the cloud. But if you already have some in-house servers, then you will probably have existing backup infrastructure that you would want to make use of.

This includes Data Protector, as the marginal cost of adding more clients (in the cloud or elsewhere) is usually zero.

The cheapest storage in the cloud (in early 2015) appears to be Amazon Glacier, which costs USD10 per terabyte. But if you already have a tape library (or even a single stan-dalone modern tape drive), you can easily have long-term cold storage at $0.50 per TB or less, and you probably already have some tapes.

If you already have a Data Protector cell manager license, you might as well keep using it because it will work out cheaper than any dedicated cloud-hosting provider.

Target device options

- Virtual tape library
- AWS block store images
- HP Cloud Device
- StoreOnce

Virtual tape library

If you are very, very constrained by your budget and need to be very conservative in how you do backup changes then you could create a Linux server and emulate a virtual tape library.

If you are currently backing up to a tape library, then this lets you keep the illusion of the same thing but put it into the cloud.

Create a Linux instance in an availability zone that you are not otherwise using. Install mhvtl on to it, and configure a virtual tape library with it. Mount a very large block image (persistent storage device) on /opt/mhvtl. You can now use this tape library just as if it were a real tape library.

If the Linux instance fails, then start a new instance, install mhvtl again, and change the host controlling the library. Note that media agent licenses are concurrent so if you make sure that you use this tape library only when you aren't using your in-house library, there is no additional licensing cost associated with this.

AWS (Elastic Block Store) volumes

The problem with the virtual tape library solution is that you are somewhat constrained by the size of the block storage that you are using. But with an external control device, you can attach and detach Elastic Block Store (EBS) volumes on demand as required. You can add slots to the external device by adding additional block stores.

Create a Linux instance in an availability zone that you are not otherwise using. Write an external control script which takes the DP command arguments and attaches and detaches EBS volumes to the Linux box. Create an External device, using that script.

HP cloud device

If you are using the HP cloud, then this is almost a no-brainer – you don't even need to provision a server. For the other cloud providers, it depends on the bandwidth you get (and the cost of the bandwidth!) to the HP cloud whether this makes sense or not.

Details on how to create and use HP Cloud devices are on page 318 (in section 14).

StoreOnce low-bandwidth replication

The previous three options don't offer a way of using in-house tape drives.

If you have a way of breaking up your backups into chunks of less than 20TB, then you can use the software StoreOnce component on an EC2 instance. It works on Windows and Linux; just make sure that you have installed a 64-bit image. The only licensing you will need is some extra Advanced Backup to Disk capacity.

An alternative is to buy a virtual storage appliance (VSA) from HP, and then creating an Amazon Machine Image (AMI) out of it. This has the advantage that it can cope with larger volumes, and it also has better bandwidth management (e.g. shaping during the day, and full speed at night).

Detailed steps on this approach are given on the following pages.

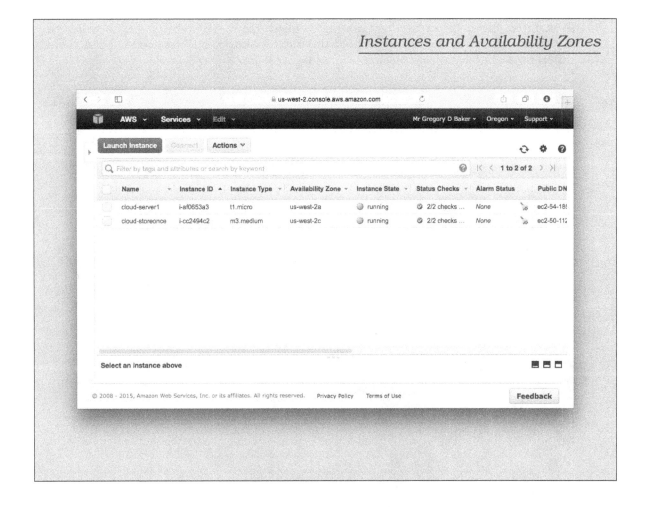

Instances and Availability Zones

The screenshot shows a very small cloud environment with just two cloud hosted virtual machines.

Most cloud hosting environments provide different availability zones. An availability zone is supposed to be a somewhat distinct location, separate to other availability zones. Usually there is very good bandwidth between different availability zones in one region.

In practice, availability zones may be isolated into separate buildings, or might only be in separate wings of the same building. It depends on the data centre where the region resides.

Since the bandwidth between zones is usually quite good, there is usually no penalty for putting the backup system into a different availability zone, and usually there is a significant advantage: two availability zones are unlikely to go off-line at the same time.

In the example above I've created an instance called `cloud-storeonce` which will be a media server and StoreOnce server to hold the backups for `cloud-server1`. I put them into different availabilty zones: us-west-2a vs us-west-2c.

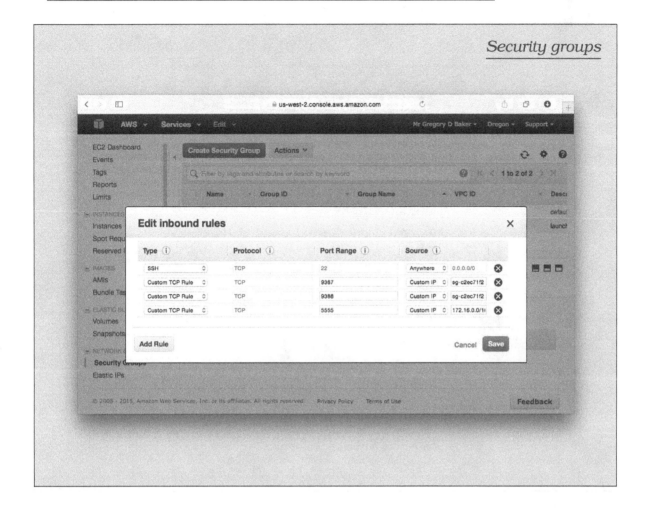

If you are connecting to your Amazon environment through VPC (virtual private connect) then you may well find that the security rules allow all traffic anyway.

But if you put the media agent and StoreOnce server into its own security group, remember to allow TCP port 5555 in (so that the cell manager can connect to initiate backup jobs). It is often also convenient to allow in TCP ports 9387 and 9388, particularly if you want to seed data to minimise data transfers in a backup.

```
●  ◉  ◉              ⌂ gregb — ec2-user@cloud-server1:~ — ssh — 80×24
no-port-forwarding,no-agent-forwarding,no-X11-forwarding,command="echo 'Please l
ogin as the user \"ec2-user\" rather than the user \"root\".';echo;sleep 10" ssh
-rsa AAAAB3NzaC1yc2EAAAADAQABAAABAQCEAT30xewB3hoDKb0xL+fUcUuvQ8G+mOwc5eoPJbdaRfN
SV8nFwfn+prfZtEXappvseLE7R9lxNJMTVxTyry+vw1Abu0n61JPKIm8OdxSrqHmHRxP1KiSawvztMqD
aEdTaehehQ5zuNaqD+vsS9dfS3uaT28xBgl2grSIWwMXMKM8z/Lxm5nn0L6KgSp9Q8n9wypaIHzjUUQN
h++BbOOR38K3Mc/DU6G0kbbLMq6bdPCn9zFq8p1z7Q+SfwogfuBoZSdRxl91MPTSmvT2TuQmauqw+pwd
RVdLxJONnYdkH25dcTv12SACprG77MEk//zf8zXiV2KxaavAP7WiGBsA9 amazon-west
~
~
~
~
~
~
~
~
~
~
~
~
~
~
~
~
~
"~/.ssh/authorized_keys" 1L, 550C
```

If you want to push the installation of the Data Protector client software to your cloud hosted virtual machines, you obviously need to have the ability to SSH in as root. The default images on Amazon do not allow this. You have to log in as `ec2-user` or similar.

The `ec2-user` has the rights to run `sudo`, and so can edit root's files. In the screenshot above I have run

```
sudo vi /root/.ssh/authorized_keys
```

I then deleted the modifiers on the key (including the command as it was preventing direct login. Alternatively, I could have added another public key to the file without restrictions.

After this, I confirmed that I could `ssh` in from my Linux-based installation server without a password. Since I had set `OB2_SSH_ENABLED=1` in the installation server's FILE(.omnirc), the installation was able to carry on as normal.

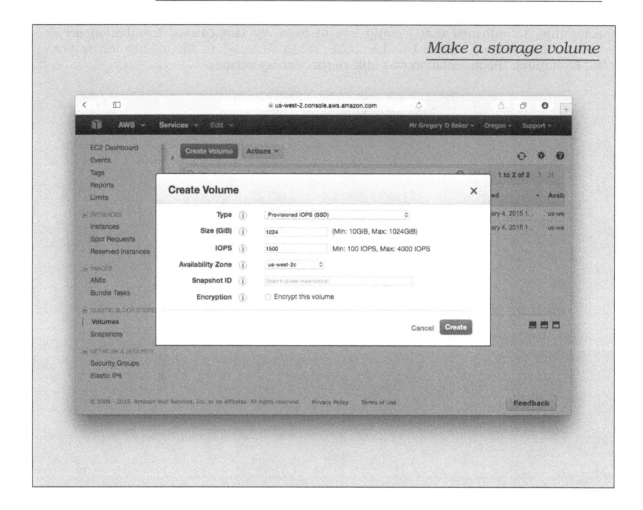

Make a storage volume

We will need some location to put the StoreOnce device. In general StoreOnce devices are very I/O intensive. When they are on rotational discs, they cause a lot of disk seeks.

So to get the very best performance it is worthwhile creating a volume with sufficient provisioned IOPS (as shown above), but this is very expensive.

Note also that Amazon have a limit of 1TB for these volumes, so you may need to create several volumes and put them into a RAID set if you need more storage space than this.

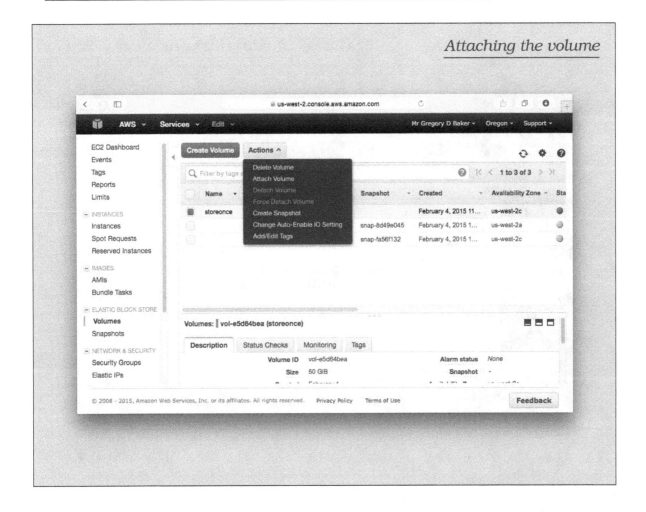

This volume that you have created needs to be attached to the server that you will back up to. One of the nice features of the cloud is that if the server failed for any reason, you could just reattach this volume to its replacement. You would only need to make a small adjustment to the definition of the StoreOnce devices (using `omnidownload`).

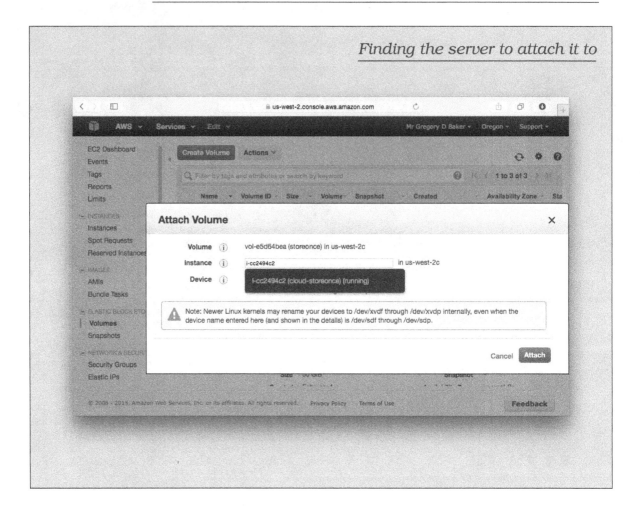

If you have named your media server's instance, then you can search for it by name here. Otherwise you would look up the instance number somehow else.

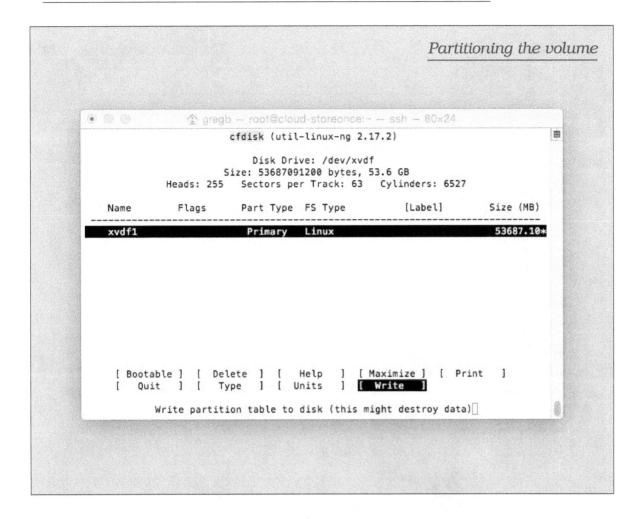

By default the volume will attach to the instance on the device file /dev/xvdf. You need to put a partition table on this device. The easiest utility for doing so is the cfdisk program, where you will create a primary partition spanning the whole disk (if one terabyte is sufficient for you), or an LVM partition type if it is not.

Format, mount and start

```
[root@cloud-storeonce ~]# mkfs /dev/xvdf1
mke2fs 1.41.12 (17-May-2010)
Filesystem label=
OS type: Linux
Block size=4096 (log=2)
Fragment size=4096 (log=2)
Stride=0 blocks, Stripe width=0 blocks
3276800 inodes, 13107192 blocks
655359 blocks (5.00%) reserved for the super user
First data block=0
Maximum filesystem blocks=4294967296
400 block groups
32768 blocks per group, 32768 fragments per group
8192 inodes per group
Superblock backups stored on blocks:
        32768, 98304, 163840, 229376, 294912, 819200, 884736, 1605632, 2654208,
        4096000, 7962624, 11239424

Writing inode tables: done
Writing superblocks and filesystem accounting information: done

This filesystem will be automatically checked every 22 mounts or
180 days, whichever comes first.  Use tune2fs -c or -i to override.
[root@cloud-storeonce ~]# mount /dev/xvdf1 /mnt
[root@cloud-storeonce ~]# /opt/omni/lbin/StoreOnceSoftware --configure_store_root --path=/mnt

The daemon has been initialized. The store root has been set to: /mnt.

[root@cloud-storeonce ~]# /opt/omni/lbin/StoreOnceSoftware --create_store --name=InCloudStoreOnce

The store InCloudStoreOnce has been created successfully.

[root@cloud-storeonce ~]#
```

The partition that you just created will not have a file system on it, so you'll need to create one with `mkfs /dev/xvdf1`.

This then can be mounted on `/mnt` (with `mount /dev/xvdf1 /mnt`).

The Data Protector GUI can do the next two steps, or since you would already be on the command line they can be done on the server itself:

```
StoreOnceSoftware --configure_store_root --path=/mnt

StoreOnceSoftware --create_store --name=InCloudStoreOnce
```

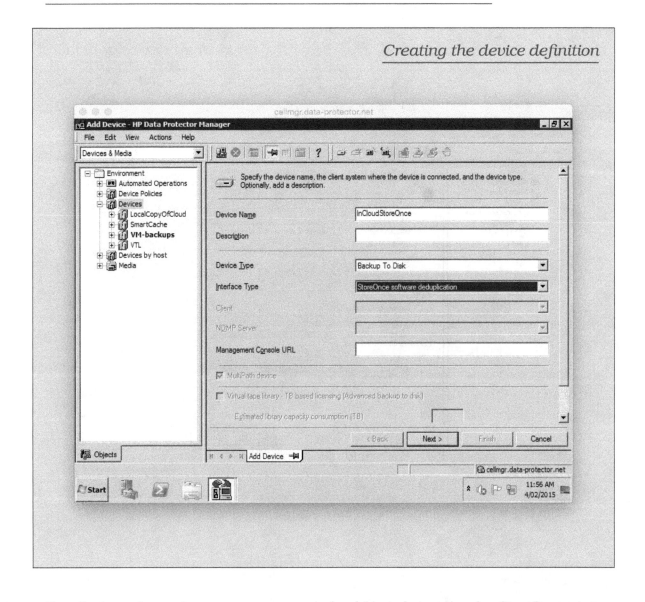

Creating the device definition

Now that you have storage space on your cloud hosted server and a StoreOnce store created, you can create the Data Protector device definition for it.

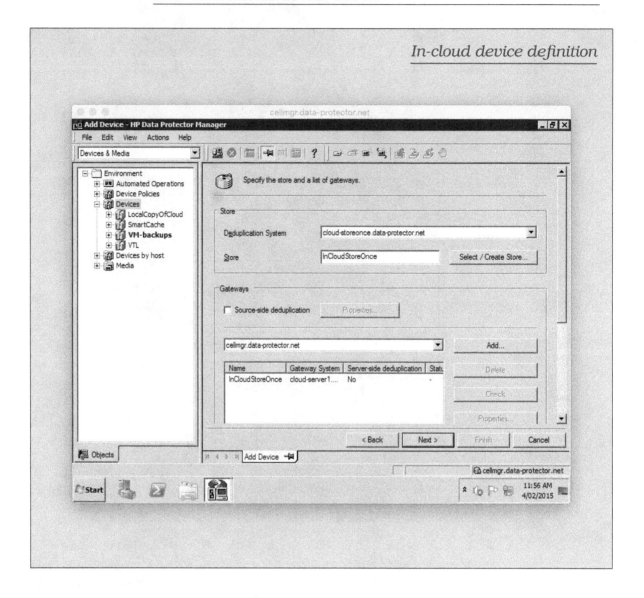

This StoreOnce device should have the cloud hosted server as it's de-duplication system. Obviously there needs to be a gateway in the cloud. If you are charged for bandwidth across availability zones, then you will probably also want to create a source-side de-duplication gateway, or other gateways (one for each availability zone).

It's not necessary to create a gateway from your internal data centre to this cloud server, unless you want to replicate to the cloud from your datacentre.

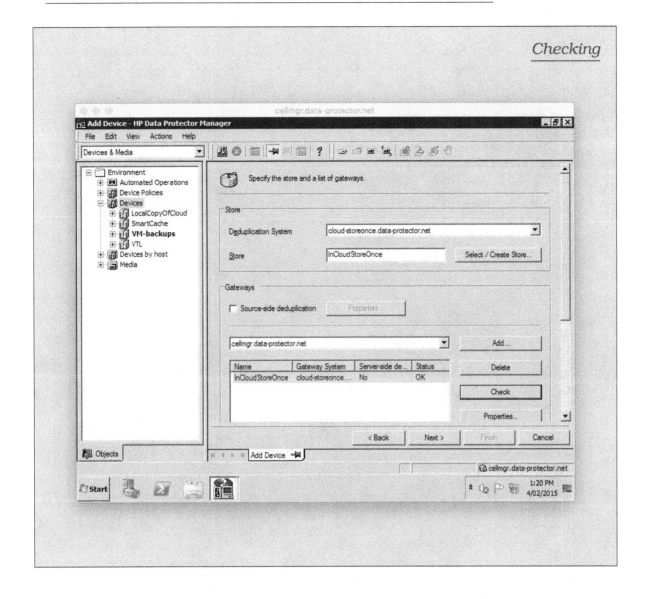

Now is a good time to validate that your security groups are configured correctly by clicking on the Check button and confirming that each of your gateways can talk to the StoreOnce device.

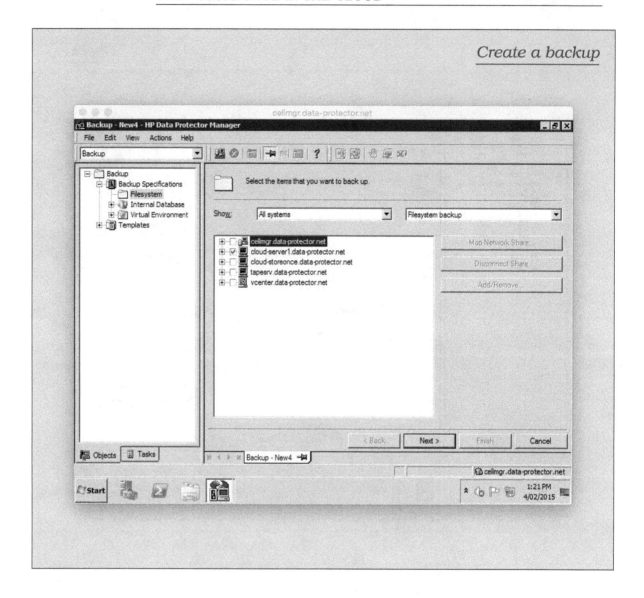

Now you can backup your cloud servers without worrying about bandwidth utilisation.

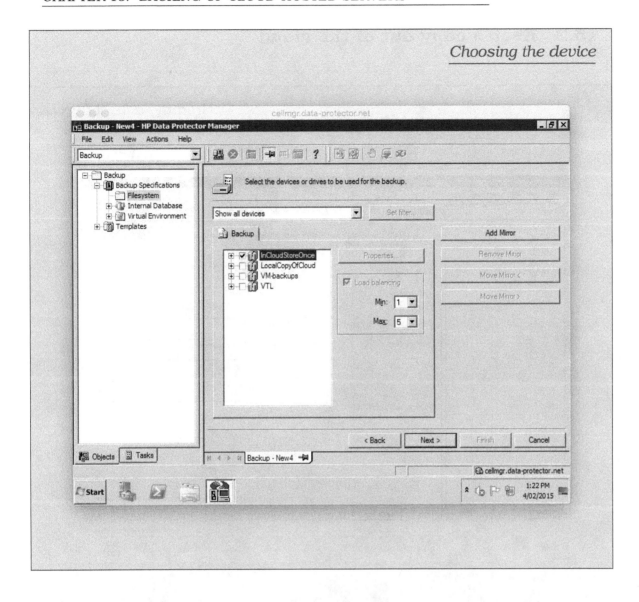

Choosing the device

Simply configure backup as you would outside of the cloud, but make sure the only servers involved (disk agent, media agent and StoreOnce server) are all in the same region.

15.2   Keep a copy out of the cloud

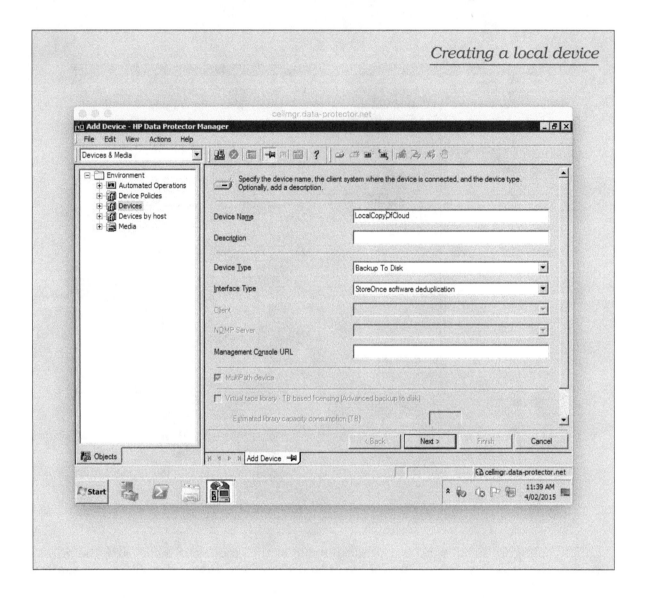

Taking backups which were done in the cloud and replicating them back to your data-centre is conceptually no different to taking a backup of a remote site, as done on page 188 (in section 9.2).

The StoreOnce device can do very low bandwidth replication. The end result will be a copy of all your cloud hosted servers' backup sessions in a convenient format that your office or data centre where you can copy it off to tape for long-term archiving.

I tend to give a name like **LocalCopyOfCloud** so that it is very obvious where the data in that store came from.

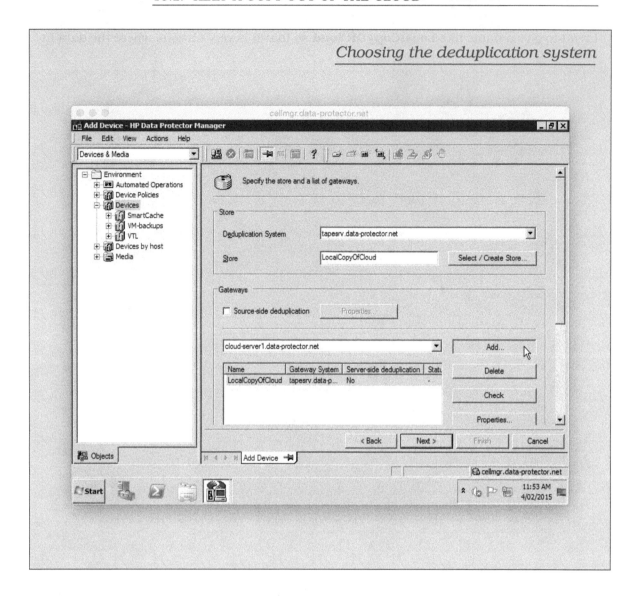

After creating a store outside of the cloud in your datacentre, you create a gateway on the cloud hosted server to connect to the datacentre StoreOnce.

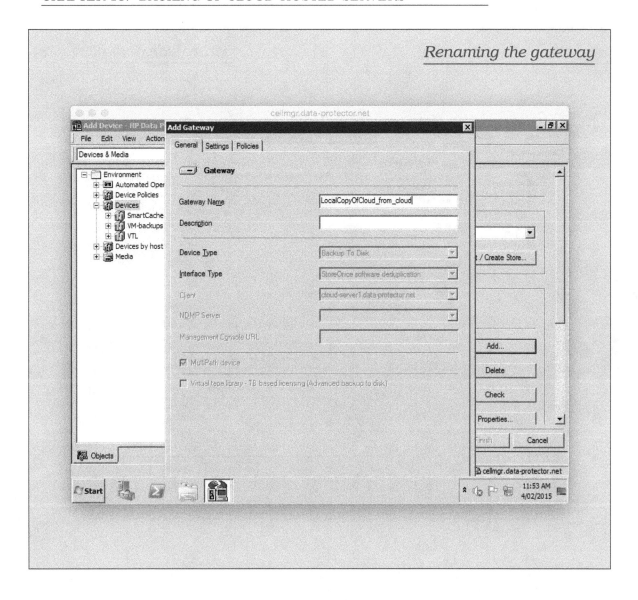

If your cloud hosting provider charges you for downloads, as Amazon does it can be very expensive to make a mistake writing to the wrong gateway. For this reason I always rename my gateways to make it very clear what they do and where they are. In this example I have called it **LocalCopyOfCloud`from`cloud**.

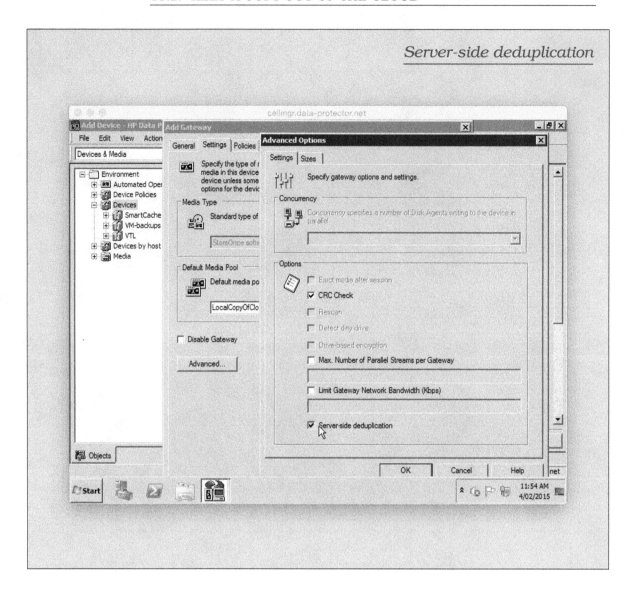

And most importantly of all: remember to tell Data Protector where the de-duplication needs to happen. In this case it needs to happen in the cloud, so that as little traffic as possible is sent out of the cloud.

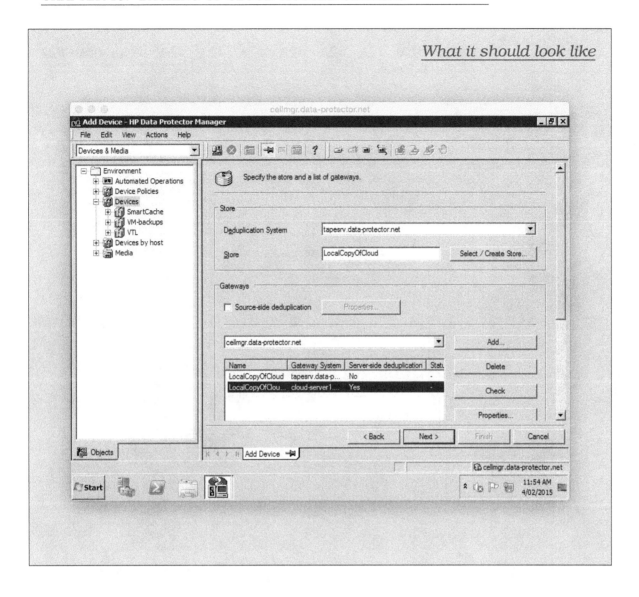

You want to see something like this. There should be two gateways at least, and the one which is sitting on the cloud hosted server should have a `Yes` in the *Server-side deduplication* column.

Remember to press `Next` and `Finish` on the next screen.

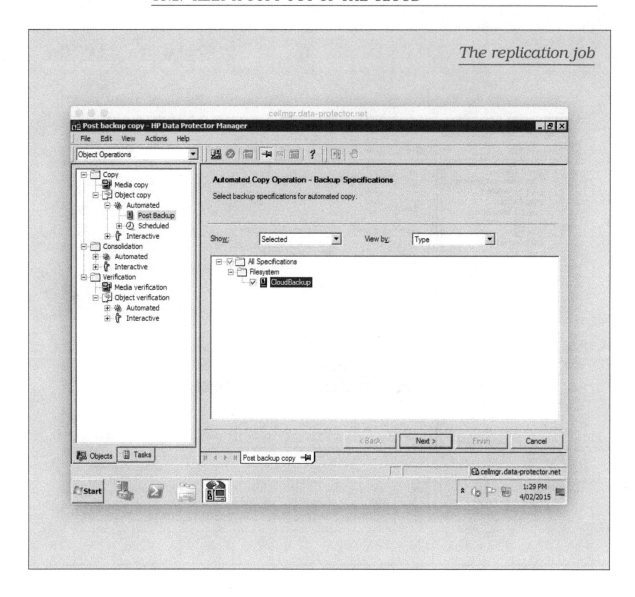

The replication job

There is nothing particularly different about the post-backup copy job that you will create. You could trigger it after the backup job itself is run, or you could schedule to run at a time when you know bandwidth is not at a premium.

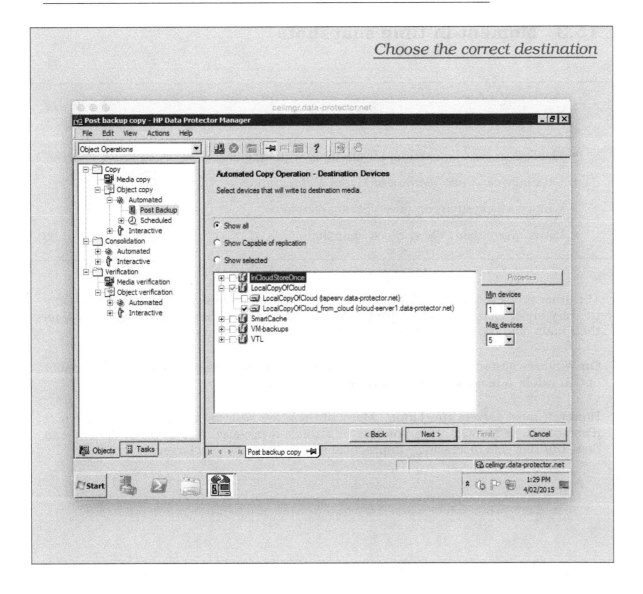

If you have named to your gateways and stores sensibly, it will be very easy to choose the correct destination device.

The remaining options on the following screens (such as number of copies to maintain and their protection) are the same as for any other copy job.

15.3 Moment-in-time snapshots

Consistent backups

- Moment-in-time is essential for anything with state (e.g. a database)
- Generally can't use VMware or Hyper-V integration
- Windows filesystem can take VSS snapshots
- Linux: use either LVM or block snapshots

The other problem is the challenge of getting a consistent moment in time backup. Only the very minor cloud infrastructure service providers are offering VMware or Hyper-V as their main offering, so virtual disk snapshot backups aren't an option.

On Windows systems there is VSS, so a file system backup taken with a VSS snapshot option will be a reasonably consistent moment in time.

However, most servers run Linux. Many of them are running a database of some sort (PostgreSQL or MySQL). It is possible to arrange a pre-exec to dump the database to disk, but this gets increasingly impractical as the database gets larger.

LVM Snapshots

- Pre-exec figures out which volume is being backed up

- `lvcreate --size` *SNAPSHOTSIZE* `--snapshot --name` `snap_of`*SNAPSHOTNAME* `/dev/vg`*XXX*

- `mount /dev/vgXXX/snap_of`*SNAPSHOTNAME MOUNTPOINT*

If you are backing up a btrfs filesystem (which is supported on the Linux agent: you can see it listed in /opt/omni/.util), then you can use its built-in snapshot capabilities.

But even ext3 and xfs filesystems can do snapshots with the help of the LVM layer. This technique dates back to the early days of HP-UX, but it works on modern Linux boxes (and probably on modern HP-UX boxes as well). You will need to do four steps:

Make sure that you have some spare space in the volume group which contains the volumes you are wanting to back up. Use vgdisplay and look for the lines about Free PE (free physical extents).

Make a backup specification (through the Data Protector GUI if you want to) including all the filesystems you want. Don't tick the host, tick each of the filesystems, even if you want all of them.

In the pre-exec and post-exec fields of the filesystem defaults (not the pre-exec and post-exec for the whole backup job) put `snapshot-preexec.sh` and `snapshot-postexec.sh`.

You can get these from http://www.ifost.org.au/dataprotector/lvm-snapshot/snapshot-preexec.sh and http://www.ifost.org.au/dataprotector/lvm-snapshot/snapshot-postexec.sh

The snapshot-preexec.sh script looks at the parent process which spawned it (which will be the vbda process) and finds the `-volume` parameter. Then it strips off the /mnt/backup part of it, and figures out the logical volume that the original filesystem is mounted on. It calls `lvcreate --snapshot`, runs `fsck` and then mounts that snapshot volume. So by the time the `vbda` process starts trying to read the `/mnt/backup/xxx` filesystem, the filesystem is mounted.

The LVM snapshot **pre-exec** is as follows:

```
#!/bin/sh
##################################################################
```

```
# (c) The Institute for Open Systems Technologies Pty Ltd, 2014
# This script is designed to be a pre-exec for a Data Protector filesystem
# object.
# Instead of backing up (say) /var, modify the backup specification to
# backup /mnt/backup/var and set this script as the pre-exec.
# (And to tidy up afterwards, use its post-exec partner)j


# These two parameters are defaults. You can use the environment variables
# for a backup session to change them.
SNAPSHOT_PREFIX=${SNAPSHOT_PREFIX:-/mnt/backup}
SNAPSHOT_SIZE=${SNAPSHOT_SIZE:-10m}

##############################################################

# The parent process' command-line shows which filesystem we are backing up.
# It will look like hostname:/file/system/path
# We need to find the right line of PS output, get rid of everything up to
# the :/ and get rid of anything afterwards.
ps -fp $PPID
REQUESTED_TO_BACKUP=$(ps -fp $PPID | grep vbda \
        | sed -e 's/.*-volume //' -e 's/ .*//')
LIVE_SOURCE=${REQUESTED_TO_BACKUP#$SNAPSHOT_PREFIX}

echo Taking a snapshot of $LIVE_SOURCE and mounting it to $REQUESTED_TO_BACKUP

SOURCE_DEVICE=$(mount | grep "on $LIVE_SOURCE type" | awk '{print $1}')
echo $SOURCE_DEVICE is mounted on $LIVE_SOURCE

CLASSIC_DEVICE=$(find /dev/vg* -lname $SOURCE_DEVICE)
echo $CLASSIC_DEVICE is a symlink to $SOURCE_DEVICE

VOLUME_GROUP=$(dirname $CLASSIC_DEVICE)
echo I will make a snapshot using volume group $VOLUME_GROUP

SNAPSHOT_NAME=$(echo $LIVE_SOURCE | tr / _ | tr -dc '[0-9a-zA-Z_]')

# Make sure everything is written to disk
sync
lvcreate --size $SNAPSHOT_SIZE --snapshot --name snap_of$SNAPSHOT_NAME \
                                    $CLASSIC_DEVICE
mkdir -p $REQUESTED_TO_BACKUP
fsck -y $VOLUME_GROUP/snap_of$SNAPSHOT_NAME
mount $VOLUME_GROUP/snap_of$SNAPSHOT_NAME $REQUESTED_TO_BACKUP
```

The LVM snapshot **post-exec** is much simpler

```
#!/bin/sh
```

```
################################################################
# (c) The Institute for Open Systems Technologies Pty Ltd, 2014
# This script is designed to be a post-exec for a Data Protector filesystem
# object.
# It is designed to tidy up after snapshot-preexec.sh
###############################################################
# The parent process' command-line shows which filesystem we are backing up.
# It will look like hostname:/file/system/path
# We need to find the right line of PS output, get rid of everything up to
# the :/ and get rid of anything afterwards.
REQUESTED_TO_BACKUP=$(ps -fp $PPID | grep vbda | sed -e 's/.*-volume //' -e 's/ .*//')
SNAPSHOT_DEVICE=$(mount | grep "on $REQUESTED_TO_BACKUP type" | awk '{print $1}')

echo Unmounting $REQUESTED_TO_BACKUP
umount $REQUESTED_TO_BACKUP
echo Removing $REQUESTED_TO_BACKUP directory
rmdir --ignore-fail-on-non-empty -p $REQUESTED_TO_BACKUP
echo Removing snapshot
lvremove -f $SNAPSHOT_DEVICE
```

Of course, the backups will be recorded as being of /mnt/backup/. Disaster recovery won't work properly (because it will never see your root filesystem as being backed up). It's a pity that there isn't an easy way of updating the internal database to make it think that it was a different filesystem backed up.

Using Amazon EC2 snapshots

- Install Amazon EC2 tools

- Backup /mnt

- Create pre-exec and post-exec script

The alternative to using LVM snapshots is only available in the cloud. This example works at Amazon, but it could be adapted to work with many other cloud providers.

Essentially, we will snapshot the root disk, mount the snapshot and then backup the mounted snapshot.

If the Amazon EC2 tools are not already installed and configured in the environment, you will need to install them. Most of the Amazon-supplied AMIs have these already in-place, but the Redhat-supplied ones don't.

First, create a backup job that will backup /mnt (even though the server doesn't have a mounted filesystem there). If necessary, just edit the data list:

```
FILESYSTEM "/mnt" cloud-server1.data-protector.net:"/"
{
}
```

Then add pre-exec and post-exec scripts as shown over the following pages.

Amazon AWS Snapshots (Pre-exec)

- Find the EBS boot volume

- Take a snapshot

- Make an EBS volume from the snapshot

- Mount the newly created volume

The following script is available at http://www.ifost.org.au/dataprotector/ec2-snapshot/snapshot-preexec.sh

It assumes that your instance has one EBS volume that it boots from, and no other attached storage.

The first couple of lines will only work on the Amazon cloud. The EC2 instance queries a special Amazon address to find out its own details – its instance id (e.g. i-121255) and its zone (e.g. us-west-2c).

Then we flush as much out to disk as we can (with the `sync` commands), and then freeze I/O on the root filesystem. Anything that tries to write to disk will block until after the snapshot is completed. Read operations will still work. We run a busier loop checking to see if the snapshot is ready.

After that, we turn the snapshot into a volume, and attach that volume to a device which will probably be free. There will be an error in dmesg about the lack of a partition table on `/dev/xvdf` but it doesn't seem to matter.

Finally we mount `/mnt` (ready to be backed up) and remember what volumes we just created.

```
#!/bin/sh

# First, get our instance ID from Amazon
INSTANCE=$(wget -q -O - \
 http://169.254.169.254/latest/dynamic/instance-identity/document \
      | grep instanceId | cut -d'"' -f4)

# Next, find out zone we are in, for the volume creation later
ZONE=$(wget -q -O - \
 http://169.254.169.254/latest/dynamic/instance-identity/document \
```

```
        | grep availabilityZone | cut -d'"' -f4)

# This script only works for single volumes at the moment
VOLUME=$(ec2-describe-instances $INSTANCE \
        | grep BLOCKDEVICE | awk '{print $3}' | head -1)

# Flush everything we can out to disk
sync
sync
fsfreeze -f /

# Create a snapshot of our root volume
SNAPSHOT=$(ec2-create-snapshot $VOLUME | awk '{print $2}')
until ec2-describe-snapshots $SNAPSHOT | grep -q completed
do
  sleep 1
done


fsfreeze -u /

# Turn that snapshot into a volume
NEWVOL=$(ec2-create-volume --snapshot $SNAPSHOT -z $ZONE| awk '{print $2}')
until ec2-describe-volumes $NEWVOL | grep -q available
do
  sleep 5
done

# Connect that volume
ec2-attach-volume $NEWVOL -i $INSTANCE -d sdf
until ec2-describe-volumes $NEWVOL | grep -q attached
do
  sleep 5
done

# Mount it
mount /dev/xvdf /mnt

# Now we can back up. Remember what we had though
echo $SNAPSHOT > .snapshot-to-remove
echo $NEWVOL > .volume-to-remove
```

Amazon AWS Snapshots (Post-exec)

- Unmount the volume

- Destroy the volume

- Clear the snapshot

The following script is available at http://www.ifost.org.au/dataprotector/ec2-snapshot/snapshot-postexec.sh

After the backup, the post-exec removes the mount, the volume and the snapshot.

```sh
#!/bin/sh

SNAPSHOT=$(cat .snapshot-to-remove)
NEWVOL=$(cat .volume-to-remove)

umount /mnt

# Detach the volume and wait until it is gone
ec2-detach-volume  $NEWVOL
while ec2-describe-instances $NEWVOL | grep -q ATTACHMENT
do
  sleep 5
done

ec2-delete-volume $NEWVOL
ec2-delete-snapshot  $SNAPSHOT
```

Index

www.ingramcontent.com/pod-product-compliance
Lightning Source LLC
Chambersburg PA
CBHW062049050326
40690CB00016B/3029